FULL TIME AUTHOR

HOW TO BUILD, GROW AND MAINTAIN A SUCCESSFUL WRITING CAREER THAT YOU LOVE

EILEEN COOK

CRYSTAL HUNT

Published by The Creative Academy for Writers

www.creativeacademyforwriters.com

Disclosure: Where there are products or services we like and use ourselves, we may have included an affiliate link. It's a win-win: you get something that we love, and we get a small amount of money that we will blow on champagne and books.

ISBNs

978-1-7772919-6-9 (Mobi)

978-1-7772919-7-6 (ePub)

978-1-7772919-5-2 (Paperback)

978-1-7772919-8-3 (Hardcover)

978-1-7772919-9-0 (Audiobook)

Although the author and publisher have made every effort to ensure that the information in this book was correct at publication, the author and publisher do not assume and hereby disclaim any liability to any party for any loss, damage or disruption caused by errors or omissions, whether such errors or omissions result from negligence, accidents or any other cause.

CONTENTS

PART III

YOUR MARKET

PART IV

YOUR PRODUCTS

PART V

YOUR AUTHOR BRAND

PART VI

YOUR BUDGET

A note about spelling…

All three of the founding members of The Creative Academy for Writers live in Canada, and we made a conscious decision to use Canadian spellings throughout our series of guides. Because… well… it's who we are, eh?!

A note to our American readers and other friends from around the world: we welcome U in Canada :) Thanks for your willingness to learn new things and play nice with your colourful Canadian neighbours.

While we always appreciate readers letting us know about errors in our books, pretty please double-check Canadian spellings before you tell us we're wrong.

We've left American spellings intact in quoted material.

xo Crystal, Donna and Eileen

To all those family and friends who believed and supported our dream of being writers, and to all the authors who came before us, lighting the path and showing us what was possible if we were brave enough to reach for it and stubborn enough to keep reaching.

For Jack Whyte, who inspired me first through his stories… and later by asking me what I was writing, enough years in a row at SiWC, to make me believe my answer mattered. This one's for you. ~Crystal

For Judy Blume, who was the first author I wanted to emulate and whom I still admire for her skill, grace and all-around awesomeness. ~Eileen

INTRODUCTION

The good news is there is no one right way to build an author career. The bad news? There is no one right way to build an author career. Which means you're faced with piecing together your own road map to the author life you want.

The two of us (Eileen and Crystal) have had completely different writing and publishing experiences. And of all the authors we know who have made the leap to a full-time author career, no two have done it the same way.

We're going to tell you a little bit about our pathways to full-time so you have a couple of examples. And you can hear the stories of many other authors by listening to the podcast interviews at strategicauthorpreneur.com.

Eileen's story

I'm *that* kid. The one who dreamed about being a writer from a young age. My family remembers me playing author, banging away on an old typewriter, before I could even spell. (Granted, my spelling still isn't great.) As soon as I understood that someone made up the stories I read,

I knew that was what I wanted to do. I always had my face in a book and my head in the clouds, making up stories.

Then I did a bad thing. I grew up. Or, to be more precise, I confused growing up with losing sight of my dreams. I decided I had to be practical. I had to get a *real* job. So I did. I went to university. I got a couple of degrees. I started a professional career. I was even pretty good at it. I told myself this was what responsible adults did.

But here's the thing. I still liked telling stories.

I decided to start taking writing more seriously. I began writing on a consistent basis, not just when the muse struck me. I started actually finishing projects instead of starting manuscripts and then abandoning them when they got complicated. I took classes. I asked for feedback. I started getting better. I sent things out. I got rejected.

I got rejected a lot.

Like, *a lot* a lot. So much that I decided to quit. That almost worked. But there was that problem again: I really liked telling stories. I had no idea if I would ever reach my dream of being a full-time author, but I knew if I quit trying, it would never happen. So I tried again.

I got rejected again. (That's how you know this is real life versus a canned, feel-good speech.) I kept trying, and eventually I secured an agent. Nine months later, she sold my book. We sold film rights. The book sold in nine countries.

Then the publisher dropped me because they weren't going to publish in that genre anymore. *Sigh.*

So I kept trying. I sold another book. Then another. My first agent left the business, and I found a new agent. I've had editors leave the business, and I've been reassigned. I've gotten contracts and lost them. I have over a dozen books in print at this point in my career. Some sold for very small figures. A few sold for six figures. This is my job. And it is a *job*. There are good days and bad days, but there is absolutely nothing I would rather do. Things continue to change and evolve. I'm now writing non-fiction as well as fiction. I mentor other writers. Being a professional full-time author is about being flexible and persistent. And it's about holding onto that dream and knowing that if you give up on it... it will fade away.

Don't let that happen.

Crystal's story

Like Eileen, I was that kid with her nose in a book All. The. Time. I perfected reading while walking (yes, before cell phones) so that I could read not just on the bus but while walking *to* the bus. I read in the bath, in class—shhh, don't tell my teachers—and as often as I could get away with it, I read all night under the covers. Somewhere there is a tape recording of me telling my preschool teacher I was going to be a writer.

So, naturally, I became a health psychologist. I thought that was more likely to lead to steady work. A career. Which, society tells us, is what responsible adults want. Except under all that responsible-adult stuff, there was still that pigtailed little me who wanted to be a writer. She managed to sneak her opinion in around the edges of things. While completing my master's degree, I taught courses to other college students about academic writing. I was the go-to final-edit person for everyone's papers. Every school break, I wrote, rewrote and *rewrote* the romance novel I'd started when I was 15.

But after finishing my master's, that pigtailed little girl got really loud. Imagine a petulant toddler, arms crossed in front of her, shouting *no* back at you every time you trolled the job listings. So I decided to give her a shot. I took a job working nights as a cocktail waitress (before that was called being a *server*) so I would be free to write during the day. And since I'd always loved rhyming kids' stories, and had inherited a daughter by this point, I started with kids' books. I sent out stories. I got rejection letters back. And then I sent some more. The petulant toddler sat down with my smart, stubborn, persistent adult self, and together we decided there had to be a better way.

In 2007, indie publishing was nowhere near as mainstream as it is now. But it was a way, and I could see how it could work for me. So I embraced it. I published a picture book, then another one. Then two more... and suddenly I had a publishing company. I was working with a bunch of other people, teaching courses and workshops, helping other folks who wanted to indie publish, and speaking at conferences about making books apps and eBooks and all kinds of fun things that combined books and technology and business management. Each thing led to something else, like a trail of breadcrumbs. I followed those crumbs deep into the forest of the publishing world.

I got an offer to write some books for an educational publisher in Korea, so I wrote early-reader chapter books on contract. I wrote my own chapter books. I wrote blog articles for money—and for fun—and learned how to do all the things involved in the business side of being a writer. When other people asked for help or coaching, I exchanged my time and knowledge for money or services I needed to advance my own writing career. (Grown-ups call this consulting.)

Along the way, I kept coming back to that same romance novel in my holiday time. And I kept on writing. And, finally, that romance author who loved her happily-ever-afters came out to play too. I let the little girl inside me grow up.

I have been making my living from writerly things for the past 15 years, and every year has been different from the one before. That little girl has collected more than 40 different titles on her bookshelf in all kinds of formats. And my author career is still evolving. Because the only truly stable thing about an author career is *change*. It's so fantastic to never, ever be bored.

But enough about us. Let's talk about you.

Throughout these next sections, we'll help you weave your choices together into a picture you like—a vision that makes sense for *your* life, skills and priorities—with a series of Your Turn exercises that help you get those ideas down on paper so you can start turning them into a business plan. Those blank notebooks you've been hoarding? You might want to grab one of them now. You might even want to crack open that special notebook you were saving. Because this work we're about to do? It's worthy of the *best* notebook you've got.

And if you prefer to save that notebook for something else, keep reading as the next thing we'll share is the link to our fillable workbook and business plan resources.

Your Turn

- Take a moment and write your story so far. When did you first think about becoming a writer? What steps have you already taken? What challenges have you overcome? Who has supported you along the way?
- Now write the next stage of your writer journey. Imagine how things might unfold in the future. How will you respond to challenges? What success will you have?
- Look at how other writers have reached their career goals. Some authors discuss this in their bios, or you may know some personally. If you don't know any writers, check out the following podcasts for inspiration:
- The Strategic Authorpreneur podcast
- The Self Publishing Show podcast
- The Creative Penn podcast
- Six Figure Authors podcast

HOW TO GET THE MOST OUT OF THIS BOOK

This book isn't *just* a book. We really wanted to set you up for success so we added a few extras to the mix to make your journey easier.

The complete Full Time Author resources package can be found at: https://creativeacademyforwriters.com/resources/fulltimeauthor.

While you *can* use some, all, or none of the additional resources listed below, best results will likely be had by using the whole planning system together the way we intended. Be brave and stretch a little outside your comfort zone—we think it'll be worth it!

But ultimately the choice is yours. Do whatever makes your heart happy.

#1 Full Time Author: Your Turn Workbook

All the Your Turn exercises from this book in a digital, fillable workbook format.

This is an editable Google document that you can download to your computer or save to your own Google drive and use to complete your own author business plan in document format. It is designed to pair perfectly with this book as each section in the book maps to a section in the document. We'll walk you through filling it out step by step through the Your Turn exercises, sharing resources and ideas for next steps along the way. This is the format that Eileen loves most as she can answer the questions right in the document, or if she wants to use her journal, she can use the question list as a prompt for easy review.

Start by filling out the workbook, and as you make your way through, you'll also be prompted to fill in various sections of the Business Plan Google Sheet.

#2 Strategic Authorpreneur Business Plan Google Sheet

An interactive business plan template complete with built-in tracking spreadsheets and accompanying explanation video so you get a tour of how it all works.

Spreadsheets are Crystal's happy place, and while she loves her journal, an interactive, auto-calculating, super-functional spreadsheet is what generally inspires her to use the "mind blown" emoji. This is the document that can be used to track your progress towards all the goals you set for yourself, and it also serves as a high level view of your data and habits through the year.

You can find the Full Time Author: Your Turn Workbook, the Strategic Authorpreneur Business Plan Google Sheet and all the other resources for this book at https://creativeacademyforwriters.com/resources/fulltimeauthor.

Inspirational advice

You'll notice some inspirational notes and wisdom from some of our author friends sprinkled throughout to help keep you going. These were written just for you, and are included here with an extra dose of support in case you need a boost.

Complete reading list

We also mention a lot of other books and resources that you can use as a jumping off point to dig into various topics further. To make it easier to follow up on that, we've collected them all up into a handy list for you in the Resources section of this book, and they have also been included at the end of the workbook as a checklist!

We know this is a big book. Your career is a big deal, and we wanted you to have everything you need now, *and* everything you'll need to help you plan each new round of leveling up.

For now, just focus on taking things one piece at a time, and don't be afraid to ask for help when you get stuck. Do only what you need, and circle back around to the other parts later—if and when you're ready.

Wherever your author adventures take you, we hope there will be something in this book to help point you in the right direction.

THE CREATIVE ACADEMY FOR WRITERS

Looking for a full-time support system for your journey?

Hanging on to your dream of being a full-time author can be hard. Friends and family may not understand that it can take years, even decades, to build up to a full-time career. If they are not writers themselves, they may not understand the siren's call of the fresh notebook, the lure of the blank page, the endless possibilities that await you in the worlds you create. (Show of hands: how many of you have at least a half-dozen empty journals in your house right now? And how many have at least one that is "too nice" for everyday use—one that you're saving for some special purpose that hasn't yet revealed itself to you?)

They don't get it. And that's okay. Because *we do*.

We writers need someone to believe in our dream and hold us up when we feel like letting go. Choosing to write takes courage: courage to continue to try when the words won't come. Courage to share your work with others and invite their feedback. Courage to send it off into the world through agents or editors or by indie publishing your story. And the world has too many people who will tell you your dream is foolish.

Instead of encouraging you, they will go out of their way to discourage you. It's easier for them to tear down someone else's dream than to work toward one of their own. You need to surround yourself with the *right* people.

That's why we started The Creative Academy for Writers. We wanted to create an inclusive place that fostered big dreams for writers and provided practical guidance to reach those dreams. We wanted to build a community of like-minded people, offer encouragement and practical support, and assist people in taking the next steps on their writing journey. We wanted to be that voice in your ear that says "you got this" when you feel like you very much don't.

This book is a part of that journey, but it's not the whole picture. If you aren't already a member, we hope you'll consider joining us online at creativeacademyforwriters.com. We have a wide range of live and recorded events, active forums, masterclasses, guest speakers and a lot of support regardless of where you are on your writing journey. Many of the "deep dive" resources we mention in this book are freely available to you there.

It's free—yes, you read that right—and a community is always stronger when it grows to include great people. And don't worry. We're making some space on the shelves for you. There's always room for more great stories.

PART I

AUTHOR, KNOW THYSELF

1

IDENTIFYING YOUR PRIORITIES

Being an author is only one part of your life. It should support you, fill you up, give you satisfaction in all kinds of ways. But there are many other aspects to who you are that will shape the author you want to be and the life you want to live. We believe it's important to create a whole lifestyle that serves you, and that means knowing a bit about yourself outside the writing—so the career you build can reflect your vision, mission and values.

Identifying the things that matter to you and the areas of your life you want to protect is an excellent thing to do *before* your planning begins. Maybe you have a spouse you love, and that relationship is central to your happiness. Maybe you have a dog that needs regular walking and plenty of cuddles. Maybe you're a busy parent of five energetic young kids who need food and water and quality time every single day. Maybe you don't have any of those, but you know your mental health depends upon having quiet time each day to rest your brain and body. Maybe your body does great when you spend an hour or two per day at your computer, but any more than that will have negative health consequences.

Whatever these priorities are, it will help you to make note of them so you can keep them in mind as you work through the coming sections on planning your path forward.

Your Turn

- What is important to you in your life? These could be values, people, activities, pets.
- Write down what matters to you—anything you want to keep in mind as you plan your author journey.

2

UNDERSTANDING YOUR WHY

Knowing your *why* will help make all the following decisions in this book easier. If you know why you love writing and why you want to make a career out of it, you can make sure you craft an author life that keeps that joy alive. If you are trying to decide between two options, then you can pick the one that is more in line with your true purpose.

> *The best advice I can give is the single hardest lesson I had to learn—that first and foremost, I am a writer because I love writing. It is the companionship and purpose writing gives that infuses my life with meaning. Don't let that get lost in the noise of publishing. Hold on to that one sacred truth—I am a writer because I love writing—whisper it like a prayer and let that love be your true north as you continue on this path.*
>
> — LIZA PALMER, INTERNATIONALLY BESTSELLING AND EMMY-NOMINATED AUTHOR

Some people write to connect with others. Some simply love the act of writing. Some writers love to craft and create, and words are their chosen medium. Some writers are in it for the fame and glamour and glory. Some writers find it helps them to process their thoughts or share their knowledge or indulge their passion for research in a particular area.

There's no right answer to this question. The only thing that matters is for you to know *why* you are writing and what you love about it so you can inform your decisions as you work through this book.

Your Turn

Make some notes in your journal, answering the following questions:

- What do you love about writing?
- How does telling your stories make you feel?
- Why do you think it's important to tell your stories?
- When you think about *not* writing, what is it you miss most?

Extra credit reading

Not sure about your why and want a resource to help you take a deep dive into this exploration? There is a great book by Simon Sinek called *Start With Why* that can help you figure it out.

3

DEFINING FULL-TIME AUTHOR

There are plenty of different ways you can define the term *full-time author*. Once upon a time, being a full-time author may have meant sitting up in your garret, sweating for hours over whether to put that comma here or there or take it out completely.

When that work was penned, off it would go to a publisher who would arrange for publication. Your books would show up in bookstores as though by magic, and you would be whisked out of your garret—or artsy downtown brick loft—and off on an all-expenses-paid book tour to launch your book and begin earning out your hefty advance.

But if we're being honest, that way of life was only ever available to a very small number of individuals fortunate enough to have the support to ensure their meals were delivered, their clothing laundered, and their earthly needs met while they whittled away at their words. Those lucky individuals also had to find a traditional publisher willing to back them fully and "launch" them into literary society.

For most of us mortals with jobs and bills and kids and way too many real-life responsibilities, there are usually a few more pieces to the puzzle.

In this book, we're going to help you identify the various pieces that you *could* fit together to build your own vision of a full-time author career. Some will appeal to you, some will most definitely not. Some won't be available to you in the early stages, but new doors will open as you "level up" and hit new milestones over time. We recognize that you may be indie publishing, going the traditional route, or trying some mix of both (often referred to as the hybrid publishing path).

When we talk about being a full-time author, we include the following pieces of the publishing industry puzzle in that definition:

- Writing
- Editing
- Publishing
- Marketing and promotion
- Advertising
- Social media management
- Platform building, branding and networking
- Business management
- Blogging
- Podcasting
- Intellectual property management
- Collaborations
- Teaching/facilitating/coaching/mentoring

Since you're in the driver's seat on this road trip, you get to decide what the trip looks like and which hot spots you're going to visit along the way!

Your Turn

We'll dig into each of those puzzle pieces later, but for now make a couple of quick lists in your journal or workbook that we will come back to later in the process. What we're looking for right now is your gut reaction.

- Which of those pieces from the list above seem like fun to you? Do any strike you as an instant *Hell, yes!* when you think about it?
- Which of those things seem scary or intimidating or overwhelming to you, even though you might think they are a good idea?
- Do any of the items on the list trigger a strong *nope, nope, nope* reaction in your mind or body?

4

UNDERSTANDING WRITING AS A CAREER CHOICE

There are a lot of wonderful things about being a full-time author, and we're going to dive into these below in more detail. You're your own boss. No set schedule. No requirement to wear pants. No one microwaving fish in the communal break room so the whole office smells like a cannery.

On the other hand, no boss means *you* have to make all the decisions. No schedule means it can be really easy to find deadlines and priorities shifting. No requirement for pants occasionally means you don't remember the last time you left the house or wore anything other than PJ bottoms. No one microwaving something in the break room means you're on your own with no co-worker to complain about—or with—and you may miss that camaraderie.

Both of us love being full-time authors, but it comes with challenges. Publishing is a fickle business. It's a business without guarantees. One book may be a hit, and the next book may tank. Your current editor may say she will buy everything you write, and then quit, leaving you with a new editor who is less keen. You may be a number-one indie bestselling author and then the winds change, and a new genre takes fire, leaving you behind. And creativity can be tricky. You may be consistently writing a book—or two or five—a year, and then suddenly life gives you a kick in the nether regions and you find it difficult to produce. (Yeah, 2020, we're looking at you).

Nothing, not even your dream job, is all good or all bad. Knowing what the pros and cons are can help you decide if you'll enjoy full-time status in this field.

5

CELEBRATING THE UPSIDES OF BEING A FULL-TIME AUTHOR

The good news? There are lots of upsides to being a full-time author. Let's look at a few of our favourites.

You are your own boss

This is huge. While you're not likely to love everyone you meet, the requirements for interaction in a full-time writing career are minimal, and you can decide who you want to interact with, and how, and when. Heck, most of your day-to-day co-workers are your imaginary friends. You get to choose your team, and you choose how and where your world intersects with the public. You are the boss—so you make the decisions, and you live with the consequences, good and bad. The upside? People can give you advice and recommendations. But you choose who to listen to.

Flexible schedule

As the boss, you are in charge. You can build your own schedule to suit your lifestyle and temperament, and you can change your mind any time circumstances change. You can adjust your schedule to suit your child-care needs, you can flex around your spouse's work schedule so you can still spend quality time together, you can book off certain times of the year so you can travel or indulge in a special hobby. If you're a morning person, you can wake yourself up at five and get to work. (Just be quiet because we're likely still sleeping.) If you're more creative in the afternoons or evenings, then you can schedule your focused writing time then.

Flexible location

You may have heard the phrase or seen the meme: *Writers—working from home before it was cool.* So, so true. This is Crystal's 18th year of working from home, and she still loves it. While Crystal currently has her dream office to work from, this is the first time in 18 years that she could say that. Most of her 40-plus books were written at kitchen tables, in coffee shops, bars or restaurants or sitting cross-legged on a blanket in the park. Eileen is still figuring out what will make her office a dream. (Alas, Ryan Reynolds has yet to put in his resume as her personal assistant.) However, she's finding that different books require different environments. She's written some on a desk in a corner of her home, others in an office, and a fair number of words in the giant comfy chair by the fireplace.

Freedom to grow and change and evolve

Your author career can—and will—evolve with you. You will be constantly learning. You will meet interesting people who invite you to be part of cool mutual endeavours. Opportunities will come your way that you never even thought to put on your wish list. And because you are the boss of your own author career, you can grow and shift and change direction as you need (or want) to. Your career can—and should—adapt to ensure you're living your most satisfying life. Not the other way around. We have each reinvented ourselves multiple times, and most authors we know have changed genres or focus areas or switched around the puzzle pieces that make up their author lives at any given time.

No dress code

Seriously. Crystal has typed a good portion of this manuscript in PJs (the ones with the clouds barfing up rainbows, or the plaid pants with a "This Day We Write" T-shirt, depending on her mood and the level of professionalism required). Eileen wants points for wearing actual clothing, but she's given up on the concept of "hard pants" and has developed an aversion to zippers during the pandemic. There is really a clothing requirement only for public appearances: if you're doing a virtual launch, meeting with a colleague via Zoom video chat, or interacting with your adoring public. Even then, most people aren't too demanding, and as long as you've got pants on and you've showered, you're fine. The savings on buying and maintaining a professional wardrobe can pay for the editing on your next book! Or pay for all those fancy blank notebooks you're hoarding.

Huge potential

Unlike many careers that have set salaries and pay-grade schedules (many of which come with a hard cap), your earning potential as a writer is hugely variable. We know a select few writers who make seven figures a year, quite a few who make a solid six-figure income, and still others who consistently earn the same or more than they did in their previous day jobs. We also know many authors who earn a much more modest income but are happy with that. Writing has both the advantage that there is no set income and the disadvantage that there is no set income. We choose to see the positive in this situation. In other words, the sky's the limit. But the only number that truly matters is what you need to support your lifestyle of choice.

Long-tail income

Once you have written and published your stories, those intellectual property assets can earn you money… *forever.* We are still getting paid for books we wrote *years* ago. Royalties are a truly beautiful thing, and with each book you write and publish, you layer in another set of products that will just keep earning over time. Unlike jobs where you get paid by the hours you put in, book royalties just keep on giving. And once you create that story, you can turn your intellectual property (IP) into assets of many forms: eBooks, print books, audiobooks, podcasts, TV shows, video games. There are so many ways to repurpose your creative IP. And each new book you release brings in new readers for your older books.

No one can tell you *no*

It's not up to anyone else to determine your future. With the accessibility of indie publishing and the plethora of tools available to help you do a good job of publishing your own works, there is no one who can tell you not to go after your dreams. Remember when we said hard work, stubbornness and just not giving up were key? Yeah, that.

Your Turn

- What benefits of being a full-time author resonate the most for you?
- What makes you feel sparkly and excited when you think about doing this career on a full-time basis?

6

RECOGNIZING THE CHALLENGES OF BEING A FULL-TIME AUTHOR

While there are lots of upsides to this career, it's not all sunshine and roses and champagne. There are plenty of challenges you may encounter, but being aware of them before you dive in will help you overcome them.

You will always be learning

You might think that in the quest to becoming a full-time author, at some point you will be *there*: you know, that place of total mastery where you know all there is to know on a topic. Sorry to burst your bubble, but an author career is one in which you will *always* be learning. Just like in medicine or engineering, things are always changing. Society changes, our readers' preferences and expectations change, and the publishing industry changes rapidly as new technologies, opportunities and trends emerge. This means there will be periods of time where you very much feel like you don't have mastery. Times when you don't know what you're doing and it feels too exhausting to learn. But you *can* learn it. (Seriously, we believe in you!)

Everything is always changing

You are always changing. You are the source of the stories, and you'll be balancing your life, your interests and the opportunities that come your way. You'll want to explore different ways of writing or write on different subjects. You will grow and improve your skills and take workshops and learn from every book you read and every author you meet. And the industry will constantly change around you. The only thing we *can* count on is change. Well... death and taxes too. But we're saving those topics for later in the book.

You will never "got this"

When you hit those bumps in the road where things fall apart for a minute or a month or a year, don't panic. Those bumps are inevitable. None of us ever totally "got this." It doesn't mean you're a bad writer. Or that you should quit. Or that you're doing it all wrong.

Look at your choices and behaviour when things fall apart so that if there *is* something you can control to help turn things around, you take that opportunity to make a change. But remember that in the writing and publishing world, kismet, luck, serendipity—also known as being in the right place at the right time with the right book—can have a big impact on career trajectories.

We'll talk more about this in the section near the end called Rewriting Your Author Career. But for now? Show up, keep writing the books, keep doing the work, and don't give up. The only way you can guarantee total failure is to stop showing up for your dream. And that is the one thing you truly do have complete control over.

You're on your own

We've talked about the benefits of being your own boss, but the truth is that you're also your own co-worker, administrative assistant, intern, and cute guy who delivers the mail. All of that alone time can make a person, well, lonely. Yes, you have your imaginary friends and perhaps a pet or two who will listen to you talk though an issue, but each author's ability to cope with all the isolation varies. Ensure that you're building a community so you don't realize a few weeks have gone by and the only conversation you've had is with your dog. (Even if your dogs think you're a genius, like Eileen's do.) Set up regular outings or meet-ups with others to build and keep an active social circle. These individuals don't need to be writers, although at times you may enjoy talking shop with people who do the same type of work as you.

> *Writing full time can be extremely isolating. An online community is great, but it's important to see real live people, too. Stay in touch with friends and former co-workers through coffee dates, lunches, or walks. Volunteer, take an exercise or art class, or consider writing in a coffee shop for an hour or two... If you're able to attend conferences or festivals, they're a great way to overdose on socialization for a weekend. They'll make you appreciate your solitude all the more!*
>
> — Robyn Harding, #1 international bestselling author, *The Swap* and *The Party*

A consistent and stable paycheque? Sorry, no.

While we do believe it's possible to strategically build a full-time author career that affords you the ability to pay your bills consistently—and even experience the occasional windfall—it's not the kind of industry where you can depend on getting a paycheque deposited to your account every couple of weeks just for showing up and doing your job. You might get an advance with a traditional publishing contract that is supposed to last for years. Or maybe you have a nice stable income for one year from a writing grant you received, and nothing for the next year. Maybe you build up a consistent publish-and-release schedule as an indie, and your ads are rockin', and your monthly income has been stable for a year (or three). Then the ads platform you based your whole business plan around changed, and your income drops by 50 percent overnight. There will be fluctuations. The only thing stable is change. We'll keep banging this drum.

Your Turn

- Which of these challenges makes you nervous—or outright afraid?
- Are there other things that you are worried about when you think about a full-time author career? What are they, and why do they scare you? (*Hint:* The more specific you can be with your answers, the better able you'll be to plan strategies to combat these fears.)

7

DESCRIBING YOUR DREAM JOB

Eileen remembers thinking, *If I only had more time, I would...* Then there was a pandemic, and it turns out that having more time wasn't necessarily her biggest problem. The other issue was that she had only so much energy and enthusiasm. Eileen wants to speak French. She likes the idea of travelling to France and starting a fluent conversation with the server at a restaurant, while the people around her think she's a clever, cosmopolitan woman. While having this conversation, she's also wearing a very chic outfit, likely with a hat.

Eileen is capable of learning French. But it's going to take time. It's going to be difficult. And the truth is she'd rather sit and read a good mystery novel than practise conjugating verbs *en français*. She can either let go of her bilingual fantasy (but not the one about the waiter) or she can let go of reading the book. She can't have both. She has to make choices.

You will have to make choices about your career, and you need to be specific and clear about what exactly you want. One of the biggest mistakes we make is being vague. Think of it like going on a road trip. If you don't know your destination, all you're doing is driving around aimlessly, looking at the world's largest ball of string or outdoor teacup and running the risk that you won't have a rest stop when you need one and will have to pee in the bushes.

The smart author knows where they want to go, what they need to get there, and what the next step in their journey will be. You don't need to know every step, just what you need to do *next*, and who you need to speak to in order to fill in the blanks.

Let's start digging into exactly what you want your dream job to look like.

What genre of stories would you like to write?

Some writers know exactly what genre they love writing in. But while it can be faster and more direct to choose just one genre, it is not a requirement for success. And you always have the freedom to change lanes down the road. Eileen has written non-fiction, children's books, YA, adult thrillers and even the occasional romantic comedy. Crystal has written children's books, non-fiction, contemporary romance, paranormal romance, and romantic suspense. There's no right answer here. However, we recommend that you be aware of the costs of splitting your focus. For those of you struggling to choose where to focus your efforts, the section entitled Your Market will walk you through some exercises to help narrow your focus.

For now, if you're not sure what you want to write, do a quick inventory of what you love to read. Are your bookshelves covered in mysteries, romances, biographies, or thrillers? You may spend years steeped in the genre or genres you choose, so picking something you enjoy will go a long way toward keeping you interested over time.

What length of stories are you comfortable with?

We will dig into story length more when we get to the products section of your business plan, but for now just think about the length of the stories you most love to read—and to write. Are they flash fiction? Short stories? Novellas? Or epic fantasy and historical tomes, the longer the better?

Your Turn

- In what genres do you want to write?

For each genre you listed, answer the following questions:

- What do you love about reading that genre?
- What do you love about writing that genre?
- Is there a particular length you are most comfortable or excited to write? Why do you love writing at that length?

8

DEFINING YOUR CAREER GOALS

What is your end game? What goal is driving you forward with your writing career? Just as our characters need to feel driven in order to continue to move forward when the going gets tough, so do you. It's important to have an understanding of what you want to accomplish and why so that you can chart the best path to reach that individual goal. There is no right or wrong answer here, only what matters to you.

Some writers have an income goal: $25,000 per year or $50,000 per year, or $10,000 per month or $1000 per day or $1 million per year. The right amount is exactly what you need to live the life you want, and we personally know writers making *all* of those amounts (yes, even the million-dollar-plus ones).

For others, the goal is a certain status milestone, like being able to put *USA Today bestseller* or *New York Times bestseller* on your book covers.

Or maybe you want to win an award, like a Giller Prize or a Hugo.

It could be a number of works you want to produce and publish. Or a certain number of book sales you want to hit—"one million copies sold" has a nice ring to it. Or perhaps there's a certain publisher you want to sign a deal with.

Maybe it's the number of budding authors you'd like to inspire through the writing workshops you teach, the classroom visits you make, the conference keynotes you deliver.

Or maybe your goal is to see your books turned into a movie, TV show, or video game, or to have someone famous play you in the movie they make about your life as an author.

Do you envision yourself as a go-getter indie author, or a traditionally published author working with a "Big Five" New York firm?

Maybe your ultimate career goal is simply to spend your days exactly the way you want to, doing something that you love on your own terms —and you're open to what that looks like.

And maybe it's all of the above! That's okay too. You're unlikely to be actively working toward all of them at the same time. Your goals will come in and out of focus. But knowing what milestones you'd like to have on your journey will make it much easier to make those day-to-day decisions about where to spend your time, money and energy.

Your Turn

- Do you have a goal—or several goals—for your career? Brainstorm a list of ideas.
- As writers, we know motivation is important. We know our characters won't continue to pursue their goal given all we're going to throw at them. It's the same in real life. Look at the goals you listed above and then discuss why those goals are important to you. What's your motivation for those goals?

9

RECOGNIZING YOUR STRENGTHS AND WEAKNESSES

Writer—know thyself! We're going to talk later about strengths and weaknesses facing your business, but it's important to know your personal strengths and challenges because you're the core of that business.

Eileen used to teach job-seeking skills to individuals, which included practice interviews. Two of the tried-and-true questions that came up for people in interviews were "What are your strengths?" and "What are your weaknesses?" Job searchers were always trying to figure out answers that were true, but that could also be seen as an asset. Eileen would tell people that the employer doesn't necessarily expect you to answer with full honesty. A job interview isn't the time to state that one of your biggest weaknesses is that if you're not interested in a project you'll put it off forever.

But this time? This time, we want you to be *really* honest. You're the only one who will see this, and since you're the boss, your job isn't at risk. Consider who you are, both as a person and as a writer.

Knowing yourself—the good bit and the bits that you may not want to share with the whole world—allows you to create a plan that maximizes your strengths and compensates for any areas of weakness.

Eileen has created a Writer's Self-Evaluation tool that may help you with this process. While it's designed to look at both your traits as a writer and the business of publishing, for this section you can focus simply on the issues related to your strengths. You can find the evaluation online at https://creativeacademyforwriters.com/resources/fulltimeauthor.

Your Turn

- Create a list of what you feel are your greatest strengths. Be specific, giving examples of when you've used or demonstrated this strength. Now is not a time to soft-sell yourself.
- List your greatest weaknesses. Again, be specific: when have you shown these weaknesses? Are there things, people or situations that make you more likely to demonstrate one of your weaknesses?
- Ask a group of close friends or family members what they feel are your greatest strengths and weaknesses. (It can be helpful to ask people who know you in different aspects of your life.) This isn't a time to challenge their assertions. (*"I'm not really* that *good at public speaking."*) Now is just a chance to understand how other people see you.
- Write a short description of yourself in the third person, as if you were describing a character in a book. Stand outside yourself. What would you say are this character's strengths and weaknesses? What motivates this character? In what situations do they excel? Where do they sell themselves short?
- What parts of the writing and publishing process make you feel sparkly and excited? Do you get jazzed up when it's time to plot out a new book, or when designing bookmarks to promote your books?
- What parts of the writing and publishing process do you avoid? What parts make that dreaded *"I just can't do that"* feeling wash over you?

10

BUILDING YOUR SKILLS AND CAPACITY

Once you have identified your skills in the exercise above, you can compare this against the list of career skills you identified in the Writer's Self-Evaluation. In the areas where you're missing skills, you have a choice to make. You can either learn those skills or contract others to perform them.

This choice between learning and contracting comes down to a few factors:

Love of learning

Crystal is an informational vacuum. The woman *loves* to learn new things. She's surrounded by books, podcasts, courses and interesting people. More importantly, she has an openness and a willingness to learn. Many people, when confronted with something they don't know think, "I don't know how to do that! I could never do that." (Eileen shyly raises her hand here.) Crystal and people like her think, "Interesting, I don't know how to do that... *yet*." They're okay with being not good at something while they learn. This doesn't mean that Eileen can't learn, because when she has to, or when it's been something she's interested in, she can do it. However, she knows that she will procrastinate when it comes to tasks she doesn't *want* to learn. Procrastination is a fancy term for putting your dreams and plans on hold, and it is best avoided whenever possible.

Commitment to craft

A full-time author understands that this is a constant journey. There is no crossing the finish line. This is one of the best things—and sometimes the most frustrating thing—about being a writer. You need to commit yourself to constantly learning more about your craft. Reading other writers to learn what you can from them, taking courses, listening to feedback, going to conferences, taking a class—however you like to learn, vow to yourself that you'll never stop trying to be a better writer. And while you can hire folks to mentor you or help make your work shine, there is no way to buy the skill of being a better writer! That one you have to earn.

Frequency of use versus time investment

If a skill is missing from your skill set, analyze how often this skill is going to be important in your career. For example, you'll have to *update* your website a lot more often than you'll have to *build* your website. You'll use basic grammar more often than you'll design a book cover. If a skill will take a lot of time to learn and be used only infrequently, it may make better sense to hire out that skill—unless you've got a mad passion for it.

Finances

Consider your budget. You may not be able to afford to contract for certain services. There's nothing like not being able to pay for something to inspire you to roll up your sleeves and figure it out on your own. This is why tutorial videos on YouTube exist! Crystal will be the first to admit that she developed her thirst for learning publishing-related skills over a long period of extremely tight budgets and limited options.

Time

Despite our best efforts to bend the space-time continuum, there are only so many hours in a day. Or as Eileen's grandmother used to say, "You can't put ten pounds of coffee in a five-pound bag." If you are limited on time, you may not have the luxury of learning a skill yourself. You may determine that because time is a limited commodity, you are going to spend it on other activities—writing another book, spending time with your family, doing research, etc. Or you may be focused on leveling up your author career more quickly, in which case the option of trading money for time might be appealing.

We'll do some more specific analysis of key skill areas when you get to setting your specific priorities for the next quarter or year. For now, let's get a general sense of your interests and preferences, because this will help as we progress through your business plan.

Your Turn

- Review the information from your Writer's Self-Evaluation and make a list of what areas you need to level up to get where you want to be.
- Which of these areas are you interested to learn more about in the near future?
- Which of these areas are you interested to learn more about one day, or you have time, but not right now?
- Which of these areas do you know you'd like to hire someone to help you with in the near future?
- Which of these areas do you know you'd like to hire someone to help you with down the line, once you have the funds available?

11

TIMELINING YOUR FULL-TIME JOURNEY

How long will it take you to become a full time author? Well, that all depends on which elements of a writing career you are trying to blend together, how far you are in the journey already, and how much time and energy you have to dedicate to your efforts.

> *Remove the word "aspiring" from your vocabulary. If you process life through written words, then you're a writer. Whether you're published or not, now or ever, that truth doesn't change—you're a writer. Don't let anybody ever tell you otherwise.*
>
> — SUSANNA KEARSLEY, NOVELIST

For most authors, three to five years is a *starting place* for a timeline. But it's not unusual to take a decade or even longer to really get established. While there are stories of authors who hit it big with one book, that's the publishing-world equivalent of winning the lottery. A nice dream, maybe, but unfortunately, that's not how it works for most of us.

Life is all about choices. What's important to remember is that only you need to make a value judgement on your choices. Or at the very least, the judgement of others shouldn't matter.

Let's consider those writers we know who earn six or seven figures a year from their writing. Sounds like a dream, right? Who wouldn't want that? But here's the thing. Those writers work *hard* for that money. They spent years studying the genre. They took courses and immersed themselves in indie-publishing strategies. They write *a lot*. They learned about ads and built their mailing lists and daily ensure their ads are working. Most of these authors have periods—sometimes years at a time—where they spend ten to 16-plus hours a day working. They may have given up evenings, weekends and vacations to build momentum in their careers. While their current schedule may make it look easy, often it took years or decades of steady work to get to that point.

The idea of all that hustle will fill some folks with excitement. It will turn other folks completely off the idea of being a full-time author. There's no question that to be a successful full-time author, there is a great deal of hustle required. But there are as many ways of becoming a full-time author as there are authors. It's up to you to decide what that hustle looks like, how you spread out all those hours you're going to put in—over months, years or decades—and what you add or subtract from your own life to make it all work. Only you can decide how intensely and how quickly you want to build your career.

How long to go full-time as an indie author?

In the indie space, there is a whole community of self-published authors built around the concept of 20BooksTo50K. The Facebook group is run by founder Michael Anderle and Craig Martelle and has upwards of 45,000 members at the time of writing. The idea behind that concept is that if you have 20 published books, each book has to generate roughly seven dollars per day in profit to get you to a "full-time salary"—if $50,000 per year is your target full-time salary. Remember, you'll actually need more than that in revenue to cover publishing expenses and promotional investments and still take home that 50 grand.

Four to six book per year is a *very* ambitious writing and publishing schedule, so most people will be looking at a minimum of five years to build to that level. And if you're writing epic fantasy that comes in at around 120,000 words and requires a ton of world-building and research, you might be able to write only one book per year. Series are generally easier to promote and sell to dedicated readers. If your books are all stand-alone titles, it can be even harder to scale up your income. If you're thinking you'd like to write a series, you may find Crystal's book *Strategic Series Author* helpful. And be sure to check out the section titled Leveling Up Your Author Career for ideas on how to increase word count and productivity.

If you are an indie author, your limitations won't be imposed by the publisher's agenda and budget. They will be determined by your own writing and publishing capacity, including how much time and money you have to invest and how well you are able to execute your plans. If you plan to take the leap into full-time as an indie author, you generally need to fund six to twelve months of writing and publishing expenses. You will pay out your editing, cover design and promotional or advertising expenses up front, and you won't see revenue from a book until at least a couple of months after launch because of the delays in royalty payments from your distribution channels. You want a bit of a cushion on top of that because there are always fluctuations in book sales and income over time and across books. And on your first few books, building momentum can take much longer. Once you have several books —especially if they are in a series—this gets easier. (Note we did not say *easy*, just easier).

How long to go full-time as a traditional author?

In the traditional world, it can take a year or two to get your first book published, from the time it's acquired to the moment it hits the shelves. And many publishers—especially in some genres—won't publish more than one book per year from a single author. If you don't yet have an agent, it will take time to find and secure one of those as well. Most authors don't receive advances that allow them to leave their day job right away. Instead, they see their advances slowly grow over time, assuming that their book sales stay high.

You will need to weigh your ability to invest time and money against the timeline you're hoping for as a full-time author. This is why many people don't rush into being a full-time author—and why it's smart to build up your momentum over time and not quit your day job too early. You want the freedom to make the best choices that will benefit you long-term.

If you are a traditional author, you have the benefit of a publishing team behind you, and you won't have to cover those costs. However, this team has their own goals and agendas, and you may not always be the priority you feel you deserve to be. Advances are typically paid in stages (upon contract, on acceptance and delivery of the manuscript and on publication) and royalties—once you earn out that advance—come twice a year. Even a large, pop-the-champagne, six-figure advance is likely paid out over two years, or more if it is for a series, so what seems like a windfall can take a long time to show up in your bank account. As a result, you'll need to have a cushion to survive those gaps in payment. And you'll still have expenses: your author website, headshots and other expenses will fall to you even if you are traditionally published.

You'll notice a theme in this book: that things are constantly changing, and writing is not an easy career to build. Heck—if it was, everyone would play with their imaginary friends full-time! If you're not in a place to make the leap to full-time writing now, it doesn't mean you won't be able to do it later. Right now, you might need a more certain primary income than a writing career can provide. But you should still get started! You can build up your skills and your catalogue and take steps toward your full-time career every day. Your timeline and expectations are as flexible and changeable as your life circumstances. And when the time is right, you'll be able to make that shift. You got this.

How much time do you have to dedicate to growing your author career?

One of the prime factors that determines how quickly you can grow your author career is how much time you are able to dedicate to your writing, editing, publishing, promotion and business admin tasks on a regular basis. Generally speaking, if you have more time to dedicate every day, you can move things forward more quickly. However, many authors have discovered that having all the time in the world doesn't automatically advance things. The work has to be done, the motivation to keep yourself on track has to be summoned, and the universe still has to align to find you the right ideas, agents, publishers and support personnel. A lot of authors flounder when faced with an open calendar, so quitting your day job to go full-time doesn't always translate to a huge change in output. In fact, the pressure of all that time with no distractions can actually hinder your creative efforts.

How many spoons do you have available?

Forward momentum is not always about how much time or money you have you advance your author career. The most prevalent limitation is actually the energy—both physical and mental—that is available to dedicate to your writing and to getting back into that chair every day to tackle the next priority.

Humans come in all shapes, sizes, makes and models, and our minds and bodies are unpredictable. Our energy reserves will fluctuate depending on sleep, nutrition, world events, our personal lives, our social connections and our mental and physical health.

If you are dealing with physical or mental illness, or any kind of lifestyle challenge, you may find that some days it's much easier to do what you'd like to be doing. Other days, it simply won't be possible to move forward.

In 2003, Christine Miserandino, an award-winning blogger and patient advocate, coined the phrase *spoonie* when she was describing to a friend what it's like to live with a chronic illness. She wrote an article that described spoon theory. This idea is based on the metaphor of each person having a set number of spoons to use each day. The spoons represent an individual's energy reserves for that day. For some people, it might only take one spoon to get through the activities of daily living, while for others it might take most—or all—of their spoons. And if you "borrow" against tomorrow's spoons, the consequences can be far-reaching and unpleasant.

Why are we talking about this? You are the only one who knows how many spoons you have available to dedicate to growing your author career. And this will impact your timelines, options, plans and daily routines.

Never let anyone tell you what being a career author should look like in *your* life. You are the only one who truly knows what you need and what you are comfortable doing in pursuit of your goals. You are the expert on *you*. And you are still the *boss*.

Full-time, part-time or occasional author?

Even though we've called this book *Full Time Author,* it's really about leveling up your career. After all, you may not actually want to go full-time and quit your day job. That's okay! There are no fixed goals here except to get what you want out of your life and move toward your dreams. We've broken out the general approaches in three main groups that we will refer to throughout this book—usually in the context of creating timelines and prioritizing different things.

Full-time or Full-time equivalent

These are authors who dedicate 100 percent of their work time to being an author and all that entails. They dedicate *at least* 30 to 40 hours per week to their writing and publishing business. That doesn't necessarily mean they have quit their day job or have nothing else going on in their lives. It just means they are investing the same number of hours per week in writing as they would in another full-time job. (1500-plus hours per year @ 30 hours per week)

Part-time

Writers who are able to invest less than 30 hours per week to their author business are generally considered part-time. Again, these hours could take place on evenings and weekends in addition to your regular job or parenting and caretaking responsibilities. Or maybe you only have the energy for 15 hours per week, but you're giving it whatever you can. (780-plus hours per year @ 15 hours per week)

Occasional

These folks are approaching their career in a professional way but aren't able or willing to put in regular hours every week. They work on things when they're inspired or when they get a break from other commitments, but they are not necessarily making steady weekly progress. (Variable hours)

Your Turn

- Look at your time commitments for the next year—or next quarter if a year feels too overwhelming—and make a list of how much time you have available in your typical day, week, month and year to dedicate to growing your author career. It may help you to download this time grid and actually colour in the blocks according to how you spend your time. Download the resource at https://creativeacademyforwriters.com/resources/fulltimeauthor.
- There are 168 hours in a week, and 168 blocks on the sheet. Make sure you block off enough time for sleeping.
- Not sure how much time you really have available? For two weeks, track your time. Carry around a notebook or use your phone, and mark how you spend your time in ten-minute increments from when you get up until you go to bed. Look at what things currently take up your time.
- Based on what you learned from your analysis or time tracking,

how many hours do you have available in an average day, week, month and year to dedicate to leveling up your author career? Are there activities you could eliminate to free up time to focus on more important things? Do certain tasks take more (or less) time than you expected?

- How much energy do you have to dedicate to growing your author career? It may help to use spoon theory to visualize this. How many of your available spoons are taken up by the activities of living your life?
- For this next phase of your author career development, are you a full-time, part-time or occasional author?

12

PLAYING THE LONG GAME

Building yourself a successful author career is as much about *not quitting* as it is about being talented or lucky or successful. When we talk about what it takes to develop a writing career, what often comes to mind are traits like talent, hard work, being good with words, having a keen eye for errors and penning an excellent turn of phrase. But that's not the whole picture.

> *Know what you want and go after it with everything you've got. And if you don't succeed, change your approach and try again. And keep doing that until you achieve your goals. 'Failure' is only a chance to learn and do it better the next time.*
>
> — JAINE DIAMOND, AUTHOR OF *DIRTY LIKE ME* (CONTEMPORARY ROMANCE)

You will need to be tough and stubborn. You will need to dig in your heels and refuse to give up. You will have to be tenacious, tireless in your willingness to learn, brave enough to reinvent yourself as needed, and strong enough to develop a thick skin to help you through the tough patches when you are learning that you will never be able to please *everyone*. And then learning it again. (Sometimes again and *again*.) You'll have to hone a sense of humour so you can laugh when you feel like crying. You will have to be creative and self-aware and clever about how you stitch together all the elements of your successful writing life.

Don't panic. We're not about to set you adrift to figure out all this on your own. We're going to be right there with you, walking you through the key things to keep in mind as you put together your career development plan. Then we'll talk about all the things that will try to derail that plan—and how to keep yourself stubborn enough not to quit, no matter what the world throws at you.

You may be wondering: if it's all so tough, why bother at all?

Well, it's not *all* tough. Some parts are pretty freakin' awesome, in fact.

There are many different reasons why people pursue the dream of being a full-time author. And while it's not all glitz and glamour and martinis with lunch, it is a pretty fantastic way to live.

How will you prevent burnout?

Knowing that you're in this for the long term, you will want to set yourself up for an author lifestyle that you can maintain and that works with your personality. If you don't, you will put yourself at a greater risk of burnout and potentially cut your career short.

Eileen is excellent at making plans and then making time to work every day on the priority project until it's done. She is fiercely protective of her weekends and her evening knitting and murder podcast time. Her approach is to work steadily toward a goal until it is accomplished, and in the traditional publishing world, her focus was on writing one new book per year. Now that she is combining indie publishing with traditional, her new focus is on writing both a fiction title and a non-fiction title. But she still uses a slow-and-steady approach to content creation.

Crystal cycles through periods of intensely focused productivity and periods of totally unscheduled and unfocused resting and recharging. She responds well to strict deadlines and tends to batch the writing, publishing and promotion phases of her year so she's not switching between so many tasks and so there are "seasons" in her author journey. Making sure the writing periods are as free as possible from teaching and business commitments lets her drop into the stories or non-fiction content and make plenty of headway all at once. She refers to herself as a "binge creator."

Both Eileen and Crystal are open and flexible to responding to opportunities. They evaluate if a new project or opportunity makes sense and are willing to pivot as needed (or wanted). This doesn't mean they're getting distracted, but rather that they are responding and changing as needed.

We're not telling you how we work because we think our way is the *right way*. We simply want to show you a couple of different examples of how an author lifestyle might look. There is no right way to be a full-time author. What matters is that you become an expert at identifying your priorities and setting strong, healthy boundaries to help you reach your goals while avoiding the ever-looming spectre of burnout.

Your Turn

- What are your character traits that will serve you well on your quest for a full-time author lifestyle?
- Have you ever experienced burnout? If yes, journal about what your symptoms were and the clues that suggested you were

reaching burnout stage (whether you paid attention to them or not).
- What decisions or actions have led to your previous experiences of burnout?
- What steps will you take to help prevent burnout in the future?
- Make a list of ten things you can do fairly regularly to "fill the creative well," sustain your energy and keep the ideas flowing.

Extra credit reading

Here are some great options for extra credit reading in the area of personality that may help you craft your ideal career. Bonus: these are all super helpful for developing book characters as well!

- *The Four Tendencies* by Gretchen Rubin provides an interesting framework for exploring how your personality will impact your preferred methods of planning, learning and self-management.
- *The Enneagram Made Easy* by Renee Baron and Elizabeth Wagele delves into nine different types of personalities in an easy-to-understand fashion. Once you've figured out your own composition of types, you can make decisions that are a good fit for your personality.
- *Strengthsfinder 2.0* by Tom Rath helps you discover your CliftonStrengths and recognize what strategies for leadership will work for you—whether you are leading yourself or a team.

13

CELEBRATING SUCCESS

Along your author journey, you will pass all kinds of mile markers and important moments that will result in you happy-dancing around your kitchen.

Most authors have a fantasy of how they will celebrate "the moment." The moment might be when they finish a manuscript, when the book is published, when they sell *X* number of copies, or when they hit the *New York Times* list. All of those are good reasons to celebrate. Perhaps you plan to take a vacation, buy yourself a fancy gift, or open that bottle of champagne you've been saving for just this occasion. Imagine us raising a glass along with you. (We're great sports that way.)

We encourage you to celebrate *more*. Life is short. Projects can be long. Taking time to enjoy the moments when things go well helps you enjoy the journey. There's a tendency to celebrate only the larger wins—like finishing the manuscript—while ignoring the regular achievements like hitting weekly or daily writing goals. Even worse, some people don't celebrate even the big goals because they've already transferred their eyes to the next prize.

Here's the problem: there's *always* another prize ahead. We know writers at all stages of their career. It's easy to say that you don't even care about getting published, that all you want is to finish one book. But once you finish it, you start wanting to publish. Once you publish, you want to publish more. You want more sales, more readers, and more money. There's nothing wrong with this desire for more. That's what will drive you forward. But you do need to celebrate along the way.

Why is celebration so important?

It creates a domino effect

Taking time to recognize what you've accomplished has a domino effect. Knowing that you will celebrate a milestone can motivate you to keep going on the days when things feel impossible. Reaching that milestone underscores the sense of accomplishment you feel. That results in a double whammy: it builds your confidence that you are the kind of person who gets things done, *and* it reinforces your appreciation of what you've done. And if all of that doesn't have you wanting to give yourself a gold star, know that recognition and celebration create a positive loop, giving you additional motivation to stretch toward the next milestone.

It does a body good

Celebration releases endorphins—nature's fun chemical! Your brain loves a nice hit of endorphins. This is why some people enjoy running. Your brain works harder if it knows some of those endorphins are coming along. If you deny yourself the chance to have them, you may find it harder to keep going.

It builds community

Writing is a solo activity, but the writing life is easier when you've got community. (There's a reason we built The Creative Academy for Writers!) Community can provide you with resources, support, and guidance. Sharing milestones allows the people around you to celebrate along with you. And you know what a shared celebration is? A party! You never know how sharing your goal will inspire others. Seeing someone else celebrate their goal may be just the motivation they need to keep going. So your party isn't selfish—it's sharing the love.

It's an opportunity to learn

Celebrations offer a chance to reflect on what you've done. You can gather data: how long did it take you to reach that goal? What resources were most helpful? Are there resources you don't have that would have made a difference? Were there distractions or challenges you could reduce or eliminate in the future? If you take the time to learn from your success, you can create an environment that makes success more likely.

How will you decide what to celebrate?

Determine what is in your control

You want to celebrate what you have the power to make happen. For example, "signing with an agent" isn't in your control. But sending out a hundred queries *is* within your control. It doesn't mean you can't celebrate those wins that are outside of your control, but you want to focus on things that your efforts impact.

Create small, achievable wins

Breaking down a larger project into smaller, more easily achievable goals allows you to create a habit of "winning." Your brain actually learns that you're the kind of person who sets a goal and then achieves it, which makes you more likely to persist when things become challenging.

Set affirmations

The book *Scrappy Rough Draft* by Donna Barker discusses the science behind setting affirmations and explains how these can help you to reach your goals. You can use affirmations to set yourself up for those future celebrations.

Stay flexible

We discussed at the start of this book that one of the characteristics you need as a full-time writer is the ability to be flexible. Things will change: your goals, the marketplace, the publishing business and everything in between. (Remember in 2019, when we all carefully made plans for what we were going to do in 2020? Cue hysterical laughter.) Planning regular check-ins with your goals allows you to pivot as needed. At The Creative Academy for Writers, we run 12 Week Year planning retreats (free to attend!), where writers have a chance to reflect on what they did in the last quarter and clarify what they will work toward in the next 12 weeks. No matter how fast things are changing, we can usually get a handle on three months at a time. These retreats are recorded and always available to members, so no matter where you are in the 12-week calendar cycle, you can jump in and work your way through the latest planning session.

How to celebrate

Now that we've sold you on the idea that celebrating wins is a necessary part of the process, how do you go about doing it?

Announce it on social media

The next best thing to having good news is sharing it. It's okay to toot your own horn and enjoy those likes as they come into your feed. (And spread the love: when you see others celebrating, take time to cheer them on too.)

Mark the moment

Take a picture of yourself and write a journal entry about how it feels to have achieved this moment. Save it for the days when you need to reread it.

Say thank you

Gratitude is one of those things that just keeps paying forward. If someone helped you by doing a beta read, or making dinner so you could write, send them a note thanking them and explaining how they are a part of this success.

Take time for yourself

Maybe it's a hot bath, a long afternoon with a book, or a walk with your dogs, but give yourself the gift of relaxation. Part of any celebration is having a moment to breathe and enjoy it.

Cook a great dinner, bust out the fancy dishes and invite friends over

This is your personal Thanksgiving, so make a meal worth the occasion —or have someone make it for you!

Keep champagne in the fridge

You don't have to spend a fortune, but keeping some sparkling wine around for an impromptu celebration is never a bad idea. Crystal likes to keep a few mini bottles of bubbly in the fridge, labelled with her next "champagne milestones," as a fun way to stay motivated. Eileen has declared this genius and intends to do the same.

Write out what you accomplished and hang it in your office

Visual reminders that you have a habit of winning are great encouragement. Some writers have their published books nearby. Others frame covers, and even more have some type of vision board where they post quotes and reminders of the journey so far.

Give an acceptance speech

Look in the mirror and give an "Oscars" speech about what this accomplishment means to you. Doing this aloud makes a difference.

Once you've celebrated the heck out of your achievement, set your next goal and *go for it!*

Your Turn

- List five to ten ideas of how you would like to celebrate milestones as you work toward your goals. Create some that are free or low-cost as well as some that might be a mini luxury to mark the larger hurdles.
- Journal about what you've already accomplished in your career. It's valuable to pause and realize what you've already worked so hard to do. Look at what helped you along the way. Explore the challenges you faced and how you defeated them. If you want to share your wisdom, consider writing a blog article

about what you learned and accomplished so that others can learn.

- Write a personal thank-you note to someone who has helped you along the way. It may be a friend, family member, former teacher or critique partner, but pause to let them know how much their support has made a difference for you.
- Consider creating not just weekly "to-do" lists, but also "ta-da" lists. We often have long lists of what we need to do, but if you happen to accomplish something that wasn't on your original list, be sure to put it on your ta-da list. It both marks how and where you spent your time and gives you credit for what you've done. When that pesky imposter-syndrome sidekick pops up, show them your ta-da list of things you accomplished to move yourself closer to your goals.
- Create a 'happy file' for yourself where you collect up nice reviews, emails from readers and other things that help you remember why you love being a writer.

14

DEALING WITH ENVY

At The Creative Academy for Writers, we believe strongly that the wins of other writers are meant to be celebrated. The story business is not a zero-sum game in our view. We all win when one of our merry band wins. You want to ensure that you see other writers not as competition but as fellow travellers on the journey. We can learn from others' success, and it can inspire us to new heights.

Alas, there are people who will respond to your success with negativity. You need to know how to handle these situations. It can be easy to hide your light because you don't want to deal with people being upset with you.

There are writers who feel that writing is like pie, and that if you get a nice thick slice (with whipped cream, no less), there will be less for them. Perhaps they are upset at themselves because they haven't reached a goal they wanted, but it comes out as anger at you. That is not your problem. That is something they need to work out on their own. They may respond by openly being negative. "It must be nice to have [insert your win here]." Or "You didn't deserve [insert win] because [lame reason]."

Another kind of negative response is passive-aggressive behaviour. The non-compliment compliment: "Hey, if you're happy with that cover, I'm sure some other people will like it too." Or "It's a great book if you like those formula romances. I mean they're not, like, 'real' books, though, are they?" (Crystal has to take a deep breath just reading that sentence.)

It can be even more hurtful if these negative comments are coming not from other writers but from friends or family—people who you believed had your back. Just as with writers, there are likely personal reasons why people have this response. It could be that they like seeing you in a particular role, especially one that doesn't allow you to be successful. It's possible they haven't reached their dream, so they want to tear yours down, so they don't feel so bad. Again, the reason for *their* behaviour isn't *your* problem. However, unlike with other writers, you may need to work through the relationship if you want to keep that person in your life.

What if you're the one feeling envious?

It's been called the "green-eyed monster" which sounds vaguely friendly, but envy is not your friend. It's natural to look over at what another author is doing or receiving and have all kinds of feelings about it. Maybe they won the award you dreamed about, or their first book received an eye-popping advance. Maybe their book promo somehow went viral and their book is downloading at speeds that rival a rocket ship. What you need to remember is that this isn't about them. This is about you.

We compare ourselves to others as a way to benchmark if we're happy or dissatisfied with our own progress. If comparison helps fuel you and encourages you to set targets then that's great, but if it leads to negative feelings and frustration let it go. Publishing is not pie. One person's success does not mean there won't be a slice left for you. When you catch yourself trash talking another writer (either to others or to yourself) stop and figure out what is driving that envy. Then correct your course and put the focus back on your own journey where it belongs.

Tips for dealing with negativity

Remember that you deserve to have good things happen to you

You've likely worked very hard for your success. There may be elements of luck involved, but luck happens when you put yourself out there for opportunities and do the hard work to prepare for those moments.

Understand that their hate means you're doing something right

This may be small comfort in the moment, but if people are envious of you, it's likely because you've done something deserving of envy! The more success you achieve in your profession, the more likely people are to notice—and then create their own stories about your success.

Be a person who offers a hand up

If you've had success, help others when you can. This doesn't mean that you don't set boundaries, or that you have to (or should) spend your time or energy on those who don't support you. However, if you are grateful for your success and invest in helping others when you can, it may make you more comfortable enjoying your success.

Don't be afraid to be direct

"When you say X, it makes me feel like you're not happy with my success." Or "I'm not sure why you would say X." The other person may not be aware of how their words impact you or come across.

Remain professional

It can be tempting (oh, so very tempting) to search out chances to get back at people who hurt you. The Internet is full of stories of authors who went after someone who gave them a bad review or entered into a Twitter death battle of insults. This never looks good and rarely ends well. This is the time to channel your inner Taylor Swift and think "haters gonna hate." Or you can take a more positive Michelle Obama approach: "when they go low, we go high." And it's perfectly normal—and a heck a lot of fun at times—to gripe with friends over a glass of wine about poor treatment. However, publishing is a small world, and you want a good reputation. Your behaviour will directly impact your brand and your career trajectory.

Make it a learning moment

Unwanted criticism is just that: unwanted. Having said that, there may be an opportunity to learn something from what someone has said. Take the time to pull your ego out of the situation for a moment and reflect. Is there anything you can learn from what someone has said? Is there anything you would do differently if faced with a similar situation again?

Ignore and avoid

If people have nothing to add to your life but negativity, then let them go! Feel free to block them on social media so you don't have to see their posts. Limit time you spend with them in real life. One of the most freeing things to realize is that you can't control what other people say—but you can control how much emotional energy to give to it. Eileen keeps a card a friend sent her. On the front is a picture of a box labelled "My big box of I don't give a f*#@+." Crystal has a collage of monkey images on her wall with the tag line "Not my circus, not my monkeys." When you find yourself spinning on something someone else said or did, you're allowing them to take up space and energy in your brain. You have way better uses for those very precious resources.

Motivate yourself

Some people find negative feedback motivating. They take it as "You get upset when I'm successful? Well, watch this! You're really going to be worked up when I hit that *New York Times* list." If this works for you, harness your irritation to your benefit and use it to push toward your next goal.

Build up positive relationships

One of the very best things you can do is surround yourself with people who are happy when you're happy. People who will cheer you on when you succeed and are the first ones to show up with balloons and champagne when you hit that next milestone. You can't underestimate the value of having the right people in your corner. We have a lot of these great people in The Creative Academy for Writers. We'll be waiting there to cheer you on, for sure!

Your Turn

- Journal about how you've dealt with negativity in the past. Are you happy with your response, or do you need to learn some new coping strategies?
- Create your own "not your monkeys" box where you can put negative feedback you need to ignore. Or create another ritual in which you release yourself from thinking about negativity.
- Create a list of people you *do* have in your corner and ensure that you're investing in those relationships. It can be nice to send a handwritten note letting your supportive friends know you appreciate them.
- Make a list of three places where you can find supportive people who will be excited for you as you level up. Try to choose groups with authors at all levels of career development because you can learn from those further along the path and give a helping hand to those who are following in your footsteps.

15

PUSHING THROUGH IMPOSTER SYNDROME

Sometimes the person heckling you as you travel your path to success isn't someone else. It's you.

Imposter syndrome is the persistent inability to believe that one's success is deserved or has been legitimately achieved as a result of one's own efforts or skills. Basically, despite evidence of your competence (published books, great reviews, etc.) you believe that your success is due to luck, and that you don't deserve what you have achieved. Imposter syndrome also comes with a sense of impending doom: a belief that it is only a matter of time before everyone around you realizes you're a no-talent hack.

This can be particularly troublesome for writers because so much of the writing process happens in our minds. If we don't have confidence in our work, it's harder to put ourselves out there. It's hard to put our butts in the chair. And each new book we write or teaching opportunity we pursue can be a particular kind of torture.

Heightening this insecurity is the fact that everything in publishing is made up of unclear milestones. Yes, you sold a book—but was it to the *right* publishing house? Or was it for *enough* of an advance? Yes, you wrote a 14-book series, but you indie published—so does that really *count?* Yes, you've had sales, but was it enough compared to other books? We constantly measure ourselves against other writers. We measure our words on the page against the exponentially more brilliant story we can see in our minds. And then we question if someone else could have done it better.

One of Crystal's lightbulb moments came when she was sitting in a room with a wide-ranging group of *New York Times* and *USA Today* bestselling authors from different genres, listening to them talk about their insecurities about the books they were writing. Every one of them had published more than 20 books with huge publishing houses and had been making their living purely from writing for decades. And *every single one* of them was openly haunted by *imposter syndrome.* We share this knowledge not to make you feel hopeless that the feeling will ever go away, but to remind you that almost every author feels this—no matter how successful they get. It's just something you have to push through. Understand that while it may come with the career you've chosen, you can't let it stop you from moving forward.

In order to battle your imposter syndrome, you will need to set mile markers along the way so you can see your progress and celebrate the heck out of reaching each milestone—so loudly that your imposter syndrome will hear you and hide out in its dark corner.

We have found it can be helpful to turn your imposter syndrome into a kind of sidekick. Grab your journal, and work through the exercises below.

Your Turn

- Brainstorm a list of all the things you hear in your mind when imposter syndrome kicks in (i.e., *that last book was only a success because… you're not really a writer because…* You get the idea).
- If your imposter syndrome were a sidekick, what would it look like? Give it a physical form. Write a paragraph describing how

big it is, what it looks like, what its voice sounds like. Does it have a smell? When does it appear? Where does it hang out? You can draw it or find a picture online that characterizes it.

- Brainstorm a list of things you can say to your sidekick when you get a whiff of it lurking in the shadows, or when it's outright getting in your way. *(I know you're trying to protect me, but I got this. I know you think I just got lucky, but I worked hard on that book, I know a lot about writing, and I was ready when that opportunity came my way. I get credit for that.)* Try to come up with one statement to counteract each of the statements you brainstormed in the first step—or one that is a suitable reply to them all. Because, let's face it, when the old comments stop, new ones will emerge.

PART II

YOUR BUSINESS

16

REFINING YOUR VISION, MISSION AND VALUES

Everything you decide as you create your specific business plan will be filtered through your vision, mission and values statements. They will act as your guiding light as your business changes and grows, and every opportunity or idea or decision can be weighed according to how well they match your vision, mission and values.

While some people think a vision statement and mission statement are the same, they are actually different in a very important way.

Vision statements

A vision statement, in this case, is a statement of what an author hopes to achieve or become in the future.

> **Vision statement for Eileen's author business:**
> *Eileen Cook inspires and entertains readers, earning a full-time income while preserving time for exploration and learning.*

Vision statement for Crystal's author business:
Crystal Hunt connects with readers around the world by writing in a variety of genres and formats, and lives a well-balanced, full-time creative life that allows her the freedom to pursue her passions.

Vision statement for The Creative Academy Guides for Writers series:
The Creative Academy team creates books that support, assist and excite writers to take the next steps in their writing journeys.

Mission statements

A mission statement describes what you are going to *do* to achieve that vision. While the two statements must support each other, the mission statement is more specific and more directly actionable.

Mission statement for Eileen:
Eileen writes non-fiction designed to assist writers in improving their craft and embracing their creative selves. She writes fictional page-turners that entertain readers and leave them wanting more.

Mission statement for Crystal:
Crystal earns a full-time writing income from her book sales. As CJ Hunt, she writes contemporary romance novels set in Rivers End, a story world that makes everyone feel at home and believe in the possibility of their own happily-ever-afters. As Crystal Hunt, she creates non-fiction books to make writing and indie publishing more approachable and help writers live their dreams.

Mission statement for The Creative Academy's non-fiction books:
Creative Academy Guides for Writers provide valuable advice in an approachable way with prompts that encourage individuals to apply that advice to their own work. These books are entertaining, and they provide information to writers at different levels of their writing journey.

Values statements

And what the heck is a values statement, you ask? A values statement is also called a code of ethics. It makes clear exactly what you believe in and how you are expected to behave along the way. Remember when we asked you to list a few things that are important to you as a person? This is an excellent opportunity to craft a values statement in line with the things you identified in that exercise so that you have a clear moral compass to help guide you through your author business development.

Values statement for Eileen:
Eileen values creativity, opportunities to learn about things that intrigue her and flexibility with time.

Values statement for Crystal:
Crystal values authentic connection with readers, the celebration of diversity and the affordability and accessibility of her stories. Her creative projects foster a spirit of welcoming community.

Values statement for The Creative Academy's non-fiction books:
Creative Academy Guides for Writers do not promise easy answers or indicate that all advice will work for all writers. Our books provide information, ideas and guidance, respecting that each writer will need to craft their own journey depending on their unique self and books.

Now that you know what they are, and you've seen some examples, it's time to craft some statements of your own to help light your way.

Your Turn

- Draft up a vision statement.
- Draft up a mission statement.
- Draft up a values statement.
- Share and discuss these with the key people in your life: family, friends, other authors in your community or critique groups. Get their feedback. Are your statements clear? Is your mission statement actionable?
- When you are comfortable with your final versions, put them into your business plan document, print them off and post them somewhere you can easily refer to them whenever you reach a decision point in your career.

17

ACKNOWLEDGING IT'S A BUSINESS

Make no mistake: if you want a full-time career as an author, you need to accept that you are a business owner. You are also likely the marketing department, finance and payroll, the CEO and everything else, at least until you get to the point where you can hire people to give you a hand.

Don't shy away from the business side of things. Knowledge about exactly what is going on financially in your author business translates to power: the ability to make smart, informed decisions about every aspect of your career development. We've found there is a tendency among authors to focus on the stories and not pay as much attention to the bottom line, but this can make it hard to properly plan goals and set budgets. If you're not on top of your finances, you won't be able to stay in the business for the long haul.

The more you know about your business, the more efficiently you will take care of your "admin" responsibilities and get back to the good stuff —which is writing your books and connecting with your readers.

What kind of business structure is best for you?

You will need to decide what kind of an author business you want to run. The obvious answer here is a successful one (amen to that!) but you will need to decide that from a legal and tax perspective as well. We're not accountants or lawyers, and the costs, benefits and requirements of different types of business structures are different in each province, state and country, so it's important to talk to qualified advisors in your own area.

But when you approach your research for this, you might want to ask questions like:

- What kind of business structure is right for me in my current situation? (Think sole proprietor, partnership, limited liability corporation, etc.)
- How difficult, time-consuming, and expensive is it to change this business structure if I pass a certain income threshold or if my circumstances change?
- How much revenue would the business need to generate, or what type of operations would need to be part of the business, in order to prompt a change in business structure?
- What are the paperwork and accounting requirements for the type of business structure being suggested? Will the benefits outweigh the costs?
- Is a business license required in my municipality?

As in every area of your planning, the goal is to keep things as simple as possible while making it as easy as you can on your future self. Asking questions ahead of time and understanding the implications of your decisions will help you know when the time is right to make a change.

Set up a system to keep track of your important business-related documents. These may include:

- Business registration or business name registration
- Incorporation or partnership documents

- Tax forms, publishing contracts, W8-BEN forms or other legal documents
- Worksafe assessments
- Business license
- Copyright documentation

This system doesn't have to be complicated or elaborate. In fact, simple systems are often the most effective. The best record-keeping systems are the ones that you will use 100 percent of the time. This may be a Google Drive folder, a set of paper folders you keep in your desk drawer, a system of digital folders on your computer or any combination thereof.

Your Turn

- What kind of business structure do you currently have?
- Is it serving your needs right now?
- When was the last time you consulted a professional about this? If it's been more than a year and your business circumstances or income have changed significantly, you may want to book another consultation.
- What professionals do you have access to for information and advice on business matters? Is there a small business advisory group in your area that offers free help?
- If your business is already set up, do you have all the relevant operating documents in one easy-to-find location? If not, take some time to collect them all up now and put them together in one place.

18

MANAGING YOUR FINANCES

You will need a bank account to receive your royalties—ideally one that is separate from your personal finances. If your business is ever audited, it will be much cleaner and clearer if your business and personal accounts are separate. This does not necessarily mean you need to register a legal name for your business or set up a formal type of business structure. Just having a separate bank account in your name, or a separate credit card that you use only for business-related expenses, will make your bookkeeping easier and clearer.

You will need somewhere to store digital and physical receipts, and some kind of system for tracking income and expenses so you can accurately and confidently do your taxes at the end of each year. The tools you choose for this will depend on your comfort with technology and the size and complexity of your author business. Wave Accounting is a good app, and it is free at the time of writing. Quickbooks Online is a paid tool, and many accountants prefer clients work with that.

If you have an accountant or bookkeeper already, make sure to ask them how they would like to receive the information from you. This will save you time and money!

Tools:

- Separate or sub-account of your regular bank account where royalties are deposited
- A file folder for physical receipts
- A Dropbox or Google Drive folder—or an accounting app or program—for storing digital receipts
- A spreadsheet or free cloud accounting program to track income and expenses

If you are using the Business Plan Google Sheet there are calculators built in to help you track income, expenses, and how much you should be setting aside for tax time. The tutorial video linked from the instruction page of the spreadsheet will show you how all of this works.

Your Turn

- Do you have a system to track your income and expenses for your writing business?
- If yes, and it includes all the components you need, then skip to the next section.
- If no, review the list above and decide what tools you will use to keep track of income and expenses as your author business grows with each new release.

19

PLANNING FOR TAXES

In a typical day job, your employer deducts a portion of your wages to pay for Employment Insurance and income taxes each month. As a self-employed person, all that becomes your responsibility. You need to make sure you are setting aside an appropriate amount of income to cover your taxes. Most experts recommend setting aside 25 to 30 percent of your total income for taxes. If you're in a lower tax bracket, you may not have to use it all come tax time. If that's the case, you'll have a nest egg to seed your business growth budget for the coming year.

As your income grows, you will need to consult a qualified accountant or financial advisor who can help you make smart decisions about how to manage your income. The key here is understanding that taxes will come due, and you don't want to be caught short and scrambling when they do.

Occasionally, a book will "hit," or you'll get a large advance. If you know you have a significant income change—up or down—coming within a few months, it's wise to chat with your accountant. You may be able to make a relatively quick change to your business structure, and you may save yourself time and money by having the conversation before the payouts are made.

This is especially important if you are working with publishers or companies in other countries and dealing with cross-border payouts and tax forms. Sometimes paperwork takes a little time to process, so give yourself some breathing room.

Your Turn

- Set up a sub-account or another system to help you regularly set aside money for your taxes when they come due.
- Each month, when you enter your income and expenses, transfer a percentage of your royalties into your savings account for taxes.
- Review your business structure annually with your accountant, lawyer or financial planner to ensure you are on the right path.
- Keep an eye on your royalties and income. Do you anticipate any big changes in the next few months? If yes, make an appointment to talk to your accountant about possible tax implications now.

20

PLANNING FOR EMERGENCIES

No one want to think about emergencies, but they come up. You can call in sick to an ordinary day job, and there's an HR department to deal with staffing issues and a management team to respond to a crisis. As a writer, you may be on your own. If you have an agent or business partner, you will have someone to help you brainstorm an approach to crisis, but ultimately, it will be your responsibility to decide on a course of action.

While you can't prevent an emergency from happening, considering possible scenarios in advance allows you to prepare.

- What if you get sick or hurt and can't write or manage your writing business for a while?
- What if you have to alter your plans because you're taking care of a sick pet, spouse, kid or parent?
- What if someone sues you?
- What if you get trashed in social media?
- What if… you die?

Here are ideas to help you prepare for emergencies:

- Assemble a strong support team that can help you brainstorm challenges when they come up and give you the benefit of their experience. This team may include friends, your agent, and fellow writers.
- Consider having a team of experts you can call on as needed. Even if you do your own bookkeeping, get a name of an accountant you (or someone else) could go to if necessary. Rather than waiting until you need a lawyer, do some research when there's no stress to identify who has experience with the publishing industry.
- Identify a close friend or family member who knows where you keep your assets and information so they can make some contacts on your behalf.
- Identify a literary executor in your will who has the responsibility of managing your book assets after your death.

We originally included this discussion in the Rewriting Your Author Career section of this book. But honestly, if you leave your emergency planning for when you need it, it's coming too late. It's in the early stages that this work is most beneficial. And if you incorporate business planning and documentation into your process now, you will know that as your business grows, you are prepared to deal with whatever comes up.

Advance planning will help relieve some of the stress and anxiety that can come from running your own business.

Are you struggling with this, or feeling a lot of anxiety as you read? It can help to distance yourself. Try writing your what-ifs and instructions in the third person.

For example:

What if CJ Hunt were ill for several weeks and unable to schedule newsletters or social media?

If this happened, someone would need to be recruited or hired to help. Ask for referrals from The Creative Academy community or call Eileen Cook (author friend) who can help find someone to take this on.

Crystal's support person would need:

- *Login information for the newsletter service CJ uses*
- *Login information for the social media accounts*
- *Branded image templates found in CANVA*

This information could be found in PasswordManager, and Jared Hunt has access to that online account. It is also stored in the safety deposit box.

The easiest way plan for emergencies is to brainstorm a what-if list of worst-case scenarios. From there, you can figure out how to prepare for them—or mitigate the risk of them happening at all. These plans will effectively become your table of contents for your ICE (in case of emergency) book, so be as thorough as you can manage.

You won't come up with all your answers at once, but you can add to your index and sections as you work through and implement your business planning. New issues will arise at each stage of career growth. As part of your annual review of your business plan, review what has changed in the past year and make sure your ICE book is up to date.

Your Turn

- Start a binder, file folder, Google Doc or digital file. Label it *In Case of Emergency*.
- Start a what-if list at the front of your ICE book. You can use some of the suggestions from earlier in this section to get you started. But the more you tailor your what-if list to your own circumstances, the more effective this tool will be.

- Start a section to go with each what-if.
- Tell at least two other people you trust where this book can be found if something happens to you and you are incapacitated.

21

CREATING A BUSINESS PLAN

At this point you might be wondering, "Do I really need a full-on business plan? I mean, the plan is to write books, sell them, and cash royalty cheques. Isn't it?"

Well, sort of.

Those are all components of a successful author career. But there's a whole lot more to it than that. And the efficiency and frequency with which you do those things—as well as the size of those cheques—will likely be more impressive if you are clear and strategic about your goals, priorities, and bottom line.

Hopefully you downloaded the Full Time Author Your Turn Workbook when we gave you the link earlier in this book. But just in case you missed it—or, you know, thought you could get away with ignoring that line—we'll wait for a second while you download it now.

The main sections in this workbook include:

- **About You:** why you're the ideal person to run this business and what skills you have (you already tackled this in the previous section)

- **Your Business:** what kind of business structure you'll use, how to handle your records and bookkeeping, what kind of author business model you are working with
- **Your Budget:** a breakdown of anticipated costs and revenues, financing for your projects and business growth, and income expectations and projections
- **Your Author Brand:** the elements that comprise your unique author brand, your values as an author, how readers and peers feel about you and your business
- **Your Market:** facts about your target market (your readers), where and how you can reach them, your distribution model to reach that market, and your pricing models
- **Your Products:** your books, your catalogue of intellectual property assets, your production schedule for your books in various formats, and additional products and services you offer
- **Your Marketing Plan:** how you will make readers aware of your books, opportunities for advertising and promotion, how you will grow your audience
- **Opportunities for Growth:** opportunities that may come your way this year, how you will evaluate which ones are "worth it," and how you will grow and maintain professional networks
- **Rewriting Your Career** (otherwise known as Plan B or Risk Management): what to do if things don't go according to plan, and options if you need a reboot

Your business plan should address the bigger picture of your business. If you're using the Business Plan Google Sheet alongside the workbook, you'll also have additional tabs for tracking various activities and financial information, which we'll introduce and refer to throughout the book. Don't worry, we'll tackle each one in turn.

Are you worried about committing to a specific plan when you're not even sure what you don't know yet? Don't panic if you're not able to nail down every detail at this stage. You're still the boss. Which means you can pivot anytime you need to. And some decisions won't be necessary until the opportunity is right in front of you.

For now, we'll hold your virtual hand and walk you through every section as you figure out your answers to the most important questions. Since each section in the book directly maps to a corresponding section in your business plan, by the time you get to the end of the book, you'll have a completed business plan too!

22

CHOOSING AN AUTHOR BUSINESS MODEL

There are several different kinds of business models for authors. Knowing what pieces to include in yours will help you put together a plan that will focus your efforts.

While researching author business models, we came across a number of different breakdowns, approaches and descriptions. We've done our best here to distill those into one field—writing and publishing—and four possible add-on categories that you can layer and combine in your business model as you like.

Diversify your income stream. Being a full-time author means being a freelancer. Teaching, non-fiction, short stories, novels... all of these are different income streams. Aim for the ones that don't eat your story brain.

— Mary Robinette Kowal, author of *The Calculating Stars*

Writing and publishing (the base)

In this type of business model, income is generated solely from writing and publishing activities. While of course you will be doing more than just writing and publishing—we've included some marketing stuff on the publishing side of things—you will be focused on producing content and selling it, either directly to your audience or to a publisher that will then sell to your audience.

There are different approaches you can take inside this business model, but the key piece is your focus on producing more content. This focus is fixed regardless of whether that content is indie or traditionally published; released wide (to all eBook retailers) or exclusive (to one platform, usually Amazon); or published in multiple formats through multiple platforms. Your primary focus is on writing more and publishing more to generate income.

+ Teaching

Teaching can be a great way to supplement income from your writing and publishing activities. It can also be a great marketing tool for non-fiction writers who teach in the same subject areas as their books. While some teaching gigs are not paid, many are. And there are many different teaching settings and formats: one-on-one consulting, coaching and mentorship as well as group-based workshops, seminars and online courses or membership-based learning communities.

+ Patronage

In this business model, writing and publishing are combined with additional income from patronage of some kind. This could include paid membership sites with exclusive content for fans, grants, fellowships, sponsorships and awards with cash prizes. You can also use sites like Patreon.com to get consistent, monthly income directly from fans who want to keep you in mac and cheese so you will keep creating content they love.

+ Writing-related income

If you maintain a blog, you can supplement your income with money from affiliate referrals. Writing-related income can also come from leading a community, teaching or coaching other writers and through the marketing efforts on your own books. You may generate revenue from ads that appear on your website or blog if you are sharing content with the world. Or you may contract to do writing unrelated to your specific interests or pursuits, such as writing website copy for an organization or ghostwriting a book.

+ Non-writing income

It's a legit strategy to include a business model where your income is not entirely dependent on your writing and publishing income. Especially in the beginning, this can ensure sustainability as you build your career. You could fund yourself if you inherited some money, won the lottery or just kept your day job either full- or part-time. A spouse or family member may be helping to pay your household bills so you can grow your career without drawing income from your writing business.

Keep in mind that your business model will likely change over the course of your career. Both Crystal and Eileen have used a combination of *all* these elements and have employed a variety of business models over time. If you stay flexible and open to changes as needed and desired, you will be better able to sustain your career over time. We do recommend that you review your business model as part of your business planning process each year.

Your Turn

It's time to decide which of these business models is the best fit for you at the current time. Scan the models above and answer the following questions:

- How are you *currently* generating your revenue? Note any current sources of income you are tapping into.
- Is this the business model you want to stay with? Or are you hoping to make some changes to your business model?
- If you want to make some changes, scan the models again.
- Are any of the items on the list a *Hell, yes*?
- Are any of the items on the list a *Hell, no*?
- What business model would you like to work your way toward in the future?
- What business model can you work with *this* year?

23

CHOOSING A PUBLICATION PATH

In the past, if you wanted to become a published author, you needed to either go through a traditional publisher or, as a self-published author, pay out a huge chunk of cash and then sell the several cases of books sitting in your garage. But with the emergence of eBooks, e-retailers and publish-on-demand options, writers can now choose their publishing model from plenty of options suited to every personality and budget.

Traditional publishing

In this model, the author grants rights for a publishing company to publish their work for a period of time. The author signs a contract detailing what rights (e.g., North American, world English, foreign, film, audio) are held by the publisher, how long they hold those rights, royalty rates and manuscript due dates, among other things. The author works with an acquiring editor to shape and polish the manuscript. The publisher is responsible for all costs: editorial, cover design, marketing and promotion. They may or may not pay an advance to the author, but they will pay out royalties as per the contract, often twice a year depending on sales.

Self or indie publishing

Before we even discuss what this model looks like, we need to discuss this term. Self-publishing, or indie publishing, has different definitions. In one, the author performs all the steps of publication themselves. In another, the author directs their publishing choices but may hire out different aspects of the process. Some people use only the term self-publishing; others call it indie. In our book, we prefer the term indie publishing and describe the author as being in control of the *process* but not necessarily doing all aspects.

In this model, the author is responsible for all costs of the publishing process including cover, marketing and editorial. However, they retain full rights to the manuscript. Their royalties for sales depend on agreements with their chosen retailing outlets, such as Amazon, iBooks and Kobo. These e-retailers typically pay royalties monthly, but there is generally a two-month delay between when the book is sold and when the author receives the royalties. The author may choose to perform all parts of the process themselves, or they may contract for these services. If you're going to take indie publishing on, we highly recommend listening your way through the Strategic Authorpreneur podcast episodes (free!) which can be found at strategicauthorpreneur.com and reading the two Creative Academy guides that dig into the business side of indie publishing: *Strategic Indie Author* and *Strategic Series Author* by Crystal Hunt.

Hybrid publishing

In this model, the author selects traditional or indie for different projects. For example, Eileen has typically traditionally published her fiction, but she has chosen to indie publish her non-fiction. Crystal has indie published her romance fiction, some of her non-fiction has been indie published, and some of her children's books (fiction and non-fiction) were contracted with an educational publisher.

Authors may also traditionally publish their work and then, when the rights expire with the traditional publisher, revert these rights to themselves and indie publish those titles. And indie published authors may sell print rights or foreign rights to traditional publishers if their sales are solid enough.

Once you know these different publishing models, you can choose which are best for you *at this time*. We encourage writers to constantly check in and evaluate if their career plan is working for them, and to make adjustments or updates to their plans as circumstances change.

Regardless of which route you take, there are steps that are the same. These include:

- Research
- Writing
- Revisions (edits and copy edits)
- Promotion
- Social media management
- Book resource management (audio rights, foreign, etc.)
- Business management (digital resources, accounting, etc.)

Oh—you thought being a full-time author meant all you had to do was write? Nope. If that were the case, we would have called this book *Full Time Writer* instead of *Full Time Author*. Building a successful career takes so much more than writing the books. That's the cornerstone around which all the rest is built, but you have to address the business side of things as well.

How do you know if you should go traditional, indie or hybrid? There is no right or wrong answer here. What matters is that you choose the path that is the best fit for you in the current moment. But there are some questions you can ask yourself to help you decide the next step in your journey, and we've included them in the Your Turn section below.

Your Turn

In order to choose your publication path for right now—understanding that you may change direction later—journal on the following questions.

- When I think about the business aspects of publishing (like cover creation, layout, marketing and advertising), I feel…
- The parts of the publishing process I enjoy most include…
- When I think about the need to stay current on business trends and technical requirements, I feel…
- After reviewing the different forms of publishing above, my first reaction to each of the models is…
- When I ask others about my skills and abilities and the different forms of publishing, they say…
- Choose one of the models at random and assume for a moment that is your decision. What is your immediate reaction to that idea? Now work your way through each of the others.

24

EVALUATING YOUR BUSINESS WITH A SWOT ANALYSIS

If you've worked in the professional world, you've likely heard the term SWOT analysis. Many businesses do this on a regular basis or when considering expansion, and we think it's a perfect addition to your annual business planning and to your planning for any kind of growth.

SWOT refers to *strengths, weaknesses, opportunities* and *threats*. It's a way of determining next steps by considering not just yourself, as you did in the self-evaluation, but also the environment you're operating within.

Strengths

What strengths do you have in combination with your business?

Above, we asked you to think about the strengths *you* bring to the table. But it's also important to think about the strengths of your overall business model and how you work as the CEO of your own company. It's important to identify those strengths so you can build on them—and rely on them when things are challenging.

Different approaches have different strengths. For example, if you are leaning toward teaching on a part-time basis while you write, a strength may be that you have a reliable income that allows you to pay for advertising. Going with an indie approach means that you can change your cover with limited lead time if you want to capitalize on a trend. A traditional model has the strength of a built-in team with experience.

Consider how your individual strengths fit with the business model and publishing model you're pursuing. If you have read the biography of Steve Jobs, you know he was a complicated individual. But there is little doubt that he was the perfect CEO of Apple. His flexibility of thought and focus on quality made him excel in his job and helped take that company to new heights. If he had been CEO of a more traditional company like Microsoft, he likely would have been less effective. In fact, there was a time when the Apple board replaced him because they thought he was too comfortable with risks, but they ended up bringing him back.

Weaknesses

What weaknesses exist in the business and publishing models you've chosen?

Every model has strengths, but it also has weaknesses. And every asset has a flip side that presents a weakness to be addressed and overcome. For example, let's look at genre. A strength of writing in romance is that romance readers are voracious—they read and buy books at a fast pace. A corresponding weakness, however, is that readers want a lot of books, and this puts pressure on the creator to provide fresh content on a regular basis. And romance readers often don't want to pay as much per book because they are consuming so much content.

Review the weaknesses of the approach you've selected. For example, if you are leaning toward full-time writing as your primary income source, a weakness will be the possible variation in income and the challenges this presents for financial planning. If instead you're considering a traditional route, a weakness will be that royalties are typically paid out only twice a year. Look at the unique mix you've selected as your ideal approach, note what weaknesses exist and consider how you will adapt and cope with these.

Also look at the intersection between your own skills and your business model. What do you bring as the CEO? What will challenge you? For example, while Crystal loves learning about new advertising strategies, Eileen tends to get quickly frustrated. She knows that understanding new and different advertising approaches is important in an ever-changing industry. However, she can quickly feel overwhelmed, which means she may not be as prepared for a change or as able to quickly take advantage of a shift. To be a successful CEO of her business, which includes some indie publishing, Eileen needs to identify this weakness and create a plan to address it. (Part of this plan is to supply her good friend Crystal with a lot of chocolate so that Crystal will continue to help her.)

Opportunities

What opportunities exist to grow your business?

It's very important to identify opportunities for growth—both for you as a creator, and for your business. If you're bored, you won't feel motivated. And unless you have some killer habits in place and the ability to ignore that boredom, a lack of motivation will start to erode both your productivity and the quality of your product.

Keep in mind that growth opportunities can look very different depending on your business model. If your business model is focused on book sales, then anything you can do to increase the quality and quantity of your writing will contribute to growth. This could mean hiring a housekeeper, renting an office space if there are too many distractions at home, or writing with a co-author. If your ideal author career includes more paid teaching time, then growth in that area will look very different.

We recommend brainstorming ideas about how to promote growth in all areas of your business mentioned above—including honing your skills! But remember: it's only true growth if it doesn't break your existing business flow. Be sure to evaluate each idea through the lens of what will multiply your results in the most efficient way based on your business model of choice. We tackle how to evaluate "opportunities" and add to your team effectively later on in this book.

Several things lead to opportunities:

Changes in the industry

We've talked above about how publishing is always changing—eBooks come in, advertising models shift, audiobooks become more popular, podcasts come into being. And who knows what is around the corner.

Changes in you

You're always in motion, developing new skills and interests. As you "level up" in the business, people will invite you to participate in opportunities that hadn't been available to you before.

Your network

Knowing more people puts you in a position to discover opportunities that are not publicly known.

Luck and chance

Someone once told Eileen that *writing is a craft, but publishing is a casino.* There is a real element of truth to this. There will be opportunities that pop up out of nowhere when you least expect them.

The successful full-time author keeps themselves open and aware so that when an opportunity presents itself, they can evaluate it—and seize it. And if they don't, they have a network of people to share that opportunity with. Because, as we've already established, sharing is caring.

Note: We dig much deeper into the *how* of leveling up each area of your business model in the section titled Leveling Up Your Author Career.

Threats (challenges)

If we're honest, we prefer the term *challenges* over *threats*. Threats sound like zombies, whereas challenges sound like something to face down and conquer. (Sure, you could face down a zombie, but it seems wiser to make a run for it.)

Challenges, like opportunities, come up for many of the same reasons. Both you and the publishing industry are changing, and for every opportunity, the opposite side of the coin is a threat or challenge. There is also an element of bad luck that rears its head and puts roadblocks in your way.

And, like opportunities—you'll be noticing a trend by now—challenges require the strategic full-time author to be aware. The sooner that you see a challenge coming, the easier it will be to respond to it. Keeping your head up means you're a lot more likely to see a hit coming. (As a US-to-Canada transplant, Eileen is very impressed with herself for making this hockey analogy.)

Your Turn

- Generate a list of pros and cons for the approach you've decided to take for your author business. What strengths are inherent in your model? What are the potential weaknesses?
- Write a letter to the universe explaining why you are the perfect choice to be CEO of your author business. What strengths do you bring? Why are you the right fit for this model? What weaknesses will you need to cope with, and how will you adapt for them?
- One way to identify opportunities and challenges in the future is to look back and see how they presented themselves in the past. Look back at your career to date and identify an opportunity you seized. When did you become aware of it? How did you respond? What would you do differently? Now do the same with a challenge in your past.

- Talk to other authors and listen to podcast YouTube interviews with other authors. What SWOT elements do they talk about on their own author journeys? Are any of those relevant to you?

PART III

YOUR MARKET

25

WRITING TO MARKET

Most likely you've heard the phrase "write to market" before—possibly hundreds of times, depending on how long you've been writing and publishing. While in some circles people use this phrase with a vague (or not so vague) reference to "selling out," we think the *selling* part is key. If your goal is to sell more books, generate more income from your writing and create a long-term and stable career as an author, then you want to write books that your readers love and that sell well in your chosen market.

This does *not* mean you need to sacrifice your personal principles, give up on good storytelling or sell your soul to the masses in exchange for a payday. It just means that you do a little research, and when you are making choices along the way, you can choose the option that is most likely to make you happy, your readers happy and your agent happy, generating the best possible return on your hours—or years—invested.

For example, if you know that readers in your chosen genre expect that the protagonist earns a happy ending, or that the villain is brought to justice, or that the question of whodunnit is answered—delivering on that expectation is the key to having them leave a great review, tell their friends how much they loved the book, and rush to buy the next one.

This does not mean chasing trends. If you hear that vampire books are hot, that doesn't mean you drop everything and add some bloodsuckers to your manuscript. If you're traditionally published, the trend may be played out by the time your book is ready to hit shelves 18 months later, even if you write like the wind. In indie publishing, you're able to respond more quickly to trends, but you still need to ask yourself the important question: Is this a trend I want to follow?

To build a career that lasts, make sure you are writing in a genre or genres that you love. It's rare to find a really successful author who doesn't read the genre they write in. You will write a better book if you enjoy the research! You need to know the expectations and popular tropes of your genre—what's been done and where the opportunities are. You will write better books if you have a solid understanding of the story arcs and literary conventions. If you're going the traditional route, knowing where your book would fit in the market will also help you identify agents and publishers that might be a good fit for your book.

> *Make time to READ. Reading makes us better writers. The more widely and diversely and licentiously you read, the richer your own words will be.*
>
> — KC DYER, AUTHOR OF *EIGHTY DAYS TO ELSEWHERE* AND *FINDING FRASER*

And if you are going to be a daredevil and break with reader expectations, make sure you do it consciously and with great deliberation. The more your book varies from the expectations of your genre, the bigger the risk that your readers may not love it, and the harder it will be to find the perfect readership.

We're not saying don't innovate—just be aware that if you choose to push the envelope, you will have your work cut out for you. Often, you'll need to allow more time to build up your stable of true fans, and in traditional publishing, that can make it harder to find the right agent and publisher for your book.

26

IDENTIFYING YOUR READERS

Identifying your readers is hugely important. If you know who your readers are, you can start to pinpoint what they expect from your stories, where they hang out, how best to market to them, what price point they expect in a purchase, what formats they like to read in and what kinds of stories will keep them coming back for more.

In this section, we're going to walk you through a few activities to help you identify your readers, create an avatar of your perfect reader, and introduce you to a few sources of data that will help you analyze your market and learn who exactly it is that you'll be writing *to*.

And yes, doing this market research is going to take some work. But if you do it (and don't cut corners), the process of figuring out your genre expectations will serve you very well and help make every decision that follows easier. It will also make it easier to sell your books because you'll know how to find readers and where to position your work.

What is your genre?

You absolutely need to know your genre. Whether you are indie publishing or pitching to a traditional publisher, it is essential to know where your books fit in the bookstore or in what category or subcategory they would be found on an online retail site. And for each genre, readers have expectations about what kind of story they're getting when they pick up a book.

What is your subgenre?

Knowing that you write thrillers, or mysteries, or romances isn't enough. You need to dig deep into the subgenre that makes the most sense for you. A medical thriller and a legal thriller are going to be very different books. There are strict conventions about how much detail to include about a murder in a cozy mystery, or how much swearing you can have in a wholesome inspirational romance. (*Hint:* None.) And a gay historical romance is going to have very different reader expectations than a paranormal romantic suspense. You need to dig all the way in and really narrow it down.

If you are writing genre fiction of some kind, it's best to focus on a specific genre for at least one book—and hopefully several—if you're planning the most efficient way to scale up your career. Be aware that if you write in several genres or subgenres, you will need to do market research for *each one*.

Your Turn

- In what genre are you writing?
- In what subgenre are you writing?

27

SIZING UP YOUR AUDIENCE

This is one area where size *does* matter. If you plan to make a living from your writing, consider the size of your market and the competitiveness of your niche. The good news? If the niche you've chosen has a smaller audience, that's not a terrible thing. It means you will know exactly who your readers are and you can make sure you dial your content right into them. However, if you have set specific—and high—income goals, you will need to confirm if there are enough readers in your niche to support that. If not, you may need to consider writing in another genre or subgenre, adjusting your income goals, or putting together a plan to find more readers. (*Hint:* This last one is *hard*).

In the traditional publishing world, NPD BookScan (formerly Nielsen BookScan in the USA, and still Nielsen BookScan in many areas outside the US) is a good source of data for publishing trends and sales numbers.

You can also get some insight into how many books are being sold in a particular category on Amazon, and how much money is potentially being earned, by using a tool like Publisher Rocket. These tools let you peek inside a category or book's estimated sales. While their results are estimates only and do not include all formats of the books or all markets, they do give you a peek into how certain categories or subgenres are performing on Amazon at least.

And if you really want to dig into the data and analytics of a particular subgenre, then K-lytics is a gold mine of information.

K-lytics is a website run by Alex Newton, and the tag line is *ebook market intelligence for success.* They have a wide range of market reports on different subgenres based on Amazon sales data. Some reports are free, and others require a small fee. But if you're serious about making your living from book sales and choosing between various genres or subgenres that interest you, it doesn't hurt to learn which ones are more likely to be profitable and check out your competition. The detailed reports include cover comparisons, keywords and subcategories, blurbs from the top 100 books in a subgenre and more. It's a fantastic way to understand the market without gathering all that info from scratch.

Your Turn

- Do some research and see what information you can gather about audience size. How big is the market for your genre and subgenre?

28

GETTING TO KNOW YOUR READERS

Do you have any demographic information about your typical reader? What age group is most likely to read your books? Is there a specific income bracket, demographic or level of education you can expect? What does the average day look like for your reader? Are your books for working professionals? Children? Busy moms with toddlers at home? Career women looking for an escape from their day? Thrill-seeking adventure junkies? How many books do they read per day? Per week? Per year?

> *Don't try to please everyone with your story. Pick one person you want to please (this can be yourself) and write for that person alone.*
>
> — Laura Bradbury, bestselling author of the Grape Series

Can you construct an image in your head—or find one in a magazine or online—who represents your ideal reader?

If you're not sure who your readers are, can you ask them some questions directly through email or social media? What kind of data do you have access to through your mailing list stats or regional sales numbers? You should look for information about:

- Location
- Age
- Gender
- Income
- Educational level
- Religion
- Ethnicity
- Marital status
- Number of children

While you may not be able to answer all of these questions up front, especially if you are at the earlier stages of your career, answer as many questions as you can. And if you can't get your own data by reaching out to your readers through your mailing list or social networks, reach out to your author network and ask if you can buy an hour of someone's time who writes in your niche to talk about some of their audience demographics.

If you don't have access to any of the options we mentioned before, then you can enter your website (if you get a lot of traffic) or the websites of a few well-established authors with similar genre targets into the search bar at Alexa.com and see what information you get. While ongoing access is pricey, at the time of writing there is a free trial. If you know what info you want, you can probably get what you need within the free trial period.

29

GIVING READERS WHAT THEY WANT

What are the expectations of readers in your genre when it comes to story conventions?

Read a lot in your genre and look for patterns. What elements must you always have in your story? What must you never have? What are deal breakers to your audience?

What point of view are the books written in? Are there usually multiple POV characters, or is the story told from a single protagonist's point of view? If you are writing a murder mystery, does your subgenre usually include the villain's POV or just the main character's? Are most of the bestselling books in your genre written in first-person POV? Third-person POV? If there is a mix, make a note of that, and you can go with your own preferences.

What elements do you want to include in your story that might be interesting, different or original? Will these break any of your genre conventions?

Join a writer's group that is specifically focused on your genre. Now that the whole world has gone virtual, you can choose from online groups all over the world!

Consult those genre-specific resources, and if you aren't sure about something, put it out to the group to weigh in on.

The best way to find answers to all these questions is to read a lot in your specific niche and figure out what people are consistently doing and not doing. Read the top ten or 20 books in your subcategory as a starting place. If you are indie publishing and going Amazon exclusive, be sure to check the top charts on Amazon for titles. If you're going wide, check the other stores—Kobo, Barnes & Noble, and the *USA Today* and *New York Times* bestseller lists—to see your competition. If you are traditionally publishing, you will likely want to check those wide sources since most traditionally published books are not exclusive to Amazon.

Then read their reviews. What do the negative reviews focus on? What do the positive ones highlight?

Once you know what your readers expect, you can create a checklist for yourself and use it to review your manuscript and make sure you've hit all the highlights, and avoided any deal breakers!

Your Turn

- What are the expectations of readers in that genre when it comes to story conventions?
- What must you always have?
- What must you never have?

30

DECIDING THE LENGTH OF YOUR BOOKS

Writing to market means learning your genre conventions and sticking to them. Or, if you're going to be a daredevil and break the rules, it means understanding the consequences and doing it on purpose!

Even though digital publishing gives you more freedom to publish books no matter how hefty they might be in print, readers have learned that certain types of stories come in standard lengths. For the most part, they will expect your books to conform to those standard lengths.

Here are standard word counts for different genres:

- Commercial and literary fiction: 80–110,000
- Sci-fi and fantasy: 100–115,000
- Romance: category romances 40–55,000; full length 80–100,000
- Middle Grade: 20–55,000
- Young adult: 55–75,000
- Mystery: 75–100,000
- Thriller: 85–100,000
- Memoir: 80–90,000
- Western: 45–75,000

These are rough numbers, and it's important to know they may shift. It's also important, if you are writing something shorter than the standard in your genre, to establish this clearly for readers.

Just as there are genre expectations about how long your books will be, there are standard terms in the book industry that identify a story's length. Here are some standard terms and word counts you can use to classify your story and communicate what to expect to your readers:

- Short story: less than 7,500
- Novelette: between 7,500 and 17,500
- Novella: between 17,500 and 40,000
- Novel: more than 40,000

Your Turn

- What length (or word count) are books in your genre and subgenre?
- What words or labels would you indicate those lengths to your readers?

31

UNDERSTANDING READER BEHAVIOUR

What formats do your readers prefer?

Are your readers into audiobooks? Large-print editions? eBooks only? Do they consume more than one book a week—or even a day—and read only on e-readers? Maybe they love paper books but mostly buy paperbacks, or only hardcover. You need to know what formats of your books your readers are buying so you can release your books in those formats and market to your existing audience with most success.

Where are readers getting their books?

If your readers are mostly older folks on fixed incomes who get their books from libraries and prefer to read eBooks, that is going to change the way you market your books. For example, you'll want to make sure your eBook distribution channels include libraries.

Are your readers mostly reading through companies that offer subscription services like Kindle Unlimited, Kobo Plus or Scribd?

Do you have a large fan base in certain countries? What information do you have about where your books sell well?

How often are readers reading and buying new books?

Do you know how many books per day, week or month your audience reads? This is a great question to ask your list! The good news is that when your readers read more than you can provide, it's a great opportunity to try collaborative marketing, do newsletter swaps and guide readers to deals and discounts on other books like yours. If readers are only reading a book a month, they can probably afford to pay more for each book and are more likely to purchase books outright. If you are targeting readers who read a book (or more!) per day, then your audience is likely taking advantage of libraries and subscription services.

How do readers find out about what books to read next?

Are your readers on social media? Do they prefer to review books on Goodreads or find their next book on LibraryThing? Are they members of book clubs? Do they like to read in transit?

Do your readers get book referrals from friends? Do they buy whatever is on the bargain rack at Indigo or on sale on Amazon? Are they reading in Kindle Unlimited and responding to Amazon's recommendations on what they should read next based on their buying history?

The more you know about your audience, the better able you will be to put your efforts into the right kinds of marketing.

Your Turn

- How do your readers find their books?
- In what formats do your readers prefer to consume their books?
- How many books per week, month or year do your readers consume?
- Through what platforms do your readers buy books?
- Do your readers use libraries and subscription services?

32

BUILDING YOUR READER PERSONA

Many authors find it helpful to envision an actual person reading their book so that when they make decisions along the way they have a very clear picture of who they are talking to. You may have seen these described as reader personas or reader avatars. Basically, you're just trying to turn the amorphous idea of an "audience" into something—or someone—tangible.

Your Turn

- Take the answers to the questions above and write up a reader persona—or personas if you write in different genres or have a split audience.
- Write a paragraph describing your ideal reader and then find an image (or two) online to represent them. When you're ready to make a decision about your story, look at that description. Would that ideal reader say *Hell, yes!* to your decision?

- If you have identified more than one target group, develop a persona for each. For example, if you write YA, you will have some teen readers and some adult readers, so it's helpful to acknowledge those two groups separately.
- Once you have your written summary, give them a name (we'll call her Sara for now), find an image that you think represents your ideal reader and put it somewhere visible near your workstation. Anytime you aren't sure what choice to make, ask yourself: What would Sara say?

If you're struggling with this, we have a recorded masterclass available in The Creative Academy for Writers that will help walk you through the process.

Once you have filled in the Your Market section of your business plan, you're ready to get up, stretch your legs, gaze out the window for a minute, refill your beverage, and move on to the Your Products section.

PART IV

YOUR PRODUCTS

33

VALUING YOUR STORIES

More than anything else, it's the books that matter. They are the heart and soul of your publishing business.

Go ahead. Take time to highlight that sentence. It's an important one. Between publishing, promotion, reader outreach, social media engagement and public speaking gigs, it can be easy to forget that your main products—the things that actually keep your customers coming back for more—are your books. And they are at the centre of every author business model.

In order to effectively manage your author business, you need to be very clear on the kinds of books you write, how long it takes you to write them, what formats your books are published in, where they are sold and for how much money, how much of that revenue you get to keep, and how they are received by readers.

Yes, your books are also your creative darlings. But once they hit the marketplace, it's no longer about how you felt when you created them or what you hoped they'd do when they went off into the world. It's about whether or not people are buying them.

Your books are your products, and they are for sale.

Your Turn

- What kinds of books do you write?
- What is your goal with your books? Why do you write that kind of book?
- What is your "special thing"—what makes you stand out compared to other authors in your genre or subgenre?
- Go to the Products tab in the Business Plan Google Sheet. Use it to make a complete list of all the titles you have already published and all the formats that each book has been published in.
- Make note of how many copies of each book has sold and, if you can access the information, how many in each format.

My best advice to writers starting out—or even those who have been at it a while and might be feeling frustrated with their lack of progress—is to learn to embrace the revision process. A book consists of a lot of different parts and it takes time to develop all of them. A first draft will only include some of the things that will land in your finished book, and likely a few that will get tossed out along the way. Consider each revision an exploration as you seek out the layers that will eventually make up your final draft. Some details may only reveal themselves after you've sorted out others. But if you tackle it step by step, you will ultimately build a better book.

— Nephele Tempest, Literary Agent with the Knight Agency

34

PLANNING YOUR PRODUCTION SCHEDULE

Your production schedule is an important part of your business plan because releasing your products into the world translates to cash in your bank account. It's all well and good to say that you want to write three books this year, but can you actually make it happen?

Quantity

In traditional publishing, editors typically want their authors to create a book a year. (The exception here is some romance editors.) Some authors write more than this. There are certainly authors juggling different aspects of a career. They may put out one romance per year and also one romantic suspense. They may write adult thrillers and contemporary YA.

In indie publishing, authors are much more likely to release multiple projects over the course of a year. It's important to balance the number of books you *want* to write with the number of books you can write with *quality*. It's hard to gain a fan in the first place. Getting them back will be next to impossible once you've disappointed them, so you need to make sure every book you put out is the best you can possibly make it.

One book at a time?

Some schools of thought insist that you should work on only one book at a time—that juggling different projects means losing your focus. However, what works for one writer may not work for another. There are many writers who successfully work on multiple projects simultaneously. If they get stuck on one, they flip to the other, so that they are always moving forward on something. Sometimes this means writing in two different genres to keep things straight in your brain. Crystal and Eileen both write fiction and non-fiction so that there aren't two competing storylines in their heads at once.

You will need to decide what works for you as a writer. If you're unsure, you may be best served by having only one project under a deadline. Then you can see if you can complete another one at the same time. If you discover you can't, you can more easily drop the non-urgent project and still hit that deadline.

Your goal is to set yourself up for success instead of frustration and ensure you aren't tempted to quit too early in the process.

There are two ways to approach your writing schedule. One is to figure out how long it takes you to write a book and then multiply that by the number of books you want to write this year. The other way is to identify how many books you want to write and then work backward from that.

The good news? Regardless of which way you approach scheduling, the information you need and the steps you take are basically the same.

How long do you need to budget to write a book?

Once you make a plan for writing—instead of writing only when the muse strikes—you have to know how long it will take you. If you traditionally publish, you may sell a book on proposal, which means the publisher will want that book turned in by a set date. So how do you know if you can do it?

Step 1: Know how much you can write on a weekly basis

If you haven't tracked your word count before, now is the time to start. You're not looking for your best-week-ever numbers, but numbers you know you can hit on a fairly regular basis. (*Hint:* The Words Tracker tab on that Google Sheet we made you is set up to help you do this.)

Step 2: Know your target

Various genres and formats have expected word counts. A novella might be 20,000 words. A full-length fantasy novel is likely between 90,000 and 120,000 words. A category romance is typically 45,000 to 55,000 words.

Step 3: Know your process

Do you write a draft all the way through and then revise? Or do you write and revise, write and revise as you go? There is no wrong way. Just be sure you understand your typical approach.

This is where you have to do a little rough math. No stress. Even Eileen, who loathes math and spreadsheets, can do this. You got this.

Planning projects based on writing speed
Eileen knows she writes an average of 10,000 words a week, and a full-length novel in her genre comes in at around 80,000 words.

Eileen also knows her process: she typically needs between two and four weeks to think through a plot and characters before she starts.

So, it should take her around four weeks to plan and then eight weeks to write a book. Twelve in total, right?

Ha ha ha ha ha ha. Oh, that was fun to imagine. This may work for some writers, but not Eileen. She knows that at least half the words she writes will be no good, and she'll end up chucking them out. As a result, she'll add an additional four weeks to write those—hopefully better—words. Now we're at 16 weeks.

At this point, Eileen can look at the upcoming 16 weeks. Does she have a conference in there? A family visit? A big holiday? If she does, she likely needs to add a week for each major disruption. And past experience tells Eileen that there will be something else to derail things. (There's always something: a cold, an emergency vet visit after a raccoon attack, etc.) So she adds another week.

If you're doing the math along with Eileen, we're now at 18 weeks. She'll need four to six weeks for revision, so that's now a total of 24 weeks. If she wants feedback on her book from beta readers, she needs to give them a couple of weeks to read and then book another couple of weeks so she can make any revisions. That comes to a grand total of 28 weeks.

With all of this laid out, Eileen can chart her progress weekly. Is she on schedule? Ahead? Behind? Charting her progress allows her to ring alarm bells if she starts slipping and either make plans to address the issue or, in a worst-case scenario, give others a heads-up that she's not going to meet a deadline.

Planning projects by working backward from the time available

Crystal knows that she has the capacity to complete about four good hours of research, plotting and writing in a given workday, and that the remaining three or four hours should be spent on business management tasks, editing, publishing tasks and the marketing and promotion of existing books. She also has an author assistant who helps her for 20 hours per week with editing, marketing, and all the indie publishing tasks associated with new releases so that she can focus on writing.

Crystal is most successful when she has two projects on the go at the same time, one in fiction and one in non-fiction. This way she can flip back and forth depending on what project is flowing and so that different times of day can be dedicated to different tasks. Crystal also knows that she can write about 15,000 good words per week.

We start with 52 weeks in the year.

Subtract four weeks over the Christmas holidays for year-end and next year's business planning.
Subtract four weeks over the summer break for some outdoor time and camping.

Subtract four weeks over the course of the year for long weekends, Easter break, a conference or two and whatever else pops up.

This leaves 40 work weeks to put into the production schedule.
40 Weeks x 15,000 words = 600,000 words in the year

Only about 500,000 of those will end up in the finished products after editing and rewrites.
Her non-fiction books (this giant one not included!) average about 50,000 words each.
Her fiction books are split between novellas around—25,000 words each—and novels—50,000 words each.

To figure out her production schedule, Crystal must take the available word counts and decide which projects from her possibilities list to tackle this year. She can choose an order in which to work on things or, if there are certain products that need to be released at specific times that year, she can set up a rough release schedule and work backward from there. If all her projects are novel-length romances or fiction books, in theory, she would be able to complete ten projects this year.

Note: There is a Production Schedule tab in your Business Plan Google Sheet. It'll help you do all the math. Sit down with your calendar, fill in the number of days each week you anticipate having to work on writing and editing, and customize the sheet with your data.

Step 4: Create your production schedule

Now it's time to review the list of possible projects you brainstormed in the first part of this section. You will want to prioritize your projects based on how you'd like to level-up your career this year. Which book does it make the most sense to focus on right now? Which one is most likely to find a home if you're publishing into the traditional market?

For example, if you are working on both an upmarket, stand-alone women's fiction novel and the next book in your successful cozy mystery series, you'll need to go back to the goals you outlined in part one of this book to know which is the better book to focus on first. If your goal is to achieve a solid income and increase royalties, and you don't have any room for risk in your household budget this year, it might make the most sense to work on the next book in your series, which you know you can sell. If your primary goal this year is to secure an agent and get a traditional publishing deal, then prioritizing your upmarket women's fiction might make the most sense for you.

And remember: you do not have to completely fill your schedule or plan to maximum capacity. In fact, it's smarter not to. If you give yourself a bit of a buffer, you will be less stressed, more flexible with your time, and better able to say yes to those cool opportunities you haven't even imagined yet. We know they are coming your way!

Note: your production schedule doesn't have to be fancy or complicated. It can be as simple as writing a word target or editing goal beside each month on a piece of paper. Or drawing a monthly calendar on a page and filling in goals. Whatever works for you.

If you are working on books that take a year or more to write, you might find it helpful to do a three-to-five-year career plan to see the longer arc of career growth over time. If you're already a full-time author, you'll have much more time available to produce your books—but you'll need to use it wisely to keep that income flowing.

Your Turn

- How many books or products can you—or do you want to—produce this year? In the next three to five years? If you don't know your writing process or typical word count, start tracking it so you can get an idea going forward.
- Do the math to determine how long it takes you to write a book.
- If you want to write a book in less time, how will you hasten that production schedule? When Eileen was working a full-time job, her weekly word count goal was 3,000 words. As she gained more time, she increased her weekly goal. She also became more comfortable and familiar with the writing process and was able to increase her production. However, she's also noticed that a global pandemic—and resulting anxiety—has had a negative impact on writing production and reduced her typical word count.
- What does your ideal author's day look like? What about your ideal week? Month? Year?
- Brainstorm a list of the top three activities or times you want to protect to help you keep balance in your life.
- Brainstorm a list of three things that are not priorities for you but that pull time and focus away from the things that really matter. Is there anything you can do to eliminate or reduce the time these take up?
- Review your production schedule. Is there anywhere you need to introduce buffer time? Have you given yourself enough rest and recuperation time?

Seriously, though: did you schedule an actual vacation?

No? We highly recommend you go back and schedule in some breaks no matter how much of a keener you are. Burnout is a nasty, nasty thing, and it will gobble up your good intentions if you don't take time to recharge.

35

CHOOSING YOUR PUBLICATION FORMATS

Once you've done the hard work of actually writing the story, you can publish that content in a variety of formats and diversify your income streams. The important part is to make sure you are providing your books in the formats your readers want (we covered the research part of this in the Your Market section). Adjust your per-project budgets to reflect the additional costs associated with publishing books in different formats and remember: you don't have to do everything at once. You can always add other formats later. If you're looking for a deep dive into indie publishing strategy and an in-depth cost-benefit analysis, you'll want to do some further reading in the *Strategic Indie Author* book.

For our purposes, make some notes about the formats in which you intend to publish this year's projects.

eBooks

These are the easiest to set up and distribute and are generally the cheapest to get up for sale. You need only a front cover (not a full wrap like you do with print books), and so most people start with eBooks. It is easy to make changes or updates to eBook files, you don't have to deal with printing and shipping costs or estimates, and they are the quickest format to get to market. Often, your book can be available for sale worldwide within 48 hours of you hitting the publish button.

Print books

If your audience likes to read in print, and if you are selling to libraries, you'll want to consider setting up your books for print on demand if you're not working with a traditional publisher. Print on demand means the books are printed as they are ordered, so you're not dealing with a lot of expensive stock sitting around your office. And you don't have to deliver the books to your customers—they are printed and shipped out directly by whatever distributor you have set up with. Some genres—non-fiction, for example—have large print readership, while other genres like romance or mystery are far more focused on eBooks.

Large-print books

This is a special category of print books with larger, easier-to-read type. These are generally sold at a higher price point because the larger font increases the page count and printing cost. They can be a good way to open up your work to new markets.

Audiobooks

Audiobooks have seen a giant rise in popularity over the past few years, with audiobook sales growing by double digit percentages for eight years in a row leading up to 2020. While the numbers of listeners are still growing, so too are the numbers of audiobooks per year people are consuming. Currently, audiobook editions are quite pricey to produce, so it's best to experiment with audiobooks once you've got a bit of an audience. But if you do have some cash to reinvest, then it's an option. Many authors and publishers will actually license their book rights to audiobook companies to produce on their behalf so they don't have to spend the money, time or energy producing their own editions.

If you decide to experiment with new formats, keep in mind that each format makes the publication and the marketing side more time-consuming. Different reader pools prefer different formats, and the marketing engines that send readers and listeners to them differ widely between formats. You will need to budget extra time for each additional format you offer.

Your Turn

- Review your market research information. Which formats are most popular with your readers?
- Which formats of your titles already exist?
- Are you ready to level up by adding new formats of existing materials?
- Do a cost-benefit analysis for each title. How much would it cost to produce the product, and how much could you expect to make off each product sold? How many would you have to sell to make back your initial investment?
- Which titles will you produce in which formats this year?
- If your budget or production plan doesn't allow you to produce all the formats you'd like this year, make a note of what you'd like to tackle in the next one to three years so you have a reminder when it comes time to prepare next year's business plan.

36

CHOOSING YOUR DISTRIBUTION CHANNELS

If you are traditionally publishing, decisions about where to sell your books likely won't be up to you. Your distribution will be taken care of by your publisher and you are tied into whatever channels they are using.

If you are indie publishing, we identified your readers and their preferred purchasing outlets in the Your Market section. Hopefully now you're working on getting your books into those channels where you know your readers already like to purchase books.

Wide or exclusive?

Will your eBooks be available exclusively through Amazon and Kindle Unlimited? Or will you publish them "wide" so they are available in a variety of online bookstores?

Wide versus exclusive is a hotly contested topic in the indie publishing community, and it's a choice that will have a potentially far-reaching impact on your career and on your readers.

Some benefits of exclusive—KDP Select and Kindle Unlimited

- Your books are available to readers through Amazon's Kindle Unlimited program and you get paid for all KENP (Kindle Edition Normalized Pages) read
- Inclusion in those programs increases exposure and recommendations to readers within those programs
- There are promotional opportunities only available to KDP Select enrolled books
- Increased royalties in some markets. At the time of writing you can only get 35% royalties in Japan, India, Brazil and Mexico if you are not enrolled in KDP Select. If you are enrolled, you receive 70%
- Less to manage and coordinate in terms of price breaks or updates to book info if your book is only in one storefront

Many (but not all) authors find that they are able to build their revenue much quicker when they are first starting out by participating in KDP Select / Kindle Unlimited.

Remember that you enroll in KDP Select for 90 days at a time.

Some benefits of wide—all eBook retailers

- You're not dependent on one retailer for all your income
- You will have access to some worldwide markets that do not have access to Amazon programs, or where Kindle is not dominating the eBook market
- You have more direct control over your pricing (and consequently your profits)
- Your books can be made available to libraries around the world
- You can sell or give away your eBooks anywhere, in any way you want—including from your own website
- You can qualify to make it onto the *USA Today* bestseller lists
- It can be easier to get BookBub feature deals for wide authors (*Note:* we did not say *easy*, just easier!)

How do you decide?

Do your research, talk to other authors in your niche, and make sure whatever choice you make is an informed one that fits with *your* vision, mission and values. While you can change your mind and switch down the road, it is often frustrating and can mean setbacks in income and reader satisfaction during the transition period.

If you feel strongly about your eBooks being available through libraries, if making it onto the *USA Today* bestseller list is a career goal for you, or if you just feel more comfortable not having all your eBook publishing eggs in one basket, then wide might be a good choice for you. Just remember that it may take a bit longer at first to build up momentum.

If you're looking for some further information on "Going Wide", you may want to read *Wide for the Win* by Mark LeFebvre and check out the Facebook Group of the same name.

You will face the same choices about where to sell audiobooks as you do for eBooks—you can distribute exclusively through ACX/Audible/Apple, or through a wide distributor like Findaway Voices or PublishDrive, which distribute to more than 40 different audiobook sellers.

Print books aren't subject to the same considerations. Your print book can be available through multiple retailers and distributors with no restrictions.

Which worldwide markets?

Are your books for sale in the markets where you readers are? Make sure you enable worldwide rights if possible if you're indie published so your readers from around the world can purchase your books. If you know that most of your readers are in Canada, the UK and Australia, you may want to make sure you are selling your books through Kobo, since that is a huge player in those eBook markets at the time of writing.

Your Turn

- Make a list of pros and cons for wide vs. exclusive publication of *your* eBooks.
- For each title and format, in which distributors and stores will your books be available?
- Will you be publishing wide or exclusive to Amazon for your eBooks?

37

CHOOSING YOUR PRICE POINTS

If you are indie publishing, the purchase price of the book has a major impact on your bottom line and sales volumes. Charge too much, and you may price yourself out of the market. Charge too little, and you may not be able to support your future publishing efforts. How do you find the sweet spot?

How do you decide on the best price point?

Market research is the first way. Ideally, after reading the market research section, you did some poking around in the bestseller charts for your niche and took note of the price points for most books in your category. Be sure to check the lengths of titles when you use their price points for comparison. In some genres, full novels may sell for $7.99 while the $2.99 or $4.99 price points are for shorter works. You need to price high enough to suggest quality and professionalism while staying competitive enough that readers are willing to take a chance on you as a new writer. It's also important to do your research on the stores that will be selling your products. If you are exclusive to Amazon, compare your books to other books enrolled in Kindle Unlimited program. If you are wide, cross-check prices across other online retailers. Pricing strategies differ depending on your publishing approach.

If you managed to obtain a K-lytics report for your genre or subgenre, there is a section on price points and their effectiveness. Review that data in light of your own sales and promotion strategies.

If you are indie publishing, for each format in which your books are available, you'll need to do a breakdown of how much of each book's sale price you get to keep. This allows you to calculate how many of each product you need to sell to recoup your initial investment, and how many you need to sell to generate the kind of income you are targeting for your author business.

Is pricing in traditional publishing relevant to you?

If you are traditionally publishing, you are unlikely to have any input into your book's price point. But price point will influence how many copies of your book have to sell before you earn out your advance. If you are receiving 10 percent of the cover price as a royalty on each copy sold, how many books must sell before you "earn out" your advance and start getting additional revenue from that book?

Your Turn

- What is the typical price point for indie published books in your subgenre, of similar length to yours, that rank in the top 100 of the sales charts on Amazon?
- If you are planning to publish wide, check the pricing for similar products on Kobo, Barnes & Noble and Apple Books.
- Which price points make the most sense for your books?

- If you are traditionally publishing and you know the price point for your book, calculate what your royalty will be on each copy sold, for each book format.
- How many books need to sell to earn our your advance on each title?

38

CONSIDERING ADDITIONAL PRODUCTS AND SERVICES

In addition to your books, you may be earning revenue from other components of your author business model. This includes things like teaching, work for hire, coaching, patronage or other elements of the business models we detailed earlier. Which other components of your author business are currently earning you revenue?

Make a complete list of all sources of non-book-sale revenue you had in the last year. If you have an invoicing program, you can do this by taking a quick scan of the reports in your software or app. If you don't have a system, it's time to set one up. But for now, review your records—your calendars, bank accounts or the stack of papers in your top desk drawer—until you have an accurate and complete list of the different revenue streams coming into your business in the past 12 months. (*Hint:* This will give you a head start when we hit the budgeting section of your business plan!)

Your Turn

- Go to the Products tab in your Business Plan Google Sheet.
- List each non-book product (mugs or T-shirts, e.g.) or service (teaching workshops) you have for sale.
- How much revenue does each product or service generate on a monthly and annual basis?
- How much time and energy does it take to produce and deliver this product?
- How much time does it take to do the administration tasks associated with selling this product?
- How much do you love selling this product?

39

UNDERSTANDING YOUR INTELLECTUAL PROPERTY

Your intellectual property is a valuable asset. We often think of our assets in terms of physical books stacked in the corner of our offices, but in fact the ideas and stories we've captured on the page have value far beyond their physical forms. Copyright and contracts are at the centre of all that, and that's what this section is all about. We'll also discuss briefly what to do when your book files get pirated. (Note that we didn't say *if* they get pirated. That's because this has happened to *everyone* we know!)

What is copyright?

This is a complex area, and we are most definitely not lawyers. We are going to give you a very high-level view of copyright and why it is important to your author career, but for specific information about any copyright-related concerns, you should do your own research in your geographical area and consult the appropriate legal professionals and regulatory bodies before making any decisions. In general, copyright protection for works created after January 1, 1978, lasts for the life of the author plus 70 years.

Copyright is the exclusive legal right to produce, reproduce, publish or perform an original literary, artistic, dramatic or musical work. The copyright is usually the creator.

In the context of books, there are a few different areas you might be curious about where copyrighting is concerned.

Copyrighting your story idea

Nope. Okay, take a breath. Still with us? You cannot copyright a story idea, concept or theme. But don't panic. If a hundred authors in the same genre were given the same idea, the ways they actually told that story would be very different.

Copywriting your words

The good news? *Yes,* you can copyright the actual words that comprise your story. The process varies from country to country but mostly involves registering your copyright with some sort of official body. In Canada, it's the Canadian Intellectual Property Office; in the US, it's the United States Copyright Office. Some combination of your country and "copyright registration" or "intellectual property" in a Google search ought to quickly help you identify the equivalent body in your area.

Copyrighting your title

No, you generally cannot copyright a book title because they are considered short phrases and are ineligible for copyright.

Copyrighting a book cover

No, you cannot copyright a *style* of book cover. If someone loves your cover and makes something similar, there is nothing you can do about that. But what if someone copies your cover exactly, right down to the same fonts and placement and image? *Yes,* that could be considered a copyright violation—although it might not be your copyright that's being violated!

Technically, if you hire a graphic designer to do your cover, *they* own the rights to it unless they specifically sign those rights over to you. The author has what is called an implied license to use the art for the cover of their book and related marketing materials. But the actual cover design? That belongs to the designer unless you've signed a contract stating otherwise.

And make sure you clearly understand if your designer expects to receive credit for their cover design on the copyright page of your book. If your cover designer licensed the image, then crediting them in the copyright page helps direct people following up on any imaging licensing issues back to the creator. However, be aware that you are ultimately responsible for confirming that your cover designer has fully licensed all fonts and images used on your cover.

Copyright and images

Yes, images are automatically protected by copyright as soon as a person takes or creates them. If you didn't take the photo, and you haven't paid to license the use of that image or obtained express permission from the person who did take the photo, then it's not yours to use. Be sure to credit your cover photo sources in your books if the licensing agreement requires it, and make sure you've appropriately licensed any images that appear in or on your books.

Copyright and song lyrics

Yes, song lyrics are copyrighted as soon as they are recorded in any form. And *no,* you cannot use copyright-protected song lyrics in your books without permission. You need to acquire permission from the song's publisher—even if it's only one line. And if you intend to produce an audiobook version of your book, you will also need to acquire performance rights for a song if you want its lyrics included in the audiobook. Most often, it's easier to leave them out, write your own imaginary lyrics, or refer to well-known songs obscurely (e.g., *He watched the karaoke singers and wondered what they were "shaking off."* Taylor Swift fans will recognize what they are singing, but you haven't actually used any lyrics or the title of the song). Even song titles, while not copyrighted, can be *trademarked*.

Copyright and quotes

Yes, quotes, even from famous people, are protected by copyright unless they are in the public domain. And yes, you need written permission from that person in order to quote their words in your book. (Before you ask, we did get permission from each of the authors we quote in this book. In fact, they wrote their inspirational notes specifically for inclusion in this book!)

What is DRM?

Digital Rights Management (DRM) refers to various software technologies that control the unauthorized use, modification, and distribution of digital content like eBooks, music and films. In this context, DRM refers to an extra security setting on your books that you may choose to enable upon publication and which prevents people from sharing your book files. Sounds straightforward and awesome, right? Sorry. It's all a bit more complicated than that.

The advantage of turning on DRM is that it stops people from sharing your books. Well, it *can*. Sort of. Mostly it just frustrates readers who are trying to share the book they bought *with themselves* by putting it on a different device. And it's totally crackable, so the actual pirates who are trying to steal your book files to put on pirate sites… well, they can still do that.

Many indie authors choose not to enable DRM and decide that if their book does get pirated, they'll just take the free publicity. Others want things locked down as tight as possible. No one can make that decision for you—except your publisher if you've gone the traditional route. You'll have to do a little investigation into the standard practices in your genre and make a decision that fits you, your values and your business model.

What do you do if (or when) your books get pirated?

We've said it a couple of times already, and we're going to say it again. We're not lawyers, and this is not legal advice. The suggestions below are just places to start when one of your books is pirated.

Depending on the specifics of your publishing arrangements and the extent of the piracy, you may need to bring legal professionals on board to help you clean things up.

If you're traditionally published, you can contact your publisher and let them know what's happened. They should have procedures in place to deal with this.

If you're indie published, you will have to take a few more direct steps—assuming you want to take action at all.

What kind of a site has pirated your book?

When they actually don't have your book

Lots of sites will claim to have your book, but they actually don't. It's just part of a ruse to get people to "subscribe" to whatever scam they have going. And if you sign up to see if they actually do have your book, you may get yourself a nasty virus or fall victim to their attempted scam. That's not what you want. In many cases, it's better just to leave it alone.

When a free file-sharing site actually does have your book

If you're not signed up for KDP Select, you can decide if you want to fight this or leave it alone. You may want to just leave your book up on the site and hope that it brings you some new readers who otherwise might not find your books.

If you're signed up for KDP Select and Kindle Unlimited, you may have a bigger problem. You have promised exclusivity—and that pirated copy of your book available for free download is actually breaking your agreement with Amazon on your behalf.

If the file-sharing site really does have your book, and you want it taken down, then follow these really great instructions from Dave Chesson at Kindlepreneur. Here is the link to the article (https://kindlepreneur.com/ebook-piracy), that way you'll have the most up-to-date information even if those instructions change after this book is published.

When the evil pirates actually published your book on another eBook distribution platform

Unfortunately, it does sometimes happen that the pirates are bold enough to actually upload *your* book to another eBook distribution platform and hit the publish button. At that point, your book is being sold through their publishing account, and they are collecting the royalties on it.

If you have already uploaded your book to that platform, there are usually checks built in to the system that will identify duplicated content. These will prompt the distributor to reach out and require you to prove your ownership over the content before you can have your book listing reinstated. We know this, because sometimes reissuing your book as a new edition under a new pen name can trigger this same action.

Most people only discover piracy when they have opted in to KDP Select, and then receive a notice from Amazon that their book has been pulled due to breach of contract because it is currently for sale in another eBook storefront.

If this happens, follow all instructions in the email you received from Amazon about how to dispute the issue. Explain that it was pirated, assure them that you are following up to have it removed from the other store, and then reach out to the store where the pirates are selling your book and inform them what has happened. Generally they will pull the book from sale until the matter is resolved. You will likely need to jump through a number of hoops to prove you are the copyright owner, and you will need to negotiate with the eBook seller around what has happened (or will happen) to any royalties from illicit sales. This is the point where you might need to involve legal counsel.

It's wise to do a follow-up audit of each and every eBook store (for each of your books) to make sure your book isn't listed anywhere else. If it is, you'll need to repeat the process with each and every store where pirates have listed your book.

To be on the safe side, you may want to add "audit bookstores where titles are available" to your monthly or quarterly checklist of recurring tasks or your assistant's to-do list. While you used to be able to hire a company called Blasty to take care of this for you, they ceased operations in 2019. So for now, it up to us authors to fight the pirates as best we can.

Your Turn

- What is the process for registering copyright in your geographical area?
- Make a note of any potential copyright issues that exist in current books and formats, and in any proposed formats. What issues do you need to research further?
- Will you enable DRM on your books? Why or why not?
- Conduct a "bookstore audit" and make sure your book isn't being sold anywhere it shouldn't be.
- Add "bookstore audit" to your monthly or quarterly to-do list.

40

UNDERSTANDING RIGHTS AND LICENSING

There are a lot of contracts involved in the publishing industry, whether you are traditional or indie. If you are traditionally published, hopefully your agent has helped you negotiate your contract and understand its various clauses. Even though you have an agent, take time to read your contracts. Ask questions when you don't understand. This is your career, and you need to take ownership for it.

If you are indie publishing you may still be signing contacts with author services companies or distributors, and you may be selling subsidiary rights like audio or translation rights.

We highly recommend reviewing these carefully, and asking for assistance for clarification as needed. If you don't have an intellectual property lawyer or agent to assist you, you may want to join the Alliance of Independent Authors (ALLi) and avail yourself of the legal consultation, contract information and sample contracts they have available to members. It's an excellent organization, and well worth the membership fee.

If you have not yet signed any contracts, review the list of questions below before you sign anything. Use the question list as a jumping off point for discussion and investigation.

Your Turn

- Open up the list of all your works you made in the Products-BOOKS tab of your Business Plan Google Sheet. Include title, word count, publication date and rights reversion date and indicate which rights have sold on which works.
- Catalogue your current assets: Make sure your list of existing titles is up to date. List all the forms and formats for each title (eBook, audiobook, print book, etc.)
- What titles and formats are on the horizon that you have ideas for or are considering writing in the near future?

If you are traditionally publishing, consult your contracts and find out the following, then enter the info in your tracking sheet.

- Which rights have been licensed? And for where?
- For how long have the rights been licensed?
- What are the conditions under which your rights revert back to you?
- Does it place any restrictions on what you can write or sell?
- Are there any rights your publisher hasn't licensed that you can sell separately or use to develop products for yourself?

If you are indie publishing, you'll want to think about the following areas, then enter the info in your tracking sheet.

- If you are using an author services company, do they control the rights to your book, or do you retain full control?
- Is there a time period you are locked into the publishing contract?
- Check your distribution contracts and know the restrictions or limitations they place on you. Do they lock you in for a certain time period?
- Does distributing through one company prevent you from working with others? Are they requiring exclusivity? For which

formats of your book does exclusivity apply? For how long? How do you terminate that relationship?
- Is there anything in your distribution agreements that might limit your ability to distribute your content or run platform-specific advertising for your content (e.g., censorship guidelines)?
- What is DRM, and does your platform of choice give you control over whether or not DRM is enabled on your book files?

41

MANAGING YOUR ASSETS

If you are a traditionally published author, once the publisher takes over the production process, you might not think about retaining editable copies of your final manuscript. However, if you ever get your rights back for your book, you will want an editable copy of the finished product if at all possible, as this will save you from paying for it to be re-edited or retyped. While there are tools and services that can help you convert a PDF to an editable and formattable document, they are rarely 100-percent accurate, and they can also be costly depending on the way your original book was formatted. If you keep an up-to-date, editable copy of your manuscript, you will save both time and money down the line.

Typically, you will receive Word document copies of your manuscript twice in the publishing process: once at the end of the developmental edits and then again following the copy edits. But there is one last round of editing that is known as "galley proofs." At this point you are sent the document as it will look fully laid out. This allows you to catch any last-minute typos (and trust us, there is always at least one). You're also looking for mistakes in the layout. For example, every line may be justified in a way that several lines in a row start with I, which looks odd on the page. As the writer, you cannot change galley proofs. You simply highlight those typos or formatting issues and itemize desired changes for the editor. However, if you ask (nicely), your publisher will typically send you a Word document copy with even these revisions included. (If you ask in advance and learn that this is not an option, be sure to make a note of any changes you requested in the galley proof so you can make those changes for yourself in your most up-to-date Word document.)

> *Save everything. No matter how rotten you think a piece of writing smells, save it, back it up, move it to the next computer every time you upgrade. Because today's crap is tomorrow's compost.*
>
> — HALLIE EPHRON, *NEW YORK TIMES* BESTSELLING AUTHOR OF *CAREFUL WHAT YOU WISH FOR*

As an indie author, you'll want to make sure that you have an editable "master" of each of your manuscripts. If you're hiring someone to do the formatting and layouts of your book, and you identify typos or changes after the book has been laid out, it can be tempting to make those changes only in the manuscript's final format. It's a pesky extra step to put those changes in your last Word (or Scrivener, or Google) document as well. But let's play the what-if game for a minute.

- What if… down the line, you want to publish your book in another format? You will need the most up-to-date version of your manuscript in the format required by the new publisher or distribution company or whoever you're working with. And almost everyone can work with a Word doc.
- What if… a foreign publisher wants to license to publish the rights in their country, and they need your book in Word doc format, and all you have is a PDF? (Worse, what if all you have is the print book, which then needs to be retyped?)

- What if… the software used to lay out your book becomes obsolete or stops playing with the latest e-readers, and you need to switch to something else?
- What if… there is a great new software that allows you to easily do all your own layouts and make professional-looking books, and you no longer want to use your old, complicated software? (*Hint:* This is what happened when Vellum came on the market.)

Version control on your assets

You well-established authors have a whole wealth of creative and business assets out there. But even if you're a first-time author, it's likely that you made some progress on your book—or wrote many books—before you picked up this book. Those are assets.

We're not talking about the fancy car or the island beach house you may have picked up with that last royalty cheque (dream big, peeps). In this case we're talking about your *creative* assets. These include things like:

- Existing tracking tools
- Old draft manuscripts
- Laid-out book files
- Audiobook files
- Character sketches
- Scrivener files
- Promotional images
- Lists of past reviews
- ISBN records

And on and on the list could go. Likely, the longer you've been writing and publishing, the bigger the jumble it is. Crystal has been doing this author business thing for 15 years. She's working on book number 40-something of her own work, and she's also worked on upward of 250 projects, counting the client and student books she's helped produce.

Most of these books were finished under tight deadlines with last-minute changes, and many have been published in multiple formats and editions—often over a period of more than a decade…

An aside from Crystal:
You sweating yet? Yeah, me too. At least I sweat when I think about going back through that older stuff. The stuff I set up *before* I had a system.

You see, it used to be just me working on most things. For years I ran a one-woman show. Then the publishing and consulting side of my business grew, and I introduced a business partner (my super-organized husband), and then I added many, many contractors to my team, and then more business partners.

And we discovered that my brain works astonishingly well in the moment. I can keep everything sorted, stay on top of stuff, manage versions and file locations and keep it all good and clean and right and wonderful.

But when it came to having someone else pick up where I left off? Disaster.

And when I had to update book files for a project I hadn't worked on in months or years? Yeah, there's the cold sweat we talked about earlier. The few times I've had to do this have been… "educational." (I promised myself I wouldn't swear in this book.) These educational moments taught me several important lessons. Anyone who's read books on decluttering—yes, it is life-changing magic!—might recognize some of these tips. They apply to your physical stuff as well as your digital stuff.

Here are a few survival tips:

- You *must* have a clear system for naming and organizing files.
- You *must* use your system 105 percent of the time.
- You *must* have the rules of your system written down so that

when you take a break, you don't forget your system or why you were doing things that way.

The rules of file naming

There is a proper way to name files so they will organize themselves—a way that will save you if you accidentally slip up and store your files in two folders (or nine folders at different levels on your desktop inside other folders named "To Be Filed" **cough**). Using this naming system will maintain the order and sense of your files even when you pull them all back into one organized folder several months or years down the line. You know, when your computer finally stops working and you *have* to clean up your desktop.

Having tried many different systems of file naming, this is the one that has proven the most effective for organizing Crystal's jungle of book files:

Project_Phase_Version_Year-Month-Day_Person.extension

If you have multiple pen names, you may want to add the pen name in there, too.

Why this? You need a system that will effectively auto-sort your files, follow your workflow and allow you to see, at a glance, what the most current files are.

If you name your files consistently, it will save you time, money and frustration. We guarantee you will swear less, be less tempted to drink, make fewer mistakes and have much more time and energy for your writing. Which, at the end of the day, is what this is all about. For each book folder it helps to have:

PenName_Book Name
->Drafts
->Covers
->Interior Layout
->Current Uploaded Version
->Promotional Materials

Here's a sample of a file naming practice in action from inside one of Crystal's draft project folders:

->CJHunt_CHARMED
->>DRAFTS

- CJHunt-CHARMED-Draft-V1-2019-05-27.scriv
- CJHunt-CHARMED-Draft-V2-2019-05-30.scriv
- CJHunt-CHARMED-Draft-V2-2019-06-15-ABdevedits.scriv
- CJHunt-CHARMED-Draft-V3-2019-06-15-CJrewrite.scriv
- CJHunt-CHARMED-Draft-V3-2019-06-15.doc
- CJHunt-CHARMED-Draft-V3-2019-06-23-ABcopyedits.doc
- CJHunt-CHARMED-Draft-V4-2019-06-26-CJcopyedits.doc
- CJHunt-CHARMED-Draft-V4-2019-06-29-BetaReaders.doc
- CJHunt-CHARMED-Draft-V5-2019-07-02-CJBetaEdits.doc
- CJHunt-CHARMED-Draft-V5-2019-07-04-ARCTeam.vellum

Then there's an ADVANCE READER COPY folder that contains the source file (Vellum) and the packaged ePub, Mobi and PDF versions that go out to her ARC team or review crew:

- CJHunt-CHARMED-Draft-V6-2019-07-04.vellum
- CJHunt-CHARMED-Draft-V6-2019-07-04-ABProof.PDF
- CJHunt-CHARMED-Final-V7-2019-07-04.vellum

Then there's a CURRENT UPLOADED VERSIONS folder that contains ePub, Mobi and PDF versions that get uploaded to the publishing outlets.

-> Current Uploaded Versions

—>eBook-ePub
—>eBook-Kindle
—>Hardcover
—>Paperback

And if she makes changes to the files after that initial publication—which she always does, at the very least to update her front and back matter—she'll name her new file like this:

- CJHunt-CHARMED-Final-V8-Revisions-2019-09-14.vellum

The old "current" uploaded versions will get moved into an ARCHIVED VERSIONS folder. And the newly exported file versions will get moved into the CURRENT UPLOADED VERSIONS folder.

You can see an example of this file structure in action in the screenshot below of the shared dropbox we use for our collaborative projects.

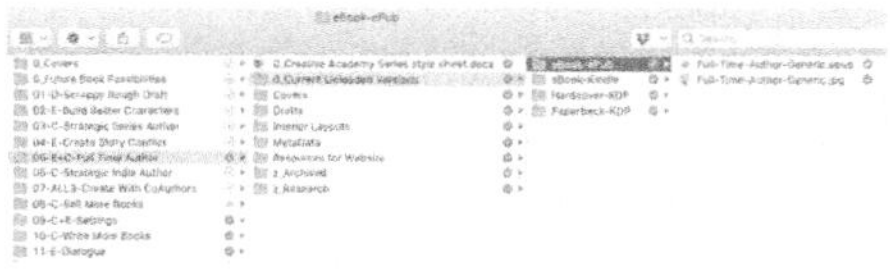

Your Turn

- Look at how you currently store your assets. Take time to learn what you have and where you have kept things.
- Decide on a file-naming convention that you will stick to.
- Create a folder structure on your computer or in your cloud service.
- Gather all your book- and series-related files from where they are currently living and put them into your new system. Rename them as required so, when the time comes to make adjustments, it's perfectly clear what the current published file versions are.

PART V

YOUR AUTHOR BRAND

42

DEVELOPING YOUR AUTHOR BRAND

There is a great deal of talk in the author world about your author "brand." What does that really mean, and how can it help—or hurt—your career?

Branding is what people think about when they hear your name or see your products or promotional materials. The way people perceive your brand impacts who will buy and read your books, what they expect from your writing and how they expect you to interact with them.

There are several different aspects of brand: visual materials like logos or promotional images or book covers; the appearance of your website, social media or other promotional platforms; the books themselves, and your voice or tone as you tell your stories; the way you interact with your readers and the public; and the way you interact with other authors. All of these can be considered part of your brand. They combine to give your audience and peers an impression of who you are, what you're all about, and what readers can expect from you through your books or promotional materials. We'll touch on each of these elements in the sections that follow and help you narrow down which ones will communicate your brand most effectively and grow your career.

Design basics

To create an effective brand, it's important to have either a basic understanding of graphic design principles or help from a professional to put together your materials. That doesn't always mean you have to hire a designer. There are some fabulous tools out there, like Canva and BookBrush, that help authors create really professional-looking visual assets from templates designed by pros. But you do need to understand what to customize on those templates in order to produce a unique reflection of your own brand. Aside from just creating things that look professional, most authors will need five key tools in their toolbox of branding bits.

This is a very visual subject area, and we couldn't cram all our video demos into this book! But there are loads of free courses out there to help you develop or improve your author branding, and we have one that you can access for free through StrategicAuthorpreneur.com. It's six modules (less than 10 mins each) that include exercises and examples to walk you through the following areas critical to nailing down your author brand.

- Design basics
- Author branding basics
- Author logos
- Author tag lines
- Fonts and typography
- Colour palettes

Your Turn

- What are five to ten words or phrases that people will think of when they encounter your brand out there in the author world?
- If you are an established author, ask several writer friends or readers what phrases they think of when they see your website or read your books. Are you happy with the answers you got? Do they line up with your vision of your brand?
- If you are just getting started on your author journey, what are some words or phrases you would like people to associate with your brand?

43

CHOOSING YOUR AUTHOR NAME

Your author name is an extremely important part of your brand. While we don't have any official stats on exactly how many authors write under pen names, most of the authors we know have at some point written under more than one name in different genres or at different stages of their careers. A pen name may be publicly acknowledged or not depending on your reason for not using your own name and there are a wide variety of reasons authors use pen names.

Originality

It may be preferable to choose a name that is not already in use by another author so you don't confuse readers or end up battling for social media profile handles and website URLs.

Clarity and simplicity

You may want to choose a name that readers can remember and easily spell in a web search.

Branding

Pen names can suggest a difference in genre. Many authors use one pen name for one genre and a different name for another. Some choose a pen name that indicates—or obscures—gender. Some men who write romance use a female pen name or initials. And there is a long history of women in what are traditionally male-dominated genres using initials or gender-neutral pen names. Make sure your pen name suits your genre—for example, Sophia Lovelace feels more fitting as a romance author pen name than a horror writer.

Privacy

Pen names can maintain your privacy by keeping your writing life separate from your personal life. People choose this strategy for a variety of reasons both general—a personal preference for privacy—and specific—an elementary teacher who writes graphic horror may not want students and parents to connect those two parts of their life.

Some countries are less open-minded when it comes to books about certain topics or in certain genres. If you are worried about the safety of travelling in the future, then you may want to use a pen name for your author activities.

How important is it to you to keep your identity secret? Many authors are open about their pen names at conferences or within writing groups. If it is very important to keep your personal identity top secret, you'll likely need to invest money to set up a corporation to sign contracts and represent you legally. Even JK Rowling couldn't keep her pen name a secret. But in most cases, readers are only mildly interested if you've got a pen name.

If privacy is your primary goal, you will want to budget extra funds for protective measures like renting a post office box with a street address to use on your newsletters and website domain registration, or to pay extra for the privacy add-ons offered by many website hosting companies.

Fresh start

Many bookstores place orders for books based on an author's previous sales numbers. As a result, some individuals who had poor sales with a traditional publisher may choose a pen name to reset their relationship with sales outlets.

The upside of selecting a pen name with no connection to your previous self is that you have a clean slate. Any challenges with your past career can be forgotten. The downside is that you also lose that connection to existing fans and readers.

Choosing your pen name

You will want to choose a name that:

- Makes sense for your genre—ask your readers!
- Fits easily on the cover of your books and is clearly visible even in thumbnail-size images
- Is easy to spell and remember
- Feels good to you! (this name will become part of who you are, and you'll need to respond to that name at public appearances and in reader emails for years or decades)
- Isn't already used by other authors
- Has social media handles and web domains that are still available

Note: Sometimes when you look up a domain from a domain reseller and don't purchase it right away, you come back to find it no longer available —or available at a much higher price. If you're looking at possible domain names for your pen names, it is a good idea to check by entering a URL directly. If all you get is an error message, that probably means no one has purchased the site. If someone owns the domain but is just holding it (either for later development or resale), you will likely get redirected automatically to another page, or you will see a "this domain is parked" message with a bunch of ads on your screen. If the owner is trying to resell the domain, you will likely see a message welcoming you to purchase the domain for X dollars. This price is usually *way* higher than the usual $5 to $20 per year that domains cost.

Pen names versus personas

There is a difference between creating a pen name for your books and creating a whole fictional persona for your interactions with your readers. While you certainly *can* do that, you will need to be aware of some trouble spots and be very careful about how you conduct yourself.

Don't create a fake identity that could cause you trouble. For example, if you're writing medical thrillers, do not choose the pen name Dr. John Smith and write a bio about how you attended Harvard Medical School. Yes, many of us want to pretend to be spies or doctors or princesses, but this isn't the way to do it.

This is perhaps obvious, but it still needs to be said: do not present yourself as being from a particular group—for example, race, culture or sexuality—that is not your own in order to capitalize on a particular trend or readership.

Also, be very aware that if you write under a complete persona and that persona eventually is revealed to your audience (on purpose or by accident), it may land you in hot water. Readers who feel very connected to your author persona can feel very betrayed when they realize that you aren't at all who they thought.

Finally, consider the energy required to maintain a persona instead of being your authentic self. It takes energy to remember who and what you are "supposed" to be, and to ensure on a daily basis that you don't slip up.

Pen names and your business relationships

Be open with your agent if you're using a pen name. In most cases, your contracts with any publisher will be under your legal name, and everyone will be aware of your real identity.

If the publisher (or another party) is paying you money under your pen name, there are banking issues you'll need to address. You may need to register that pen name as a business name in order to secure a bank account under that name. Or, if you need to separate yourself from your pen name and receive payments anonymously, you may need to use an incorporated company as suggested earlier.

If you are traditionally publishing, feel free to discuss pen name options with your editor or agent. They may have ideas about what names would work best in the marketplace.

You'll have to determine if you want to appear in public under your pen name or your real name. Be aware that flights and hotel reservations will need to be in your real name, so ensure your publicity assistant knows how to make those reservations and save you trouble at the gate!

Your Turn

- Think about all the reasons to have a pen name.
- Do you need to protect your privacy or keep your work, life and writing separate?
- Do you think you will write in multiple genres?
- Are you in need of a fresh start or a career reboot?
- Brainstorm a list of possible pen names that could be associated with each of your genres. Research each name to see if another author, public figure or social media personality is using it. Would you be able to secure a website domain with your new name?
- Once you have a short list of pen names, ask a group of readers or authors what they think. Ask specific questions. Is one easier to remember? Easy to spell? Does it seem like a good fit for your chosen genre?
- Is creating and maintaining another pen name worth the extra cost to you in money, energy and time?

44

BRANDING YOUR PROMOTIONAL MATERIALS

Whether you are traditionally published, indie published or hybrid, you'll likely be responsible for creating some kinds of promotional materials. When you're designing a flyer for your school talks, selecting images to promote your book launch or preparing slides for a presentation to your local writers' group, you want your brand reflected in everything you create.

Consistency in people's minds helps paint a clear picture in their memories.

Your Turn

- Organizing your branding assets is key. If you don't already have one, create a folder wherever you store your author files and call it Branding Assets.
- Collect the assets you have from the sections that follow (once you've confirmed you want to keep them), and make sure to

clearly label them as you go. Not only will this save you time when you need to create something new, but it'll also save time if you hire a helper or if something happens to you.

- Add instructions on where to find this folder to your ICE book.

45

BRANDING YOUR VISUAL ASSETS

Every visual asset you have, from your book covers to your website to your social media headers, should have a consistent look and feel. This is especially true for your books. Although some practical design elements and style might change from book to book, the pieces should feel like they fit together overall, even if they aren't 100-percent "matchy."

Author logos

You don't necessarily need a fancy author logo. Some people use a word mark, which is basically your name, in a specific typeface, turned into an image you can place anywhere so it will always look the same. Many sites have tools to help you make your own free logo, so do a Google search for free logo makers and you'll find an array of options. If you're looking to have a logo professionally designed, numerous companies specialize in that. And if you're feeling flush, there are many very talented graphic designers out there who can create you something truly unique. Make sure you clearly communicate your keywords and phrases so anyone you're working with understands your end goal. Show them where you will use your logo and alert them to any specific shape requirements (circle or square; portrait or landscape orientation, e.g.). It helps to show a few samples if you've found something you liked the feel of.

Your Turn

- Do you have an author logo?
- If yes, is it communicating what you want, or does it need an update? If you want an update, make a list of all the places where that logo will need to be changed.
- If no, work through the Strategic Authorpreneur module on designing author logos. Take a stab at designing one yourself or get an estimate of what it would cost to have one designed for you.

Author tag lines

A tag line is a short catchphrase that tells readers exactly what kind of books you write.

For example, Crystal uses a couple of different tag lines depending on context:

> **I write kissing books.** This is her primary author tag line. It indicates that romance is her genre of choice, and also hints at her sense of humour and her obsession with the movie *The Princess Bride*.
>
> **Come home to Rivers End and fall in love.** This is her tag line for her primary fiction series. It clearly communicates to readers that they are contemporary hometown romance novels.

The Strategic Authorpreneur course modules present lots of sample tag lines for different genres.

Your Turn

- Do you have an author tag line?
- If yes, is it communicating what you want, or does it need an update? If you think you want an update, make a list of all the places where that logo will need to be changed.
- If no, work through the Strategic Authorpreneur module on creating author tag lines. Brainstorm a list of several ideas and then get feedback from other author friends and, ideally, a few readers as well. You need to make sure you are communicating what you think you are communicating!

Fonts and typography

Ideally, you will have one or two specific fonts that you use consistently on promo materials, on your website, and on other visually branded materials. Select one font for headlines and titles and another one for plain text that is easy to read and works well with the headline fonts you have chosen. Make sure that you have downloaded the font files to your computer and save them so you can load them into any programs you are using (like Canva or BookBrush). If you're working with a designer who is choosing fonts for you, ensure that they are either available for free or for a reasonable price. Some fonts are very cool but extremely expensive to purchase.

Your Turn

- Do you have a specific set of fonts you use in your visual assets?
- If yes, have you downloaded these files and saved them somewhere handy? Do you have the names of the fonts listed in a convenient place to remind yourself and make it easier to share with an assistant?
- If no, work through the Strategic Authorpreneur module on

fonts and typography. Brainstorm a list of the visual assets you might create. Narrow down your font choices to a few favourites, and then test them out by drafting a handful of different promotional images.
- Once you've confirmed your fonts, install them on any computers you use for writing-related activities, and upload them to the software programs you use most often (like Canva and BookBrush).

Colour palettes

Colour is a powerful component of your author branding. Ideally, you will choose two or three colours to use as a base for your visual assets. These should work with your fonts, tag line and logo to set the tone for your brand. While many authors start with colours they like, consider colours that are a good fit for your genre and that signal to your audience what you're all about—just as your book covers do.

Whenever you're working with multiple colours, make sure you have selected a set that belong together as a palette. You can use a website like coolers.co, to help you generate a complementary palette and choose a range that works for you. Once you have identified your chosen colours, be sure to put the colour hex codes somewhere safe where you can easily retrieve them. A hex code is a six-digit combination of numbers and letters that corresponds to a certain colour when you type it into a computer. Technically, the numbers and letters represent the amounts of red, green and blue (RGB) in a colour. For example, the hex code for the colour on the cover of this book is #becf20, and if you put that into a colour picker, you'll get our Creative Academy green!

Your Turn

- Do you use a specific set of colours in your visual assets?
- If yes, do you have their hex codes identified and saved somewhere handy?
- If no, work through the Strategic Authorpreneur module on colour palettes. Narrow down your colour choices to a few favourites, and then test them out by making up a handful of different promotional images.
- Once you've confirmed your colours, save them in any programs that let you save your custom colours (like Canva, BookBrush or Microsoft PowerPoint).

Images

Often, your promotional images will include images or backgrounds chosen from stock websites or from within your video- and image-creation tools. Set some guidelines for yourself and your team so that you know what types of images are appropriate for your brand. For example, you may choose to use only illustrations of a certain style on your assets. Or maybe you only use backgrounds that do not contain people. Or maybe you use very saturated colours or only black and white. Note these visual and style guidelines and then you can bookmark images that fit your brand. You may also want to note any specific filter or setting you use to adjust existing images to suit your tastes. This includes the custom backgrounds you make for your video chats and Zoom calls!

Your Turn

- Do you have any rules or guidelines around what kinds of images you collect to use for your promotional assets?
- If yes, do you have these images clearly identified and labelled

so you can identify where they came from and which company you licensed them from? Are they saved somewhere handy for use and sharing with team members?

- If no, go through your favourite stock photo site or creative tool and bookmark some of the images that seem like a good fit for your brand.
- Note any rules, guidelines or specific filters that you might apply to the images to achieve your customized "look" in the future.

Your appearance

While there is nothing to say you have to colour coordinate your wardrobe to your branding colours or style, it does help to consider how you are going to put yourself together for author events where you are visible to your audience. Are you portraying the vibe you want? Would someone looking at you think fun? Professional? Artsy? Full of humour? Dark and brooding? Just as your words set a tone, so too do the outfits you choose to wear. There is no right or wrong way to dress, and we're sticking to our earlier rejection of dress codes. But some authors have a custom-made T-shirt they wear to all their events, or they always choose a certain colour of top or wear a special hat. (Hey, a wizard's gotta get his power from somewhere.) You do you! Just make sure you're consistent and communicating intentionally with your audience.

Crystal has a couple of items in each of her branded colours and often matches her dress or top to the brand she is representing. For example, since teal is her branded colour in The Creative Academy and in the Strategic Authorpreneur podcast branding, she will wear that colour when she presents on non-fiction topics. When she is interacting with readers and fans as CJ Hunt, she wears red or purple—both colours associated with Rivers End. It's easy, and most people don't even notice you're doing it. But it does create a subtle, unconscious connection.

Your Turn

- Do you have any consistent rules or guidelines for yourself around your author appearance?
- If yes, have you written them down anywhere?
- If no, go through your options and your habits and see if there is anything you could do consciously. Even a ring, necklace, or pattern or colour of shirt could easily become a signature.
- If you like to wear a specific T-shirt or an item you've had made for you, consider ordering a backup. Crystal and Eileen have both been in situations involving an extremely stressful spill or a last-minute opportunity that just happened to fall on laundry day.

46

BRANDING YOUR AUDIO ASSETS

Just like you have a visual logo for your various promo assets, you can also use a specific sound or song as an audio logo for promo videos or other multimedia content. Audio logos or signatures create consistency in your audience's mind, and music and voice can suggest powerful emotion or a feeling of intimacy. People feel like they know you when they hear your voice. If you're going to include audio elements in your promotional materials, make sure they have a consistent tone and evoke the feelings you want associated with your brand. Always make sure that any audio you use is properly licensed (and credited as required) if you are not the original creator of it.

Your Turn

- Are you using any audio assets as part of your author brand?
- If yes, have you saved those source files somewhere convenient and easy to access?
- If no, think about where you would use an audio logo and whether or not you need one. If you do a lot of videos or promo

spots, you may want to explore some stock sites and find an audio clip you like. Take it for a test drive, and then make sure it's included in your branding assets folder.

- If you are using audio from a licensed source, are there any rules, restrictions or guidelines about how it can be used? Are there any specific requirements for how you credit the source or creator of that audio?

47

BRANDING YOUR PRODUCTS

Your brand in your book covers

People really do judge a book by its cover. They will also judge you (at least a little) by your book covers. When readers and peers go to an author's website, the style and quality of the covers definitely contributes to the way they perceive that author's brand. You want to make sure that your books have professional and polished covers, and while they don't all have to "match," especially if you're writing in different series or subgenres, they should at least look coherent—like they all belong to you and fit with the logo, tag line and colours you have chosen for yourself and your website.

While your book-cover fonts don't need to match those on your other branded assets, ideally, they will at least come from the same style family or hint at your genre. For example, if your author logo is a gothic font and you are writing non-fiction books about counselling… you may have a mismatch that needs looking at. It's generally easier to change the branding on your promotional materials as your career evolves than it is to change up your book covers.

Your Turn

Look at your book covers.

- Do these covers seem to fit with the list of words and terms you identified in the general branding steps?
- Do they clearly indicate the genre of books you write?
- Do they fit together in a way that makes sense to readers? If not, you may want to consider a pen name or at least some kind of separator, like tabs for different genres, to break things up visually wherever your books appear together.

Your brand in your book layouts

The inside of your book—the way your content or story is laid out—is all part of your finished product package. People will notice if the margins in your books are too narrow, if the type is easy to read, or if the spacing is inconsistent.

Traditional publishers usually have a trained book designer who deals with all of this, so their authors don't have to. But if you are with a smaller publishing house, make sure you review your proof copies carefully, and don't be afraid to point it out if something looks off to you. Assuming you've been reading widely in your genre, you should be well positioned to notice if something is off-genre or off-brand for that publisher.

If you are indie publishing, you're in control of your layouts and how they look. Note which style settings you're using in your layout programs. Does each chapter start on the right-hand page? Are you using drop caps to start each chapter? How do you indicate section breaks? Do all the books in a series have the same order and content for front and back matter? Consistency is an important part of the reader experience. And if you are writing a gothic horror novel, don't choose the layout with the flowery script for chapter headings. That will be jarring for your reader, no matter how much you love the way it curls on the letter Q.

Crystal has a document with screenshots of each type of element as well as a text label for the layout settings she uses. That way she can visually confirm that the fifth book in a series looks the same as the second—without having to look back through all the old books each time. Whether you are doing your own layouts, or hiring contractors to help you, having a reference document like this will save you time and money while also contributing to the quality and consistency of your finished products.

Your Turn

- Do you have a pattern or settings list for the layouts of your existing books?
- If yes, have you made a note of what they are and how they work? Have you noted which layout program you used so you can be consistent next time?
- Have you changed layout programs or methods over time? Review your older titles. It may be jarring enough that you decide to put in the time and energy to update your older books so they all match. If that is the case, make a list of each book that needs to be changed and then budget the time to complete those tasks.

Your brand in your stories

The books you write are part of your author brand. They contribute to how people see you and how your readers connect with you. We already covered some of what readers are expecting in the chapter on "Your Market." In the context of branding, you are really just checking your stories for internal consistency within your brand. If you've always written historical fiction, and suddenly you jump to science fiction, make sure you have considered all the implications for your brand and for readers' expectations. Even if you are staying within the same genre or subgenre, be aware of what elements are part of your brand. If you've always written fairy-tale retellings and suddenly switch to a bad-boy motorcycle club romance, your readers are going to need a little heads-up!

Your Turn

- Besides the standard genre elements we identified earlier, are there any specific touch points that are specific to your brand of storytelling?
- Do you always write at a certain length? Or feature specific types of characters or situations? If there are any recurring elements, make note of them.

Your brand in your other products

Any other products or services you sell are also part of your brand. Do you coach other writers? Do you do school visits or give talks at writing events? Your words, your content, your professionalism—all of these are part of your brand. In the sections that follow, we'll dig into what branding looks like in your reader relationships and business relationships and how to handle conflicts when they come up.

Your Turn

- Do you have any templates or specific guidelines for your other products or services?
- Collect any existing sample assets and look for recurring elements.

- If you don't have any branding notes yet, or if you need to make some changes, brainstorm a list of branding elements you might want to use in your new products or services.

48

ENGAGING WITH READERS AND FANS

Are you interacting with fans on your YouTube channel or through live-streamed or in-person events? Are you corresponding with readers via email? Maybe it's through your social media accounts. Anytime you interact with readers and other industry professionals, you are contributing to your overall brand. Make sure that your personality and communication style are consistent and let some of that personality shine through in both your content and images. *You* are what makes you unique. If you don't let any of that out in your interactions, then it's a lost opportunity to really connect with peers and fans alike.

Engaging with readers and fans: No, they're not always the same thing

Readers and fans *might* be the same, but they're not always. A reader is a person who has picked up your book and read it. They may have liked it enough to check out if you've written anything else. If they see you have another book out, they may even pick it up.

A fan is someone who read your book and *really* liked it. They certainly checked if you've written anything else and have already ordered it. They tell their friends about your book. They may have visited your website. They check out what you have to say on social media and signed up for your newsletter so they're sure not to miss any new releases. We're not saying that fans have to tattoo your character's name on their forehead, but they just might.

As writers, we're always hoping to turn readers into fans. The advantage of fans is that they are seeking out you and your books. They are signing up to learn more and can be counted on to respond when you need them. Readers, on the other hand, are people you need to seek out and connect with. They need to be convinced to give you their time and money.

The true story of Eileen the superfan
Eileen used to be a rabid fan of the TV show The X-Files. Years ago, the show was filming where Eileen worked. By sheer luck, as she was leaving the building one day, X-Files star Gillian Anderson was coming in. Eileen's mouth fell open. She didn't have a romantic crush on Gillian, but she loved, loved this show. She had huge admiration for this actress. She wanted to express how much the show meant to her.

"I love your show!" Eileen gushed.

Gillian smiled kindly. "Thank you so much." She then waited for Eileen to move out of the doorway and let her pass.

Eileen, however, knew that she would likely never again meet this actor, so she wanted to engage in some kind of conversation. And yet she had nothing of substance to say. She smiled and nodded.

Gillian smiled and nodded back.

Eileen kept nodding and smiling.

It got awkward.

Then it got really awkward. Only so much time can pass before you have to speak. Gillian was likely considering how quickly she could escape

> *this odd woman when the first thing that came to Eileen's mouth popped out.*
>
> *"Well, good job. Carry on!" Then Eileen saluted Gillian and marched off as if she were Patton trying to rally the troops. It was not her finest moment. She keeps it in mind every time she meets a reader who likes her work.*

Dealing with fan behaviour

Writers dream of having fans. We want them. We may daydream about long lines at book signings, sitting in a coffee shop and hearing people whispering one table over: "Is that the famous author [insert your name here]?" There is no Oscars ceremony for writers, but that in no way stops us from perfecting a speech in our heads.

But the reality of fans can be a bit different. Many writers are introverts, so having conversations with strangers is awkward. We're not always sure what to say. You might even wonder if you're being punked. How do you respond to fans and deal with positive attention?

If you're sent a card or email, create a file to save them

There are lots of up and downs in publishing. On those hard days, it can be nice to look through those appreciative comments to lift you up.

Remember that fans will often feel that they know you

They've built a relationship based on hours or weeks spent with your words. You're the creator of some of their favourite imaginary friends! If you meet fans in person, do your best to be gracious and kind. If they salute you or stand frozen in front of you, blocking the door, know it comes from a place of respect.

Consider a wrangler

If you're doing an in-person event, you may enlist the help of a friend to assist with crowd management. This person can keep a signing line moving so that you don't have to be the one to say, "Time for you to leave!" I know some authors who employ assistants (or imaginary assistants) who can take the blame for things: *I'd love to read your whole book, but my publisher won't allow me to do that.* Or *my assistant is in charge of my schedule and will let you know if I can do* X. Then the assistant, not the author, is the one letting them down.

Be cautious of becoming involved in a fan's personal issues

Because fans feel that they know you, they may be inclined to share personal issues. As someone who writes YA, Eileen often hears from teens struggling with many challenges. It's *really* tempting to try and help, but you have to question if you're the best person to solve those issues.

Create healthy boundaries

You will have to decide how much of yourself and your time you wish to share with the public. In the beginning, when a novice writer reaches out to you for feedback on their first story, it's wonderful. It's evidence they think so much of your writing they want your help. But then more people start to ask: can you read this? Can I contact your agent? Can you tell me how to get an agent? How do I write a whole book? If you're not careful, you'll end up spending a lot of time helping and supporting your fans.

Decide how much of your time you can spend on fan engagement. Consider setting up resources on your website. These might include handouts with advice for new authors, a commonly-asked-questions page, or a list of resources that can point people in the right direction (and which you only have to write once). And, of course, you're always welcome to suggest they join The Creative Academy for Writers, where'll they'll find a bevy of freely available resources!

Not all fans are happy

The bulk of this section has dealt with fans who reach out to share how much they love you and your work. However, fans may also have negative responses. They may feel that you've made a bad decision about what happens to a character. (Perhaps you killed off one of their favourites, or someone made a life choice they don't agree with.) Because fans are sometimes very enmeshed in the world you've created, they may feel a sense of ownership of it. They may tell you how you've done them wrong. You will typically find you cannot convince them otherwise. You are best to respond with a neutral remark that you will take their words into consideration but that you also have to do what is best for the characters from your perspective. Our advice here is not to argue with them.

Practice safety

It's important to at least touch on the issue of safety and privacy. There are people in the world who aren't well or who don't share your need to maintain boundaries. Those are not your issues to address—your focus needs to be on your safety and the safety of your friends and family.

Consider an unlisted phone number and ensure location services are off on your phone so you aren't making it easy for people to identify where you live from images you post on social media. Consider what you post on social media. If you name your favourite local pub, people know you live nearby and may visit the neighbourhood. If you mention your child's school, someone can assume that you go there on a regular basis to pick up or drop off your kids.

And don't use your home as your return address on information available to the public—like your author domain registration or the address at the bottom of your newsletter. There are many services that let you rent a post office box with a physical address attached. You can use this for anything that requires you to share an address publicly.

Identify and keep a list of safety resources. This may involve talking with your agent or editor about how to handle any fan behaviour you find uncomfortable. They may have additional resources that can help. Your local writers' association may have additional supports. And never underestimate the value of talking to other writers, who may have more experience in these areas and can help you draft a plan of action. Finally, there are groups like Hollaback dedicated to helping people deal with harassment online—and one consistent piece of advice we've heard over and over in our research is to keep track of interactions that make you feel uncomfortable and limit your interaction with those individuals. Trust your instincts.

There's no need to be paranoid. As much as we writers like to think we're cool, we rarely get the kind of fanbase that actors or athletes can generate. However, a little bit of caution goes a long way.

Your Turn

- Set up a physical or computer file (or both!) where you can store positive feedback and emails.
- Create a FAQ (frequently asked questions) portion of your website where you can direct readers who are looking for advice on improving their manuscripts or navigating the publishing industry.
- Track how much time you spend managing fans and determine if it makes sense to hire an author assistant for a set number of hours per month.
- Conduct a safety review of your social media. How much personal information do you post on your social media? This could include specific names, location, or details about your home.
- Brainstorm strategies to engage with fans without revealing trackable personal information. For example, instead of naming your children, you could call them "Spawn 1" and "Spawn 2." Look at how often you detail locations where you could be found, details about your home etc.
- Identify and keep a list of safety resources you can call on if needed.

49

BUILDING YOUR BUSINESS RELATIONSHIPS

Writing may be a solo activity (unless you're counting your imaginary friends), but publishing is often a team sport, regardless if you are going indie or traditional. Knowing how to build and grow those important relationships makes a big difference to your success as a full-time author, and every interaction you have with peers and industry professionals will impact your brand and, ultimately, your career.

Know your place and worth

The literary agent Janet Reid once wrote, "Writers are not the beggars at the banquet of publishing." Eileen printed out that advice and posted it by her desk to serve as a reminder. There is a tendency for writers to swing one of two ways when working with others in our industry:

- Apologetic author: Some writers feel they must approach publishing professionals on bended knee. They apologize for asking for things they are due to receive and are overly thankful for any attention or time.

- Full diva: Other writers are ready to strap on a crown and start ordering people around, perhaps with an occasional "off with their heads!"

As the creator, the writer is the central component of publishing. Without our words, the worlds we create and the stories we tell, a publishing industry wouldn't exist. However, our books are made better by using the resources of people who may know more than us in different areas. This is a fancy way of saying we're critically important, but we may want to hold off on the full crown-wearing diva behaviours.

You may work with an agent, an editor, a copy editor, a cover designer and other authors. You want to ensure that these business relationships are positive. Not only will this reduce your stress levels, but it will give you the best chance to create the best book possible and build a career in which others want to work with you.

How to be a good business partner

Before you ask for help, do your research

Is this a question you can answer on your own? Can you come to a conversation with a few different options and ask them to weigh in with their expertise?

Manage expectations

Eileen can recall a time when she was shopping with her mom as a child and came across her kindergarten teacher in the frozen food aisle. She was shocked. She believed that teachers lived in the supply closet at the school. It completely rocked Eileen's world to realize that her teacher had a life outside of her interactions with Eileen. Then, all of a sudden, there she was, out in the rest of the world, wearing jeans, having her own family, buying frozen corn! That's a good life lesson to carry into publishing.

The people you interact with have outside lives and other clients. Eileen has one agent. But that agent works with more than 20 writers. While Eileen may feel that her crisis of confidence over a publication detail is of primary importance, her agent has to be weigh that against what her other clients are dealing with. And there are pictures—proof that her agent also has a family and a life. Go figure. Turns out Barbara doesn't live in the agency's supply closet. Eileen and her problems may not be Barbara's number-one priority at any given time. This doesn't mean that Eileen isn't important, or that she doesn't require her agent's time or attention, but she must manage her expectations that things revolve around her.

Respect timelines

One fact of publishing that seems to be universal, and that everyone can agree upon, is that everything will take longer than you might imagine is humanly possible. As a result, you want to respect agreed-upon timelines. If you don't, there will be a cascading impact on other people and *their* deadlines. Before you agree to a deadline, review your to-dos and schedule and be certain that you can meet it. Create a project plan so you can measure your progress against it and know if you're ahead of schedule or running behind.

If you have to miss a deadline—life does happen—let the other parties know as soon as possible that there's going to be a problem. The more advance notice they have, the easier it will be for them to shift projects about. The point here isn't simply to hit your deadlines (although do give it a good try) but rather to understand other people are also busy.

Be polite

Under the heading of things that shouldn't have to be said but apparently do based on what we've seen happen in real life: don't be a jerk. In fact, go one step further: be polite and reasonable and kind to others. This means enacting the lessons that you mastered in kindergarten but may have forgotten in your creative haze. Say please and thank you. Share occasionally. Listen to what others are trying to say before you interrupt. And when the picture you were drawing doesn't turn out quite the way you expected, don't throw crayons at other people no matter how frustrated or tired or cranky you may be.

Give back

The creative community is just that: a community. It becomes stronger depending on the people in that community and their willingness to be active members. One of the founding principles of The Creative Academy for Writers is the idea that members help members. This might take the form of support and encouragement, taking time to read or critique, sharing information, or boosting a social media post. Giving back not only makes you feel good but also creates a web of networks and support that you can call upon when the time comes. The publishing journey is a looooooooong one. (Extra o's added so you get a sense of just how long. We would add more just to get the point across, but our editor won't let us.) Gaining support and helping others along the way means that we all enjoy the trip.

Provide clear communication

Depending on your business relationships you may do most of your communication via email, text or voice mails. This means you often won't have the benefit of non-verbal visual cues to know what the other person is saying or how they're responding to your comments. This creates an extra reason to be clear with what you're saying and ask questions to clarify your understanding.

Discuss expectations and communication styles with your business partners. What are reasonable turnaround times? What's the best way to reach them with important issues? When Eileen writes an email to her agent, she often concludes by putting in bullet points any specific areas she wants Barbara to respond to. If a matter is time-sensitive, Eileen lets her agent know and provides a date by when she needs the information. If it's a more casual conversation, she will put in the subject line something like *Questions re: new book ideas (low priority)*. If she has a pressing concern, she may write *Cover issues (high priority)*. Of course, the secret here is to make sure you don't flag something as very important if it's not.

Regularly review your business processes

If you are working with a set team or regular collaborators, make sure you have a system in place to review your processes regularly and reflect on what's working, what could work better, and how you'd like things to evolve on a regular basis. For example, after we write each new book in this book series, our Creative Academy team meets to go over what worked well and what we'd like to change before diving into the next one. We ask partners and team members what they would like to see change. We do this every three months for longer-term projects, and between each shorter-term project that is more "contained."

Your Turn

- Make a list of your existing business relationships. And make a point to check in with your collaborators to see how they feel the relationship is working. If there are any issues that need to be resolved, be sure to clarify them.
- If you come to a verbal agreement with an individual that involves some kind of expectation or deliverable (e.g., a deadline, a cover), follow up with an email or text so you have a paper trail.
- Create a system to save or file important communications with key people so that you can easily find and reference it again. It's not pleasant or efficient to dig through months of emails or texts to find something you'd agreed upon.

Conflict is necessary in a good story, and inevitable in any author career. What will set you apart from the crowd and help your brand is how you choose to deal with those conflicts.

How to handle conflicts in traditional publishing

Many of the tips in this section are relevant for all types of conflict resolution. The difference in traditional publishing is that you may not select the team that you work with at the publishing house. Yes, you have the ultimate power to cancel your contract, but you likely want to think carefully before choosing that option.

Have reasonable expectations

One of the best things you can do to reduce conflict is to have reasonable expectations of the process. We all want to be our editor's number-one priority, but here's the secret—they're also juggling other authors and projects. There may be a time when you take a back seat. Yes, you want your book to be featured in *Entertainment Weekly* but demanding that the publicity team get you in the magazine isn't reasonable.

Ask questions

Publishing can be a confusing process, especially the first few times you go through the mill. It's fine to ask questions! How long will *X*, *Y* or *Z* take? What is happening with publicity? What kind of marketing support can you expect? Your agent or your editor may be able to answer many of these for you. Many conflicts arise out of confusion or miscommunication.

Know what hill you're willing to die on

There may be some issues for which you are willing to go to the mat. For example, perhaps you have a BIPOC (black, indigenous, and people of colour) character and the initial cover design depicts them as white. You may have a line of dialogue that, for you, perfectly summarizes the story's theme, and the editor keeps trying to change it. But there will be issues you will need to compromise on if you're choosing traditional publishing, because it's a team sport. Know what matters most to you so you can choose your battles. Your publishing team is much more likely to work with you if they see that you're reasonable.

Choose your location and time

If you have a conflict with someone during the publishing process, be thoughtful about where and when you address it. If you're on a group conference call, that's *not* the time to call out your agent for sending you the wrong information. Social media is *not* the place to air any grievances. You may have been wronged, but by taking that argument public (at least before trying to address it privately) means that you're likely burning a bridge—or several.

Take a breath before reacting

Hey, we get it. This is your book. The story that you've been working on for months or years. It matters a lot. However, before you get upset about a topic, take a deep breath and choose how to respond instead of simply reacting. This may mean taking some time to gather more information, research options or consult with others.

Create win-win situations

Here's the thing: everyone wants your book to do well. Remember, you're all on the same team. Now, they may not want it as badly as you want it, but they want to be a part of that success. When it gets frustrating—and it will get frustrating—remember that you have a common goal. Look for places where you can help them to help you.

Play the long game

This book is about the goal of being a full-time writer. That's about a career. A career is more than one book. This means that you also need to think in the long term. You will be in this business for a long time, and while it may seem huge, the industry is smaller than you might imagine. Consider your reputation and what you want to portray when you interact with others.

Conflict resolution 101

There are many ways that people respond to and deal with conflict. The four most basic ways are Fight, Flight, Freeze and Fawn. These are explained in more detail in Eileen's book *Create Story Conflict*, but in general, when faced with conflict the different approaches respond like this:

> Fight: You come out ready to win the battle.
>
> Flight: If possible, you avoid the conflict altogether.
>
> Freeze: You freeze and hope that the conflict goes away or that you don't become involved.
>
> Fawn: You attempt to appease the upset person and give in to reduce their agitation.

It's important to note that you may respond differently depending on the conflict or what else is happening in your life. For example, you may be very direct in a work environment but avoid conflict when it's with your partner. Or perhaps you have a tendency toward compromise unless you are at your wit's end after months of working at home during a pandemic.

Knowing your default conflict style means that you can challenge yourself if you need to grow or improve. For example, Eileen knows that avoiding conflict is her default, with a healthy dose of fawning thrown in because she hates when anyone is upset. (Unless it's in fiction—then she loves that conflict.) So, when she's faced with conflict, she knows that she will want to avoid it and that she needs to work against that. She will create talking points and a list so that she can talk to the other individual and not get flustered in the moment. Before going into a negotiation, she thinks about her priorities and makes sure she's addressing her needs and not just wanting the conflict to disappear. On the other hand, if your approach is more fight focused, you may need to pause, consider how you can be less argumentative, and ensure you're hearing the other point of view.

Learning some basic conflict resolution skills is helpful for anyone in business. There are endless resources online and several great books about this, including *Getting to Yes: Negotiating Agreement Without Giving*

In by Roger Fisher, William Ury, and Bruce Patton (2011) and *Resolving Everyday Conflict* by Ken Sande and Kevin Johnson (2015). If you haven't taken a conflict resolution course through work or school, we recommend that you read more about this to gain the skills needed to compromise when necessary and stand firm on issues that matter.

Your Turn

- Understand your current conflict resolution style. If your conflict resolution styles haven't worked well in the past, explore how and why you responded so you can learn different strategies going forward.
- If conflict is a challenge for you, identify a support person in your network with whom you can brainstorm ideas, voice your impulses and role-play any future conflicts so you can feel prepared.
- If you have to have a difficult conversation, it can help to have key bullet points you want to discuss in front of you. This will ensure that you touch on everything that is important.

PART VI

YOUR BUDGET

50

BUDGETING FOR SUCCESS

Budgeting in the creative world can be tricky. Incomes can swing wildly from year to year and month to month. Projects don't all cost the same to produce. Expenses can come up unexpectedly alongside opportunities, and it can be really hard to accurately predict both income and expenses. However, despite what you may be thinking now (oh, thank goodness we can skip this part of the business planning process)... you *can't* skip this part. Not if you want to do some leveling up.

Many authors cover their writing expenses out of their household budget or vacation fund, and we don't always want to look at those numbers in red and black on the page in front of us.

But unless you have unlimited funds at your disposal, you *will* need a budget in place to guide your spending and keep your finances on track. One of the best ways to ensure you can stick with your author career long-term is to be aware of your financial position and make business decisions based on accurate numbers that are in line with your budget. Since we're playing a long game in the publishing world and success doesn't happen overnight, the key is to make sure you don't "bleed out" when it comes to finances. You need to stay in the game long enough to catch—or create!—that big break.

In order to make good business decisions, you *must* be able to accurately answer the following questions:

- How much money do you need to achieve the goals you have set for yourself this year?
- How much money do you have available?
- Where will you get the money that you need to balance your budget?

You need to make informed choices about how you'll spend the money available to you so that you get maximum value out of the experience.

You should be able to take care of all the basics with the free Business Plan Google Sheet we've created, but if you're looking for something a bit more robust, you can use a software like You Need a Budget (YNAB) or Quickbooks. And ask your accountant if there is a specific software you need to use for your official records.

How to tackle your budget

There are two ways to approach the budgeting process. The first way is to identify how much money you need and then figure out how to get it. The second way is to figure out how much money you have and then decide what it can best be spent on. It's likely that you will end up trying both approaches before you settle on the right solution for you, and we have presented both methods here to help you decide which makes the most sense in any given situation.

Start with your ideal plan and estimate how much you think you need for the year. Then look at what you have available. If those two numbers don't match up, you'll be faced with a decision: you can figure out where to get more money *or* you can figure out where to cut back your growth plans for the year. The right approach for you will depend on your life circumstances, your financial options and the stage you're at in your writing career.

You may have noticed multiple tabs on your Business Plan Google Sheet template—we've set it up so that everything you need to plan and track is in one handy place. We've also added some magical calculation help, so if you plug the numbers into the right places, all will be calculated for you. Pretty awesome, right? We know how many writers break out into a sweat at any talk of numbers and spreadsheets. But let's be real… while we may not be excited to know our exact financial position in the early phases of our careers, it *is* fun to watch those numbers grow over time! And it's satisfying to have a clear record of your business's evolution. We really, truly want you to succeed, so we're sharing what we've put together for ourselves. Now, you don't have to figure it all out on your own.

Your Turn

- Open the Business Plan Google Sheet, and then watch the video on how to customize and update the Budget tab for your business.

51

PLANNING FOR ANNUAL OPERATING COSTS

First, let's figure out what you need to account for in your regular annual operating budget. It's smart to set up an annual budget with funds allocated for:

- Learning, skills training and professional development
- Hiring help for the tasks you need to outsource (e.g., cover design, editing)
- Tools you use across multiple projects or contexts
- Marketing and promotion (website hosting, domain fees, social media tools, advertising)
- Any other recurring costs that you encounter on an annual basis

If you are traditionally published, you might think you don't need to worry about this. It's true that a traditional publisher covers many costs, including editorial, cover design, and production. This is one of the advantages of traditional publishing. However, you still need to create your own budget so you can determine what you can spend on training and any marketing and promotion tasks you may be covering on your own. You may need to build a website this year, or buy an app to help manage your social media updates, or maybe hire someone to help you organize a podcast tour to promote your new release.

You'll figure out your recurring costs (annual subscription to accounting software, or your BookBrush account for making promo images), the costs of leveling up in your focus areas for the year (maybe you've decided to buy Vellum to format your own book files or hire a mentor to help level up your writing craft skills) and you will figure out a budget for each project on your production schedule (cover design, editing, audiobook production).

You may also have purchased lifetime licenses to software or tools. It's good to keep track of these so you remember you have already purchased them. For those tools you pay for monthly or annually, keep your eyes open for deals on lifetime licenses—so you can remove it from your recurring budget!

Your Turn

- Open up the Business Plan Google Sheet you downloaded and click on the Budget tab. Fill in as many expenses as you can think of that were lifetime purchases, or that are recurring monthly or annual expenses.
- If you are already using a bookkeeping system of some kind, review your records from the past year to fill in these blanks.
- If you don't have an accounting system, get out your credit card statements from the past year and review your writing-related expenditures.
- Note each of your expenses and allocate them to the correct column (project, recurring monthly, or annual).

52

ESTIMATING PROJECT-BASED COSTS

You will be focused on a certain number of products and projects in the coming year. If you've been following along in the book, you have already set up a production schedule for yourself. Now, you will use that plan to help you construct your budget for this year. If you are traditionally publishing, your project-specific budget may include a promo budget for your new release.

You indie publishing folks will need to know exactly what you need to pay for a good cover designer, editing on your manuscript, setup fees on publication, launch promotion, and any other tools or helpers to get *each* book published. Our handy-dandy spreadsheet has categories for several different types and lengths of projects. You can label these appropriately, and it will auto-calculate annual amounts based on how many of each type of project you're planning to do.

Any monthly fees you add to the spreadsheet should automatically calculate an annual amount.

Pro tip: If you are funding your projects through incoming royalties or your day job, make sure your production schedule matches up with your cash flow, so you have the cash on hand when you need to spend it. There is generally a two-month delay between when royalties are earned and when they are paid out for indie publishers. For traditionally published authors your royalty cheques may be even less frequent. If you're planning to scale up your ads or publish a few new projects, make sure you have access to that cash in real time. Best practice is to spend only the money you already have or know you can count on. Don't "pre-spend" royalties you may or may not get in the future—you'll need those to fund your next round of growth!

We've referred to publishing as a casino, and this is one context where that analogy is really useful. Only spend money you can do without in the current moment, because it may be months (or even years) before you reap the rewards of today's hard work and financial investment. And while we hate to say this, some books never pay off what they cost to produce. You may win big on some and lose on others. Be prepared to weather those low-income, high-expense times while you build and grow. And minimize your expenses wherever it makes sense to give yourself more of a buffer.

One of the most common challenges we find when it comes to completing your budgeting exercise is not knowing what things cost. And prices for some services range very widely—you can pay anywhere from ten dollars to one thousand dollars (or more) for a book cover. We've tried to provide ranges, averages, or current industry-standard prices in the budget template to give you a starting place. But you will need to do your research, choose tool plans and features that are right for you, and price out services from various providers to find the ones that fit your goals, genre and budget.

Your Turn

- Fill in as much as you can of the project-based expenses tab in the Budget tab of the Business Plan Google Sheet.
- If you are newer to the writing business, ask community members for budgeting tips or use some of the default amounts in the spreadsheet as guides. Don't make assumptions, however

—double-check numbers for yourself because things shift and change in this industry all the time. Make a list of all the project-based expenses you need to research.

- Work through the sections that follow, filling in more of your budget spreadsheet as you nail down answers to the questions we ask after each section.

53

INDIE PUBLISHING INCOME EXPECTATIONS

Income expectations in the indie publishing world vary wildly. A 2020 survey of over one thousand indie authors conducted by WrittenWord Media broke the reported career trajectories of those thousand authors into five categories.

- Stage One: $0–$249 per month
- Stage Two: $250–$999 per month
- Stage Three: $1,000–$4,999 per month
- Stage Four: $5,000–$9,999 per month
- Stage Five: $10,000+ per month

The average number of published books for authors who were earning less than $249 per month, according to this particular survey? *Six books.* The average number of books from authors earning between $1000 and $4999 per month was *29 books*. While this is just a sample, and there are lots of unknown variables—quality, genre, book length, publication date—there is one thing we can agree on: a lot of books were published to get to an annual income of between $12,000 and $60,000. And the survey didn't report if those income amounts were gross (before expenses) or net (after expenses).

Although we know some authors who managed to break out much earlier and start earning six figures and more with fewer than ten books, there are no guarantees about how quickly this will happen. Most people who are earning a living from the royalties on their indie-published books tend to have at least 20 titles in their catalogues. And non-fiction often generates more revenue than fiction. (It's also easier to scale up non-fiction sales with ad spends.)

This is why we focus on sustainability, decreasing your expenses, and not putting too much pressure on your books to pay your bills when you're just getting started, especially if you're focused on fiction. You need a plan that lets you level up skills and knowledge and learn as you go—and still manage the costs of producing high-quality products along the way.

When you are an indie publishing author, you are running a small business. And most small businesses take a couple of years to become profitable—and that's if you are all in, working every day on growing your business. It is realistic to assume that for the first two or three years of your indie publishing career, you will either be making very little or reinvesting what you are making so that you can grow your catalogue and build up a collection of professional, polished projects.

If you are playing it safe, plan to fund your publishing and marketing efforts for the first two to five years through income unrelated to your writing.

It can be very helpful to have these "income level" breakdowns, although you may want to adjust the levels for yourself depending on your own goals and thresholds. We like to break that middle bit up into a couple of different levels—just like we break up that second act of a story into more manageable parts in the plotting process. We don't want to get stuck in a saggy middle in financial areas either. And somehow, seven levels seems like just the right number to us—it allows us to add that top-level category. And yes, we personally know multiple authors who make over a million dollars per year. It's nice to know that's *possible*, yes?

Here is our full-time author levels breakdown :

- Stage 1: $0–$249 per month ($0–$3,000 per year)
- Stage 2: $250–$999 per month ($3,000–$12,000 per year)
- **Stage 3: $1000–$2499 per month** ($12,000–$30,000 per year)
- **Stage 4: $2500–$4999 per month** ($30,000–$60,000 per year)
- **Stage 5: $5000–$9999 per month** ($60,000–$120,000 per year)
- Stage 6: $10,000+ per month ($120,000+ per year)
- Stage 7: $100,000+ per month ($1.2 million+ per year)

Most full-time authors will fall into stages 3 to 5. One very important thing to note is whether your metrics and income expectations are gross or net—before or after expenses, taxes and other deductions. When setting income goals for yourself, how much take-home pay (net income) do you need or want? If an author makes $10,000 per month but pays out $5,000 per month on advertising and another $2,000 per month on staff and tools to help them manage their business, then their actual take-home is only $3,000 per month. But the effort and level of management involved might be much greater than someone who is comfortable creating a "Stage 4" author income and staying there.

Paying yourself

If you are an indie publishing author, it is realistic to expect it to take one to three years before you will actually draw a salary from your business (in other words, pay yourself for actually writing the books). In the beginning, most of the money you make will go back into your business to pay for the editing and publication of your next book. So you will want a clear plan of how to make it to that point. Go back to your operating budget and make sure you have planned out how to manage this transition stage.

Once you are through the transition stage, make sure you are reviewing both your personal financial situation and your business financial situation on a regular basis. We like doing quarterly reviews of the big-picture stuff and monthly bookkeeping to make sure budgets are staying on track and we're on top of all our income and expenses since they vary month to month. It helps to actually schedule this time into your calendar each month.

Your Turn

- Assess your income statements or royalty payouts from last year. How much revenue did you generate? Do you see trends in your monthly income?
- Are those amounts before or after expenses? Do the math and figure out your actual take-home pay after expenses were paid.
- At which income stage are you now? Are you happy with that, or would you like to change it?
- Where would you like to get eventually? Which stage would you like to reach this year? Make note of those goals and keep them in mind as you work through the marketing and leveling-up sections that follow.

54

TRADITIONAL PUBLISHING INCOME EXPECTATIONS

We are often asked how much, on average, a person can expect as an advance for their book. There is no easy—or accurate—answer to this. But for a first time author an advance is more likely to be in the four to five figure range than it is to be in the five to six figure range.

A publisher's advance depends on many things, including:

Genre sales expectations

The publisher will have prepared an in-house document that compiles sales numbers from books they view as comparable titles. They will base the advance in part on what these books have sold. This varies from genre to genre.

Author sales

Does the author have a backlist? What have the sales for the author's previous books looked like?

Author's platform

Does the author have a platform of readers and fans that the publisher might reasonably expect to buy the book? Does the author have name recognition or authority on a topic?

Hot topic

Does the book deal with an issue or topic that is on trend? Does the publisher feel they can capitalize on sales? Keep in mind that with traditional publishing, it will typically take a year to 18 months for the book to come out.

Size of the publisher

Smaller publishers typically have smaller budgets and offer more modest advances or, in some cases, nothing. This does not mean that a large publisher is going to offer a large advance, but they typically do offer some form of advance.

Luck

Every so often, a book comes along that an editor or publisher is really excited about. Perhaps it's the writing, or perhaps it is something they haven't seen before. There may have been an auction where other publishers were bidding for the title and drove up the price. Maybe it's just your lucky day! There is a wild-card element to advances.

Does the size of your advance matter?

There are books that receive a very modest or no advance and go on to be huge bestsellers. And some books that earn large advances don't meet expectations. When mulling over offers, authors should consider not only the advance but also what else is on the table. Smaller publishers typically offer smaller advances, but they may have a more hands-on approach that the author likes. They may choose the smaller advance in order to be a larger fish in a smaller pond.

You may also choose to work with a specific editor instead of going for the biggest advance. You may connect with a particular editor's vision and choose to work with them even if their publisher isn't able to offer you as much. Perhaps the publisher has come forward with a marketing plan that excites you, or they agree to buy all three books in a series, making a commitment that another publisher may not.

There is some logic to the idea that the larger the advance, the more committed the publisher is to seeing the book do well. Of course, publishers want all their books to do well, but if they have paid a six-figure advance for a title, they will typically invest more time and money into marketing to ensure they see a return on that investment. While having a larger advance may make you excited to have more attention on your book, be aware that it also comes with higher expectations.

Show me the money! Or how advances work

An advance is called an advance because it is typically paid in advance of the book coming out and before any royalties have been earned. (Very clever naming on their part!) Advances are typically, but not always, paid in three instalments: 50 percent is paid when the author signs the contract for the work, 25 percent when the book is accepted following the edit process (this is often called Delivery and Acceptance) and the final 25 percent when the book is actually published.

Once the book is out, the author earns royalties on each book sold. These royalties are then applied against the advance. When the author has officially earned more royalties than they were paid as an advance, this is known as "earning out" and is cause for celebration and general merry making. Royalty statements are typically issued twice a year, and the author will get a statement of how many books have been sold.

Some things to keep in mind:

- Your agent will take their cut (15 percent) off the top of your advance.
- If it's a foreign sale, the agent's cut is more likely 20 percent—10 percent for your agent and 10 percent for the foreign agent.
- You have to pay taxes on this money, so be sure to save funds for this come tax time.
- Different formats earn different royalty amounts as specified in your contract. For example, eBooks may earn 25 percent, hardcovers 10 percent, paperbacks 8 percent. And there may be

differing royalty amounts for books sold through places like Costco.

- Royalty rates may vary depending on sales. For example, you may earn 10 percent on hardcover sales for the first 10,000 sales and 12 percent after that. These bonuses are negotiated in the contract.
- You will continue to get royalties on your book as long as it is in print and selling copies.

Barbara Poelle's book, *Funny You Should Ask: Mostly Serious Answers to Mostly Serious Questions About the Book Publishing Industry* (2020) contains much more detail on what you can expect in terms of income and how income is paid out. Plus, she's funny as all get out, so it's a great read.

How to level up your advances

The very short answer to this question is to sell more books. The better the sales of your past books, the easier it is to negotiate and obtain a higher advance. The publisher is happier to pay out a larger advance to keep an author content—and loyal—if they are fairly confident they will get that money back.

There are other factors that can impact the size of your advance. You may write what the publisher deems is a "breakout" book. When they read it, they realize that this is going to be *the one*, and they may be willing to provide you with more money to secure publication. You may also change agents—an agent more skilled at negotiation may be able to nudge your advance up, in particular if your sales have been good.

Keep in mind some authors aren't concerned about the amount of the advance because they are sure they will earn out and are happy to wait until the royalty statement comes to have it. Others like to earn the income up front. If you have a track record with a publisher, it's common for them to buy a book from you on proposal: you submit an outline and sample pages, and they provide you with a contract based on that. This means you would be getting 50 percent of that advance before you've written the book. This has the advantage of giving you funds while you are writing. The downside is often a very hard deadline, because the publisher will want you to deliver that book they've already partially paid for.

Your Turn

- Assess your income statements from last year. How much revenue did you generate from advances? How much income did you receive from royalties and sales of additional types of rights (such as translation rights)?
- Do you see trends in your annual income? From statement to statement?
- Are those amounts before or after expenses? Do the math and figure out your actual take-home pay after expenses (such as your agent percentages and promotional expenses).
- Which income stage do you expect for the coming year? Are you happy with that, or would you like to change it?
- Where would you like to get eventually? Which stage would you like to reach this year? Make note of those goals and keep them in mind as you work through the marketing and leveling-up sections that follow.

55

QUITTING YOUR DAY JOB

You might be wondering why this is in the budget section and not in the chapter titled Author, Know Thyself. But ultimately, the decision to go full-time needs to be as much about the bottom line—the profits from your business and your household income levels—as it is about your willingness and ability to devote yourself to your creative business full-time. No matter how much you might want it, there are still bills that need to be paid and basic necessities to buy. Especially if you're not the only one depending on your writing revenues.

In fact, some authors find that staying at their day job a little longer than they'd planned allows them to do things like buy lifetime licenses for the software they use the most, get higher-quality help with covers and editing, and generally reduce the stress of everyday living so they can focus on—and enjoy!—their creative projects.

Others find this decision taken out of their hands when circumstances change. There are plenty of success stories that start with: "Well, I lost my job / got bought out / got injured / was forced into early retirement / got downsized… and I decided just to go for it and see what I could do." Intense need can be very motivating for some writers—and panic-attack inducing for others. You know yourself and the needs of your own household. It's up to you to recognize when your moment comes!

Let's take a look at some hard numbers and break down what specific circumstances might create your "make-the-leap moment."

Your Turn

- How much money do you *need* to make or have to cover your monthly expenses?
- How much money do you *want* to make or have to live the lifestyle you want?
- How much money do you need on hand to cover your author business expenses for the next six to twelve months? (*Hint:* Your author business budget and this year's project budgets together make up this number.)

Remember: there is always an option to do everything in a way that costs less money, but that inevitably takes more time. Don't lose heart if you're on the DIY or budget-friendly path. You can absolutely still get there—it just might take a little longer if you're throwing time at the problem instead of cash. The upside of that slow and steady path? That organic growth tends to be quite stable and sustainable in the long term, even when other circumstances change!

What are you willing to sacrifice to get there sooner?

Would you be willing to live in a significantly smaller home if it reduced your household income requirements and you could write full-time? Or would you rather have a day job (part-time or full) and stay in a particular house?

Are you willing to get up a few hours before your day job starts to work on your writing career as you build up your backlist? Or give up Netflix in the evenings? If you can only write on weekends or vacations, it will take you longer to launch a full-time author career. That's not a bad thing, but it is a choice you need to make.

Can you test drive the life you think you want?

Before you quit your job and dive right into being a full-time author, can you take that life for a test-drive?

Can you spend your vacation time from your day job living as a full-time author? Set a goal for yourself: imagine what your perfect author day or week looks like and live that as completely as you can over your vacation.

Does your work offer you the option to bank sick days and use those? Can you take advantage of a program at your work that allows you to take a sabbatical or unpaid leave of absence? Do you have the option of working longer shifts in exchange for working one less day per week? Can you use that one day per week to live your author life, see if you like it, and discover if you're able to move things forward?

Are you able to negotiate with family members or your life partner to explore what being a full-time author would look and feel like on a longer-term basis? This won't be an option for everyone, and even having the conversation about your goals and dreams can be difficult. But having the support of the people in your life is extremely important. Be sure to think about what you can contribute to make this a fair exchange. If you prepare some suggestions of how you can support your family in a different way during this time, they will be more likely to support or at least consider your plans.

Your Turn

- Think about what you are willing to give up in your life to accelerate your transition to a full-time author career. Make a list of all the possibilities to review with your household. Recruit your partner, family members or friends to help so you get a complete list of options.
- Does your work have any options for holidays, vacation, sabbatical or unpaid leave? What are they?
- Is there a time this year when you could "test drive" being a full-time author and see how it feels?

56

FINANCING YOUR AUTHOR BUSINESS GROWTH

Sometimes the budget required does not add up to the budget available. We get it. Life doesn't always co-operate with our dreams, and there are a lot of factors that influence the bottom line. Sometimes those other sources of funding just don't come through. Or a sudden change to your employment situation, family life or personal bank balance creates a need to instantly re-evaluate your plans.

Crystal's love of the DIY approach and passion for learning to do things herself is firmly grounded in a history of never having enough money to hire other people to help. And she's developed her wide knowledge of tools and software over decades of chasing "free" tools wherever possible. Eileen's decision to downsize her home was made partly to ensure that she had the freedom to retain her full-time author lifestyle despite changing life circumstances.

If the budgeting exercise has shown you that your budget and your needs list don't quite line up, here are some ways you can make adjustments to keep moving forward anyway.

There are two primary sources of funding when seeking funds to help you to grow your author career.

1) Your money

2) Other people's money

Investing your own money

Often, the easiest money to get your hands on is your own. Crystal kept her day job longer than she needed to in order to bank that extra money and fund one big year of career building and pay the publishing costs on the projects she intends to release during that accellerated leveling up year. Before that, she allocated any income from teaching presentations and workshops to her publishing fund for future projects, which motivated her to say yes to those opportunities. She saw her progress and opportunities grow as that savings account grew.

When it comes to our Creative Academy Guides for Writers series, we've set up a system where we put a percentage of our profits back into advertising, editing and publication of the next title. Although we don't personally get "paid" as much from book sales in the moment, we're trying to ensure we have the funds to take important next steps in the long term and generate consistent, stable growth over time. To build something lasting, you have to invest over time.

Ideas to gather your own money:

- If you're still working, investigate how you might put a percentage of your earnings aside to give you a cushion.
- Look at expenses. Where can you cut back?
- Look at long-term financial planning. How quickly can you pay off debts like high-interest credit cards? Should you buy a used car or a new one? Or just get a bus pass?
- If you get a windfall, use that to pay off long-term expenses. When Eileen earned a dance party–worthy advance, she used to it pay off her biggest expense—her housing—so her monthly costs could remain low, giving her more security and options.

Only you can determine your budget and decide what constitutes a need versus a want. If you live in a more expensive city, you could save money by moving away, but it might cost you social opportunities, for example. If you have a spouse or children living at home, you will need to take their interests into consideration as well. While you may be willing to cut off cable and Netflix to save money, they may feel differently.

One of the most valuable things you can do is become clear about your own financial status. What are your expenses and sources of income? How do you spend money? Are you financially impulsive, or are you a saver? What is your comfort level with financial decisions?

To better understand your own relationship with money, we recommend you read *You are a Badass at Making Money* by Jen Sincero and *The Illusion of Money* by Kyle Cease. We might feel funny talking about money, we might feel bad about wanting it—while still really wanting it—and we might even find it intimidating once we've gotten it. Jen Sincero does a great job of keeping it funny but real and challenging you to consider the role money and finances play in your life. Ask yourself: what role do you want them to have?

The gambling philosophy

It's really important to understand when something is an investment and when it is a gamble. Nothing in the world of publishing is for sure. Just because you feel like you are investing in new skills or professional help or a published book does not guarantee a return on that investment. And even if that book does pay you out over time and you recover your costs, it may take years before that happens. Investing in education or services that you believe will help you advance your career is a great thing to do. But we highly recommend that you only do this with funds you don't need back quickly. Think of it as you would a very long-term investment. Or sticking money into a slot machine. The reality of publishing is that a small number of projects make most of your money over time, especially if you find one that hits it big. Only "play" with what you can afford to either lose or not see a return on for quite some time.

But what if you don't have access to your own funds that you can afford to part with or sock away for a long period of time? Fortunately, there are other options!

Investing other people's money

Besides the money coming from a day job or book advances and royalties, other funds flow to an author such as foreign rights and audiobooks. All of these contribute toward the income you earn as a writer. However, there are other sources of money you may not have considered. Access to these may depend on where you live. The ones below include some available only in Canada, but check your home country and area for something similar.

Public Lending Commission

Authors can be paid a portion of a fund to compensate them for having their books in public libraries. Be aware there is a deadline to set up an account each year.

Canada Council for the Arts

This organization provides grants for writers for a range of activities including book research and writing. Similar grants in the US may be found by researching online.

Access Copyright

This organization provides funds for writers who may have their work or a portion of their work used in another form (such as a classroom text).

Paid speaking opportunities

There are paid speaking opportunities for schools, libraries and some conferences. In Canada, there is a wonderful program, TD Book Week, which funds children's and YA authors to present in schools.

Hardship funds

There are many writing organizations, such as the Society of Children's Book Writers and Illustrators, the Writer's Union of Canada, and the Science Fiction and Fantasy Writers of America, that offer funds for authors who may need assistance.

Scholarships and residencies

Some writers organizations offer scholarships to conferences or residencies. These scholarships may be awarded based on need or membership of particular marginalized groups. Many writing residencies offer reduced costs for writers to get away and focus on their craft.

Discounts and coupons

If you're not sure if there are any discounts available, get comfortable asking. The worst someone will say is no. Eileen teaches creative writing at a local university and as a result gets a discount from Apple when she has to buy a new laptop. Many writers' organizations, like the Alliance for Independent Authors and our own Creative Academy for Writers, arrange discounts for members on various tools and services you might need along the way.

Crowdfunding and patrons

There is a trend toward creators seeking direct support from the audiences they provide content to. So you can look at Patreon, Kickstarter or tools like Buy Me a Coffee to set up a system where your audience can support you directly.

Pre-selling books

If you're an indie author, you can actually pre-sell books to friends and family in order to raise the funds you need for the editing and publishing process. It's not easy, but it is possible. Think of it as a local or personal version of Kickstarter.

Holiday money and gifts

If you have people in your life who buy gifts for you on special occasions, let them know that you're trying to raise money to live your dream and that any cash you receive you'll set aside to pay for book editing, a cover design, or whatever your next need is. Often, people are happy to help you reach a goal if they know you're saving for it.

Barter or trade your skills

If you just can't get the cash together, think about people you know in your author networks or personal life who may have the skills or tools you're looking for. What can you offer them in return for help with what you need to move your project forward? It may be writing-related, it may not. If you have a friend who is a great editor but is desperate for child-care—and you are at home with your kids already—negotiate a trade of their editing time for your child-care time. Maybe you are great at story feedback but you don't have access to Vellum for preparing your book layouts. Offer to swap. Use your imagination and get creative. Put it out to your author networks for ideas. Just make sure that the boundaries or parameters on any trade agreements are clear and agreed upon by both parties, and ideally even written down. Open ended swaps can be challenging, so if there is an "expiry date" on cashing in on the IOU make sure both parties understand that.

Your Turn

- What options do you have to source financing for your business from *your money*? Make a list of all revenues and sources of income you can safely access and allocate to building your writing career.
- How much of your own money do you have access to in the coming year to grow your author career to the next level?

- What options do you have to source financing for your business from *other people's money*? Make a list of all possible revenues and sources of income they could generate.
- Identify anyone in your network who has the skills you are looking for. What skills do you have that you could offer up or barter in exchange for the help you need?

PART VII

YOUR MARKETING PLAN

57

REFINING YOUR MARKETING MIX

Book sales and marketing is an extremely important area to cover, and we are going to touch on various components here at a high level. We can hear you groaning all the way from here. We get it. We know the marketing is the hardest part for most authors. Many writers even choose to pursue traditional publishing arrangements because they believe their publisher will take care of all the marketing and promotion. Sorry to burst your bubble, but even if you go the traditional route, you don't get a free pass.

If you intend to take your career to the next level and pursue this full-time author thing seriously, you *will* need to embrace the whole marketing and promotion side of things. Does this mean you have to do *all the things*? Absolutely not. But you do need to decide which things will get your precious time and attention and which things you will give yourself permission to put in the "not right now" or "never" pile.

Your marketing plan could include activities in any of the following categories:

- Reviews
- Author website

- Mailing list
- Author profiles
- Social media
- Free promotion
- Paid promotion
- Paid advertising
- Awards and contests
- Other really cool stuff we haven't thought of

We dig into these areas in more detail in the sections that follow—but for now, our goal is to help you identify which components you're going to include in your business plan this year and what your budget allows for marketing. Then you can make decisions that fit your budgetary borders.

Your marketing mix

We generally get about 80 percent of our results from 20 percent of our activities. We want to adjust the dials on your marketing mix to fit you—and dial down the time wasters that don't offer as much benefit as they could. There are three primary "filters" you can use when deciding which ingredients go into your marketing mix and deserve to be part of this year's business plan. Use the information from the "Your Turn" questions above to identify which areas you want to either set up or level up this year.

Time

Decide how much time you have to dedicate to the marketing side of things each week or month. It's easy for marketing to expand and fill every waking second if you let it. But we know that the best way to market your current book is to write another one, so the goal is always to keep the promo side of things confined to the time that is *not* needed for writing your next book.

Enjoyment

Which of these elements to you enjoy? Make sure you include some of those in the mix. You are much more likely to do a task that actually brings you pleasure. While it's not realistic to think that you will love all aspects of marketing, you can choose the activities you dislike the least!

Skills

Which of these marketing activities do you already have the skills to do yourself? Which of these will require outside assistance to set up or monitor? Which of these areas could you, or do you, want to learn more about so you'll be ready when the time comes?

Money

How much does each marketing option cost? And how does that mesh with your budget? Some people budget for marketing a set amount per month or per release. And others funnel a certain percentage of their revenue back into marketing efforts. For example, we invest up to 25 percent of the monthly royalties for our Creative Academy Guides for Writers series back into our advertising. We meet each month, review our income and expenses, and decide whether to maintain, increase or decrease that amount. That allows us to scale appropriately and adapt to market changes and adjustments to advertising costs.

For the purposes of putting together your business plan and identifying possible areas to level up, we'll stick with an overview here. Some of these options may be more accessible at different stages of your career or for different kinds of publishing, and we'll try to indicate that. But most should be available to *all* authors—regardless of your publishing approach.

If you really want to level up your marketing game, we have a whole other book in The Creative Academy Guides for Writers series to help you dive into detailed strategy and planning for each of these areas—it's called *Sell More Books* by Crystal Hunt and it'll be available in 2021. We've also included some extra credit reading recommendations throughout this section so you can further explore very specific areas of your marketing and promotion.

If you are looking for more information, we have free master classes in The Creative Academy for Writers on *all* of these topics. They're available for you to work through at your leisure.

Your Turn

- How much time do you have to dedicate to marketing and promotion efforts on a daily, weekly or monthly basis?
- Are any of your marketing activities not showing the results to justify continuing with them?
- Make a note of the activities from the list above that appeal to you and might even be fun—and then add "mailing list" to that list. (Trust us on this one. Once it starts making you money and you level up your skills, you may even grow to love it!)
- Which activities from the previous sections feel like a good fit for you skills-wise at this point in your career? Which ones could you complete without having to hire help or take a course?
- How much money do you have to dedicate to your marketing efforts this year? Is this a monthly amount, a per-release amount, a percentage of revenue or a combination?
- Revisit your budget in your Business Plan Google Sheet and make sure you have filled in the budget line items for marketing and advertising.
- If you have already been working in some of these marketing areas, which do you think need some leveling up?
- Use the Marketer and Marketer-Progress tabs in your Business Plan Google Sheet to review your existing marketing efforts and refine your focus for this year's business plan.

58

LEVELING UP READINGS AND SPECIAL EVENTS

We suspect that your writer daydreams include an image of yourself standing in front of a room—or auditorium—full of rapt listeners as you read from your latest novel. This is in addition to the daydream where you're invited to all kinds of cool literary parties where your favourite authors are hanging out, drinking out of glasses with cool garnishes.

As a career author, you'll often be invited to read from your work. Every time you are reading your work in public and engaging with fans, it contributes to your brand identity and is an opportunity to connect with readers *and* sell your books. These tips will help you master it like a pro:

Plan for your reading to last for 5 to 10 minutes maximum

There's a reason we read to kids before bed. The sound of someone reading can lull people to sleep. That's not something you're looking to do. Read too long, and you'll have an audience snoozing away.

Select a reading that makes sense

You can read from the opening of your novel, or, if you're reading from somewhere in the middle, provide a couple of lines of context to your story first. "This scene takes place when the main character, Xavier, meets Yolanda for the first time."

Avoid reading spoilers

If you've got a great twist or reveal in the book, don't read it aloud! You don't want to ruin that moment for the reader later or give them a reason not to buy or read the book themselves.

It's okay not to read every line as written

You may wish to cut out some lines that deal with subplots or that won't make sense to the audience. You may also take out some of the dialogue tags ("he said," "Jared said") because when you speak aloud, they may not be needed. Highlight what you want to read or cross out what you will be skipping. You can also underline passages you want to emphasize verbally. Eileen will often write in a slash mark to remind herself to pause and take a breath. You might think breathing should be obvious, but Eileen has a tendency to forget when reading aloud.

Use silence as your friend

There may be a moment where you want to pause for emphasis. If people laugh, allow them to do so before reading what happens next. You may want to race to the end, but allow yourself to take your time.

Consider performing your piece instead of reading it

You could use slightly different voices for different characters. You may use arm gestures or facial expressions that work well with what you're saying.

If you don't have to stand at a podium or sit in a chair, consider moving around

The idea is to move with purpose instead of looking like you might just wander off. And make sure you don't turn your back to the audience, or wander too far away from the microphone if you're using one.

Practise, practise, practise

You'll be more comfortable and relaxed if you've read the piece multiple times. Practise aloud so you can feel the cadence of the words as you speak.

End with a call to action

Remember that this is an opportunity to connect with your readers *and* invite them to purchase your books. Make sure you are clear about how and where they can connect with you after the reading, and tell them where they can purchase your books. If you are signing books after your reading, share the location and duration of that opportunity with your audience.

And maybe most important of all: remember to have fun. This is your big moment. Enjoy it!

Your Turn

- Do you have any planned readings scheduled?
- Are there any upcoming opportunities that you could apply to be part of?
- Scan community events announcements, ask in your writing communities, and sign up for online newsletters for local libraries and literary associations to see what your options are.

59

LEVELING UP REVIEWS

There are two main kinds of reviews: reader reviews, and editorial reviews by industry professionals, organizations or other published authors. (Short reviews by other authors are sometimes referred to as "blurbs.")

Reader reviews

You'll see these listed on the sales information pages for many books in the form of stars and comments, and there are reader-focused sites that have huge databases of reviews. Goodreads is one of the most well-known, and BookBub has a "review this book" function that's built into the platform. There are also sites like HiddenGems, where you can pay to access their database of reviewers and they will send your books to their audience in exchange for a fee. If you plan to use one of these sites, make sure it's a reputable company that adheres to best practices for reviews. And understand that paying to access that group of people does not guarantee you favourable reviews.

Editorial reviews

Usually these are reviews from higher-profile publication or individuals: magazines, other notable authors in the genre, or even celebrities. Most often you'll see editorial reviews quoted on website pages, promotional materials or sales pages for the books. (Amazon has an editorial reviews section.) Some will even be included on the cover of the book.

Editorial reviews are important for a book's promotional campaign and may have the most influence on purchases in a traditional bookstore environment.

The power of reviews

In the digital book world, online customer reviews tend to be the most important factor when potential readers are deciding whether or not to buy your books. Reviews make your ads more effective. Many promotional sites require your book to have a certain number of positive reviews before it can qualify for promotional opportunities. More of your mailing list will purchase if you have positive reviews. And you're more likely to get invited to participate in collaborative promotions with other authors if you have a solid base of reviews.

Resource: Kindlepreneur.com has some fantastic resources on how to get more reviews, tips on what you can and can't do when asking for reviews and some great articles on how and why you might need them.

Your Turn

- Do a reviews audit by pulling up your books on all the platforms where they are for sale. How many reviews do you have on each platform? What is the average star rating?
- If you notice a trend of not-great reviews or star ratings that are lower than you'd like, make sure you take some notes on how to avoid getting reviews like that in the future.

- Do you need more reviews? (*Hint:* The answer is always *yes!*)
- Brainstorm some ways you could recruit more reviewers.

60

LEVELING UP YOUR AUTHOR WEBSITE

While it is possible to develop an author career without a website, feedback from industry professionals, publishers, and readers suggests that one of the first things they do when they discover a new author is to check their website for new books and sign up to their mailing list. For writers pursuing a traditional publishing arrangement, editors, agents and publishers will be looking for you to have a professional online presence. An author website is a cornerstone of your author brand and your sales and marketing strategy. It is one of the only pieces of digital real estate that you have complete control over, and it acts as the central hub for all your other promotional efforts. There are lots of tools to help you create an author website even if you're not a tech expert—ask for recommendations from your author friends or take advantage of one of our free master classes on this topic in The Creative Academy for Writers.

Your Turn

- Do you have an author website yet? If not, choose a course and work through it, taking notes on which platforms you might like to use.
- What is your budget for a website? Knowing your budget will help you make choices along the way. Website platforms like SquareSpace or PubSite, which are easy to use and take care of hosting for you, cost about $25 per month at the time of writing. So that's a good starting place for your budget.
- Set a recurring appointment in your calendar to work on your author website. Use the time for researching and building it at first; after that, use the time to keep it updated.

61

LEVELING UP YOUR MAILING LIST

Mailing lists are one of the things authors complain about most often. How often to send it, what to put in it, how to not feel like a slimy pushy salesperson while you ask people to buy your books… these are all common issues.

The technical side of building signup forms, maintaining your deliverability scores (which are *what* now?) and keeping everything updated can also feel overwhelming.

But this is one of the most powerful tools in your arsenal and a huge component of any stable author income. This is the asset that will help you grow faster, enable stable launch numbers and set up every new release for success as you grow that career. It will bring you exponential returns over your author career if you invest a little time and funds up front to get it all set up and working in your favour.

Mailing lists are also one of the most common regrets of established authors—once they learn what it can do for them, they wish they'd started their mailing list sooner.

Since there are quite a number of steps involved in setting up a mailing list—and this book is already getting too heavy to carry around—we will dig into this topic in greater detail in the forthcoming book *Sell More Books*.

For now, check out the numerous free master classes in The Creative Academy that deal with how (and why) to set up your mailing list. And we recommend you get your hands on the book *Newsletter Ninja* by Tammi Labrecque. That will fire you up to tackle your newsletter.

Your Turn

- Do you have a mailing list?
- If no, make it your mission to set one up as soon as possible. Mark a recurring date in your calendar called "level up mailing list." For now, those appointments will be focused on learning about and setting up your list. Later, you can use them to create content to send to your list!
- If yes, when was the last time you reviewed your onboarding sequence? Do you need to update any of your messages? Look at your deliverability scores and open rates. Are there areas in which you could do better? How regularly are you sending out? Can you make an improvement to get you more in line with this year's goals?

62

LEVELING UP YOUR AUTHOR PROFILES

When we refer to author profiles, we're talking about customized pages on different online communities and websites where fans interact and books are listed and purchased. Once you have a book published, there are plenty of places you can claim your author profiles, customize them, and connect readers to all your books in all their formats. These make it easier for readers to see what books you have written. On your profiles, they can also discover:

- Where to go to learn more about you (your website)
- How to get on your mailing list (the link to your sign-up page can go right in your profile)
- Where they can connect or interact with you (your social media)
- Samples of, or links to, your blog posts, videos, and reviews
- Buy links so they can click right through to an online store to purchase something they like

Some sites like BookBub and Amazon will even notify your followers when you release a new title.

Here are some of the main author profiles to ensure you have claimed and customized:

- Amazon.com Author Central
- International Amazon sites (France, Japan, UK, Germany, Italy)
- BookBub
- Goodreads
- LibraryThing
- BookSniffer

And there are many, many more that you can find with a quick Google search. Be sure to check if your publisher, or any author groups you belong to, have a customizable profile page available for you to claim—like SCBWI (Society for Children's Book Writers and Illustrators), RWA (Romance Writers of America), or ALLi (Alliance of Independent Authors).

Your Turn

- Have you claimed all your main author profiles yet? If not, make a checklist of the ones you haven't claimed and schedule a time to do that.
- If you have claimed all your profiles, when was the last time you updated them? Review each profile and make sure it has a link to your mailing list sign-up form or, at the very least, your website URL.
- Are all your books connected to your profiles? Are they displaying current covers? Is there anything else that needs updating?
- Does your website or email signature feature a call to action to follow you on your various author profiles?

63

LEVELING UP YOUR FREE PROMOTION

There are lots of free promotional opportunities. You can:

- Work with other authors to cross-promote your new releases or discounted books, using tools like BookFunnel and StoryOrigin
- Arrange newsletter swaps and signal boosts on social media
- Run giveaways through your mailing list or social media

There are even some promo sites we discuss in the next section that don't charge you to be included in their programs. You just need to follow their submission guidelines.

Your Turn

- Brainstorm a list of authors in your niche who might be willing to do a newsletter swap for your next promo or new release.
- Is anyone in your social networks promoting a price drop or new release right now who you could give a signal boost to?
- Do you have anything you could use as a prize for a giveaway?

A signed copy of a print book, a branded mug made on RedBubble, or an eBook version of your boxed set, maybe?

- What do you want from your readers in exchange for a contest entry? Decide if you want to add people to your mailing list or have them follow you on BookBub or any site on which you're trying to build followers.

64

LEVELING UP WITH PROMO SITES

Some promo sites are paid, and some are free. Basically, the owners of a promotional website, social account or mailing list send out an announcement of your book to their readers. In exchange, you pay money. It is even free to submit your book some promo sites—although to score a BookBub feature deal, for example, you have to apply and, if you do get chosen, pay hundreds or thousands of dollars depending on your category and worldwide region.

The upside? These deals are sent out to massive audiences. The cheaper sites may have tens of thousands of readers on their lists, and BookBub has hundreds of thousands or even millions of followers in your specific genre! In WrittenWord Media's 2020 Roundup survey of more than 1000 authors, promo sites in general and BookBub specifically were the runaway winners in terms of what promotion tactics worked best for most authors. It's worth your while to learn more about how these work.

Look for promo sites that are most specific to your genre or subgenre because it's important to keep your audience as focused as you can. That will hopefully turn more viewers into buyers, but will also keep those "also-boughts" nice and focused.

David Gaughran has a wonderful online course—free at the time of writing—called Starting from Zero, which talks all about how to run these kinds of promos strategically. Both he and Dave Chesson over at Kindlepreneur also have fantastic lists that they update regularly of all the best promo sites.

Your Turn

- Can you take advantage of promo sites, or is it up to your publisher to submit your book? (If it's up to your publisher, ask them if they have anything planned that you could help promote.)
- Make a list of promo sites that are the best match for your promotion budget and your audience in terms of your location, genre and sales channels. Some sites require you be published wide to qualify.
- Review any restrictions on discounting your books, such as KDP Select's guidelines around the timing of countdown deals or titles that have already been discounted in last 30 days.
- Schedule a price drop.
- Schedule some exposure on promo sites around that sale.
- Download the Strategic Authorpreneur Promo Planning Google Sheet to help organize your promo push and track your results.

65

LEVELING UP PAID ADVERTISING

When we talk about paid advertising in the modern publishing landscape, we're usually talking about companies that put ads for your books in front of their audience in exchange for a fee. These platforms generally include Facebook, Amazon and BookBub. (BookBub's ads program, accessible by anyone, is not to be confused with the tougher-to-score feature deals we talked about in the last section). While there are other search engines and social platforms with ads programs (Google, LinkedIn, Twitter, Pinterest, Instagram), we generally recommend that you pick one of the first three we mentioned if you hope to level up your marketing efforts through ads. Amazon, BookBub and Facebook have proven most effective for authors.

We also recommend that you choose just one platform to start with. Amazon ads can be a good one, since it's harder to spend your money on that platform. Why is this a good thing? You can learn from experimenting without worrying about spending large sums of money very quickly as you figure things out. On other ads platforms like BookBub and Facebook, you may need to invest a fair bit more cash during your learning stage.

Once you've chosen a platform, learn from the experts. Do some Google searches for resources on how to set up ads. Each company that runs an ads platform has free tutorials and learning hubs you can access. Look for one or two highly rated books on your chosen platform, although always check the book's publication date first—ads platforms change very frequently, and relying on out-of-date information can cost you.

The best, and most up-to-date, sources of information on how to use an ads platform is often available through online courses. Some of these are free, some are paid. Ask people in your author groups which ones they have found most helpful. If you're not sure where to start, we suggest signing up for this free Amazon Ads course from Kindlepreneur.com.

If you have trouble breaking into the competitive Amazon.com site in the US, you might try setting up ads in Canada, the UK or Australia, as those are newer markets with less competition. We found those were great markets in which to test ads. Finally, Deb Potter's *Amazon Ads for Authors 2020: Tips and Strategies to Sell Your Books* is a great place to start if you feel ready to tackle Amazon Advertising. It covers several of the most common markets.

Your Turn

- Are you currently running any paid advertising on your books?
- *Can* you run paid ads on your books? If you are traditionally published, your publisher may be doing this for you. Find out if they are, or if they plan to in the future.
- How does advertising fit into your annual budget? How much money do you have to work with in terms of marketing and promotion?
- Which platform do you think you would like to start with? If you're not sure, read some articles, talk to other authors about what's working for them and watch some tutorials on each platform to see which one appeals to you most.

- Take an online course from a reputable source on how to use that platform.
- Set a budget if you don't already have one. How much are you willing to spend to learn to run ads? (*Note:* We said *spend* not *invest*... because there is no guarantee that money is coming back.)

66

LEVELING UP SOCIAL MEDIA

Social media, like Instagram, Facebook, Twitter and other sites, *can* be a great way to connect with your readers. The challenge is that it takes time to build an audience, it takes time to interact with the community and it takes time to gain a good understanding of how best to use the platform. And it can be a giant black hole of time and attention if you're not careful about how you're using it. If you're going to dive into social media, keep the following in mind:

- Know what you want out of your social media time. Do you connect with authors, connect with readers, learn about what other authors are doing, or connect with librarians and teachers, for instance?
- Pick a platform you enjoy using. Ideally this will also be where the audience you want to connect with hangs out.
- Lurk for a while.
- Limit the amount of time each day and week that you spend interacting with these networks.
- Be patient and consistent. It can take one to three years of social media activity to build enough of a following to see actual results in terms of your sales.

Always ask yourself: Is this more effective than writing another book or putting time into another area of marketing?

Your Turn

- What social media platforms are you on now? Make a list. You might want to put the name of each platform at the top of a fresh piece of paper or sticky note and answer the following questions about each one:
- How much time per week do you spend on this platform?
- What outcome do you want from this platform? What's your goal?
- Have you seen a direct benefit from the time you have spent on this platform? If yes, identify what it is.
- Do you enjoy this platform? Could you remove it or put it on pause for a specific period of time?

67

LEVELING UP AWARDS AND CONTESTS

Who doesn't like winning an award? Especially if it comes with a fancy trophy, plaque, certificate suitable for framing or a cash prize. Some contest prizes even include your piece being published. We all like to feel special. And adding "award-winning author" to your bio makes you feel just a smidge sparkly. It can also influence sales numbers and the promotional opportunities you can qualify for. For example, if you or your publisher is applying for a BookBub feature, awards and accolades may make you more eligible for getting chosen for the feature slot. And if you're applying for a writer-in-residence or teaching gig, winning an award or hitting a bestseller list can be a great thing to have on your resume.

However, not all awards and contests are equal. Be aware that they are often money generators for the organization. This is not necessarily a bad thing, but if you're investing the money, you want to ensure that the award is worthwhile. Saying that you won the Crystal and Eileen Award for Being Nifty isn't going to impress any editors or agents. Winning a contest with a major organization like *Writer's Digest* is going to carry more weight.

There are writers who end up in a cycle of applying for contests and awards. It can feel great if you win, but does that win move your career forward?

Things to consider with contests and awards:

- If you're traditionally published, ask your editor or agent if they'll be submitting your novel to various contests (e.g., the Edgar, the Hugo).
- What is the cost of submitting to the contests you're interested in? Is there a submission fee? A set number of copies you must provide? Do you have to pay to ship these copies?
- Who are the judges of these contests? Do you have the opportunity to get your work in front of someone who may be able to help with your career?
- Is there a cash prize for the winners? Will your work appear in any publications?
- Do you have a budget line for contest entries in your overall business plan?
- What are the contest submission dates?
- Have you read the full submission guidelines to ensure you qualify? Do you understand any rights that you may be granting to the contest?

Depending on your level, you may also be asked to judge a contest. This is an honour, but one that comes with a time commitment. It likely has limited advantages to you other than some exposure, but it is a chance to give back to your community.

Your Turn

- If there are contests that you're keen to enter, write the due dates for submission in your calendar so they don't sneak up on you.
- If you're traditionally published, speak with your editor or agent about what contests and awards the publisher will be putting your name forward for. If they aren't willing to cover the costs of certain contests, ask if they would be willing to donate copies of your book if you cover the submission fee.

68

LEVELING UP YOUR CATALOGUE

It's an interesting fact that the best way to promote an existing book is to write another book—especially if it's part of a series. With each title you add to your catalogue, the number of ways readers can find you goes up. And once they get to know you through one book, you have a chance to convert them from reader to superfan.

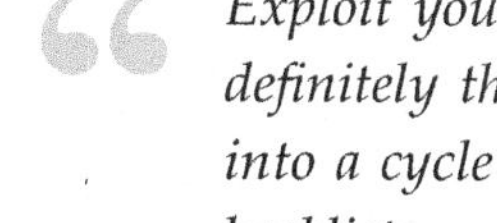

> *Exploit your backlist. Writing a new book and promoting it is definitely the best way to build your career, but it's easy to fall into a cycle of only doing that. There is value in curating your backlist, repackaging titles, preparing ads and creating sharables. As you build your fanbase, ensure they know you have other work to explore.*
>
> — DANI COLLINS, *USA TODAY* BESTSELLING AUTHOR OF MORE THAN SIXTY ROMANCE NOVELS

Note, however, that you will likely be able to grow your catalogue more rapidly if you are indie publishing because the publication schedule is entirely within your control. If you're working with a traditional publisher, talk with editor and agent about production schedule options. You may end up working with multiple publishers or releasing some titles under a pen name.

Even if you're not publishing new books, you can still level up your sales by making the most of your backlist titles.

The key here is to write the best book you can, whether it's your first or fifteenth or fiftieth title. If readers love it, they'll go looking for more of your stories. And those books will be part of your catalogue for life—and beyond!

And then set about optimizing your backlist titles for maximum read-through. You want to lead readers through your titles and the best way to do that is by making sure you've optimized your front and back matter.

What are you looking for exactly when you do this audit of your existing catalogue? Ask yourself the following questions for each book:

- Do you have a list of your other books (also known as an "also by" list) in the front and/or back matter of your book?
- At the back of the book, is there a preview or excerpt from the next book you want them to read?
- Is the call to action of where they can purchase that next book clearly phrased and placed where they can't miss it?
- Did you include a call to action to join your mailing list so you can notify them of future releases and other news?
- Did you request somewhere that they leave a review if they enjoyed your book?
- If the book is part of a series, is it clearly shown what other books are in the series, and where this one fits in the series order?
- Is there any out of date, or incorrect information, branding or covers (within the previews of other books) in your book?

While it will be harder to make changes if you are traditionally published, it's still good for you to know what readers see and whether or not each book is helping promote the others. If your publisher is considering a reprint or new edition of your book, you will be able to call attention to any issues you have identified. And for eBooks, updates are generally much more accessible!

Your Turn

It's time to conduct an audit of all your existing titles!

- Draw a "reader pathway" diagram that shows the ideal reading order for all your books.
- Now compare the back matter for each book against your diagram to make sure it's clear to the reader which book to read next.
- Clean it up, add your branding, and make this reading order list or instructions a bonus feature on your website.
- Make a checklist or template of your optimized front and back matter.
- Review each title and update your files as needed.
- Re-publish/re-upload your files to your various publication channels.

Note: if you are updating your files in advance of a planned promotion, make sure you do this at least a couple of weeks in advance as sometimes re-publishing can impact pricing or listing information. Leave yourself enough time to get any errors corrected before your promotions go live!

PART VIII

LEVELING UP YOUR AUTHOR CAREER

69

DEFINING WHAT IT MEANS TO LEVEL UP

Leveling up our author career comes in many forms. We most often think of growth in terms of adding things—more books, more sales, more fame, more career elements (such as coaching or mentoring), or more compensation for our efforts in various areas. In fact, you may have to *subtract* things from your business plan to really hit that next level of growth. Leveling up could mean focusing on your writing and hiring out the publishing and promotion tasks so you can really go to a deeper level with your craft.

In this chapter, leveling up means taking the next step toward the big career goals or milestones you identified in your mission statement. And that can look very different depending on the focus of your personal author mission.

When do you know it's time to level up?

Often it will be an emotional cue or trigger that calls your attention to the fact that you're ready to chase a new challenge or try something new. You might be feeling a bit bored with your daily routine or find yourself procrastinating instead of getting down to work. You may not feel challenged by what you're working on. Or maybe you've found real clarity about which aspects of the business you love and which ones you don't, and you are feeling conflicted about how to spend your time.

Maybe you've seen your word counts, profits or published catalogue growing and are itching to see what working to your full potential might look like. Maybe you've been offered a really great opportunity that fills you with excitement, and you are dying to say yes and see what happens. Maybe you're constantly plagued by thoughts of something that diverges from your current author business model.

Or maybe it's outside circumstances that have given you the signal—a lost job, an unexpected inheritance, a period of work-from-home lockdown time—and you have to choose what you will do next.

All of these are good indicators that it is time to roll up your sleeves, take a good long look at where you're at, and see what you can do to get things to the next level.

Your Turn

- Are you feeling bored or irritated with any particular aspects of your writing business? What parts?
- Are you feeling resentful of other authors you see making progress and frustrated with yourself because you aren't?
- Are you feeling overworked and overtired, like you're spinning your wheels?
- Do you feel like you aren't being challenged in your work anymore? In which ways?
- Do you feel like there's more potential in a certain area than you are actualizing right now?

70

RECOGNIZING OPTIONS FOR LEVELING UP

Leveling up looks different depending on your business model and the things you love most about your author career. Here are a few very different case studies in leveling up. But in each case, the author leveled up by committing to activities they loved and their unique strengths.

Adding teaching to a traditional author career: Eileen Cook

Eileen has long enjoyed the stage. In high school, she tried out for every school play. The downside was that she wasn't actually a great actress. How else could she get in front of people and have them pay attention to her? By teaching, of course!

In order to level up, Eileen did some research and legwork:

- She studied workshops and talks that she enjoyed. How did the speaker engage the audience? What things kept her attention? When did her attention lag?
- She identified her special snowflake skill in the area. Eileen can be funny, sometimes even on purpose! Humour is a great way to capture an audience's interest.

- She volunteered her time to speak at small venues to get practice.
- She reached out to conferences she liked and asked for advice. One of the first conferences Eileen ever went to was the Surrey International Writers' Conference. She asked the coordinator how speakers were chosen, what topics were popular and how she could make herself a more attractive candidate. (Note here that she didn't demand, but tried to partner with the coordinator. After several years of preparation, she did get chosen.)
- She approached one of the community colleges with a creative writing course idea complete with a suggested outline, learning objectives and sample lecture. They offered her the course, and she was able to build on that until she was teaching at the Simon Fraser University Writer's Studio.

Lesson: You may need to invest time to work up to the experiences you want, but these are great opportunities to learn and work out the kinks in a safer environment. Eileen was glad to learn in smaller library talks before taking on a keynote to an audience of 700.

Fast-tracking indie publication to generate a larger, more stable income: Michele Amitrani

Michele Amitrani is a bilingual author, English being his second language. Michele knew that in order to level up his income from his books, he would have to vastly increase the number of titles in his catalogue and prepare a number of stories that could be released on a rapid schedule to build his mailing list, grow the momentum of his sales and train himself to write and release on a more regular basis. He wanted to increase his output and income in both the English and Italian markets.

This is what Michele did to level up:

- He cleared his schedule every morning at the same time and established a pattern of daily writing.
- He publicly committed to a challenge to write and release a short story or novella every month for one year. His goals were to

improve his craft, experiment with writing in different genres popular with readers, and get more comfortable writing in English.

- He pledged to donate $100 to a charity for every month he did not hit his goals. (We're applauding him because in 2020, he did in fact hit all of those goals!)
- He committed to working with an accountability partner to hold him to his pledge.
- He identified the niche in which he most enjoyed writing, and which also seemed most popular with the readers.
- He grew his mailing list from a small handful to 1500 very loyal fans.
- He rewrote the stories he gave his mailing list for free, had them professionally edited to ensure they were in the best possible shape, and retitled them as needed to make them more cohesive as a set.
- He researched his chosen market—mythological fantasy—identified representative, high-quality covers in the genre, and found an affordable cover designer with a good reputation who could create professional covers for his stories.
- He translated his stories from English back to Italian and had the cover designers prepare both Italian and English versions. In this way, he doubled the number of available products and repurposed his existing content.
- He planned a strategic release schedule for 2021 to roll out the polished and professional mythological fantasy series both individually and as a boxed set in both languages.

Lesson: You need to make a commitment to your production schedule and hold yourself accountable. Also look for how you can maximize the products you already have on the market to grow your readership.

Leveraging an existing indie-published catalogue to increase sales and revenue: Crystal Hunt

Crystal knew that to get more eyes on her indie-published non-fiction titles, she would have to dive into the world of online advertising. But how would she know how to level up and get the maximum bang for her buck?

- She inhaled information—collecting, reading and listening to podcasts, books and courses by others who had navigated the world of online advertising.
- She asked others for help—but she ensured that she had something to offer in return. In addition, she made sure when she asked a question, it was one she couldn't find the answer to on her own.
- She tracked the methods used by different people in different subject areas, making a list of what she felt she could learn and integrate into her own plan.
- She created a budget to ensure she could execute the plan she created.
- She tracked and analyzed outcomes. Instead of becoming frustrated when an approach that worked for one writer didn't work for her, she tried to determine what may have happened. She exercised patience… even when she didn't always feel it.
- She looked at the number of reviews on the books, focused on increasing that number and analyzed the impact of that on her ads' effectiveness. (*Hint:* It helped!)
- When she felt she understood the ads systems but was frustrated at not being able to grow this side of her business as she had hoped due to lack time, she hired help.
- Perhaps most importantly, Crystal remained flexible. She understood that "what works" can change in a constantly evolving marketplace. She now runs ads for her books that ensure they get the attention they deserve. She respects her readers, and it shows. And she asks for help when she needs it.

Lesson: You can't always count on just following exactly in the footsteps of those who went before you. You need to invest the time and energy to understand what worked for them and why, all while understanding the same situation may not exist for you. If you remain flexible and committed to a process, you can stay relevant even as that process changes around you. And when you get stuck, get help.

71

IDENTIFYING YOUR AVAILABLE TIME

Before we identify *your* version of leveling up, let's first do a quick assessment of how much time you have available.

Wait. Aren't we coming at this all backward? Shouldn't we figure out what we want and then see how much time we have to do it?

In theory, you can do it that way. But we have found that if you first perform some "time freeing" or "commitment decluttering," seeing how much time you could make available will actually open up more options to you. It will help you choose how best to level up. If something on your schedule is not a *Hell, yes!*—if it's not contributing much to your career development or your happiness—then see if you can reduce or remove it to make space for all the good things that are coming your way.

Decluttering your schedule is sort of like giving a nod to the universe to indicate that you're committed, and ready to take advantage of all the cool stuff on offer—even stuff you don't know about it yet.

Okay, you've got goals to set, so let's get this party started.

How much time do you have to dedicate to leveling up your author career?

Earlier in this book, you did an exercise to figure out how much time you actually had to dedicate to your author career on a weekly basis. For it, you used the chart that tracked the hours in the week: 168 of them, no matter which time zone you're in.

Now we need to repeat that exercise, but our goal this time is to get a sense of how much additional time you have on top of all the things you're already doing in your author career.

For example, let's say your goal for this year is to write two books instead of just one. You want to double your writing output and level up your production schedule.

You will need to find a way to write faster or increase the time available to you for writing. If you are claiming more of your career time for writing, you'll need to eliminate something else from your list of tasks to free up some more of those time blocks. And if you're trying to increase your output by trying different ways of plotting your books or shifting to dictation since typing speed is your Achilles heel at the moment, then you're going to need to dedicate some time to learning how to do those things, practising them, and then getting more efficient. That all takes time. Long term, it'll be very beneficial, but in the meantime, you still have to fit those things into an already jam-packed schedule.

Your Turn

- How much time do you currently have available in each week that can be assigned to whatever your "leveling up" project might be?
- Is there anything you can remove from your current schedule or commitments to free up more time to dedicate to your leveling up? How much more time will that free up?

- Are there any items in your schedule that you could get rid of if an amazing opportunity presented itself? Make a list of those now and keep it off to the side, just in case.

72

IDENTIFYING YOUR PRIORITIES

Because you can't work toward everything at once without getting frustrated and diluting your efforts, it will help to narrow your focus to the next *one* specific goal or milestone. Most of these goals will revolve around one of two things:

1. Increasing the quality of something
2. Increasing the quantity of something

What is your next "just one thing" goal?

If you're a shiny new author with one book to your name, and your ultimate career goal is having 100 published books, your next goal is pretty obvious. You're going to write like the wind, my friend! Then you'll polish that story gem until she shines, then rinse and repeat.

If your goal is to get an agent and a traditional publishing deal, then your focus might be on increasing the quality of your book, increasing the quality of your submission package or increasing the number of query letters you send out. Or perhaps all three.

If you are more established, you have a number of titles behind you, you've built a solid and loyal readership, and you are going to make a run at the *USA Today* bestseller list with your next book, then you're going to need to focus in on that. Yes, you'll be focused on writing the best darn book you can. But equally important will be the quality of the advertising and marketing campaign you need to enact in order to achieve that. And you will need a thorough understanding of how books hit that list and what must be in place in your book and publishing strategy in order to make sure you qualify.

Extra credit reading

Gary Keller and Jay Papason's book *The One Thing: The Surprisingly Simple Truth Behind Extraordinary Results* is a great resource to walk you through the process of identifying your "one thing."

Your Turn

- Brainstorm a list of all the areas of your author business you might like to level up this year. Start with the big stuff. For example, you might want to level up your income. Or increase the size of your catalogue. Or work toward securing a traditional publishing deal. Or build a bit of a side income with editing clients.

What are your priorities?

How will you allocate the time you have available? Regardless of what type of creative businessperson you are, you are going to be faced with choosing between a seemingly endless number of tasks and "opportunities" that could all help you level up your chosen area. And there will never be enough time, money or energy to do all of them. There are certain tasks that should always be on your radar: you need time to write and edit your manuscripts, you need time to get your book into publishable format regardless of whether you are indie or traditionally published. And you will need to set aside time to manage the promotion and business side of things. But the rest of your time? That should be geared toward your number-one-priority project.

How will you plan and prioritize?

The concept of the 12 Week Year comes from the book of that name by Bryan P. Moran and Michael Lennington. The idea is that when we plan things for a full year at a time, we often end up scrambling in the last quarter as the deadline approaches. And we get more done in those three months than we do the rest of the year. The other challenge we've found is that things change every few months so that even when we plan out the whole year, we often need to make a new plan in three to six months anyway.

What if the timescale were shortened and you treated each 12 weeks as a "year"? This would let you pick a very specific focus for that time period and keep your priority tasks list clean and clear in front of you. Three months isn't too long to wait to start on that other great idea or to move to the next phase of your project, so it can be mentally and emotionally easier to stay focused on just one thing. If you align your 12-week years with the seasons, it also lets you adapt your schedule and tasks to fit the season. We've found this increases our chances of successfully sticking with our plans.

And if things do go awry at some point in your 12-week period, you have three more chances to hit it in that year, so you don't let as much time get away from you before you are prompted to hit that reset button.

Four times per year in The Creative Academy, we run 12 Week Year retreat sessions where we get together via Zoom online and plan our next 12 weeks in a group setting. We highly recommend that you join one of those. If there isn't one coming up right away, you can look through our library of recorded past retreats, work through the previous one on your own and then join us for the next live event.

Your Turn

- Review your list of areas you *might* want to level up this year.
- Think about each one in turn and make a note of how you feel about it. Are you lit up with excitement? Does dread curl in the pit of your stomach?
- Now think about the benefits of leveling up in each of those areas. Which thing, if completed sooner, would have the most positive ripple effects or make the other areas easier to level up?
- Which things, if leveled up, would put you on a more direct path to your ultimate career goal? Remember your author vision, mission and values statements from earlier? Which of these areas could you level up to become more closely aligned with those statements?

73

IDENTIFYING YOUR NEXT ACTIONS

Choose just one thing

Inevitably when we get to choosing *just one thing* to focus on for the next 12 weeks, people start to panic. Several people will say they don't want to choose just one thing. (Crystal is often one of these people. Eileen is usually checking to see if the twinkly magical being has shown up yet so she can skip this planning. Alas, no). And, of course, you are your own boss and may do as you like. But it's important to understand the consequences of dividing your focus, and what that can mean for your business. Because refusing to focus on just one thing is, in the end, still a choice.

One of the best techniques to illustrate the impact of this choice between focusing on one thing and focusing on multiple things is something Crystal heard about in an interview with author Alessandra Torre on the *Self Publishing Show* podcast. It originally came from a book that none of us can remember the name of! (Sorry, brilliant person who originated this: if you know who it is, email us, and we'll update the book. Seriously.)

Imagine two players are standing on the soccer field. Player one has just one ball (representing one career goal). Player two has three balls on the field (their three career goals). Time and energy are limited, so each player gets the same five kicks to assign to their goals. Player one knows exactly which ball to kick, so without wasting a single moment assigns all five kicks to that ball and makes it halfway down the field. Player two takes longer to decide how to assign their kicks, and eventually chooses to assign one kick to each ball, and then the two remaining kicks to their "primary" ball (career goal). While they made progress in all the areas, their energy is divided, so they are a couple of measures behind player one on the field.

There are a couple of important things to note about this scenario. Neither way is *correct*. Player one may reach the goal line and achieve their one goal first. But player two, though taking longer to reach that goal line, may complete multiple goals in quick succession.

You can do the same kind of visual exercise with spoons if we return to the spoon theory from earlier in the book. You have a notecard in front of you for each goal. Each day, you can allocate your spoons onto any of those piles you want. Some piles will build up quickly, some won't.

The most important thing is to understand that if you're choosing to keep multiple balls on the field (or multiple goal spoon piles on the table) it's going to look and feel like everyone else is making their way down the field more quickly than you. This can be frustrating. It's harder to keep your momentum and excitement going if you're comparing your progress to others. So if you are going to rock your author career player-two style, make sure you are really passionate about the goals you hold onto and careful not to compare yourself too directly with the other players on the field.

You are committing to a marathon approach, not a sprint. Make sure you keep up your strength and stamina so you can make it all the way to the finish line!

And remember to look up at the field once in a while. Otherwise, you may discover you're kicking your balls toward something that isn't even the goal anymore. Or that you've left the field altogether and are kicking your balls in random directions.

Eyes on your own test paper. While connecting with other writers is vital for learning and growing, it's easy to fall into the trap of comparing and thinking you fall short. Your journey as an author will be different from everyone else's, so stop looking at other authors' achievements and processes and worrying you're on the wrong path. You're on your own path, and that's exactly the right one.

— TAWNA FENSKE, *USA TODAY* BESTSELLING AUTHOR OF 35+ ROMANTIC COMEDIES

Your Turn

Okay, it's time to assign just one thing to each area you want to level up. Review your answers to the questions above.

- Which area are you going to focus on leveling up for this next 12 Week Year? Which one will get you the closest to your priority goal and have the biggest positive impact on your business in the short and long terms?
- If it helps to allay your panic about choosing, you may want to make yourself a list for the next four of your 12-week periods, so your brain knows you're still going to work toward those other goals. They're just not at the front of the line… yet!
- And if you're the type of person who really feels you need to level up multiple areas in the same 12 Week Year, you're in good company. In this case, Crystal's pro tip is to break your time into

chunks using your different job descriptions as a guide, and choose just one thing to level up in each area of your business.

Let's take a look at an example breakdown for this scenario:

Crystal's priority mission for 2021 is to double her monthly income from royalties by the end of the first quarter (Q1). She knows that at current sales levels, price points and newsletter list size, each book she releases generates a certain amount of income. Some books are co-authored, which means the work is shared and they are much faster to write, but revenues and ad costs are shared as well.

Identify your options. In order to reach that doubled income goal, Crystal has two options:

- Level up book sales by increasing exposure via advertising, and this can be done by increasing ad spends (quantity) or increasing the efficiency of ads (quality).
- Level up the number of titles for sale by adding another title to her catalogue.

Ask yourself if there is a way for you to scale both quality and quantity at the same time. In this case, if at least one of the books is co-written, a much quicker production deadline is possible because the whole team works together.

And if she hires out help with editing, pre-publication tasks and setting up ads, she can turn a percentage of her marketing budget into an effective longer-term ad campaign. This will yield higher quality in terms of audience exposure and higher sales from better quality ads and read-through on *all* the books in the series. Paying for help also leaves Crystal more time for creation of new products.

Assign a priority task in each area of your business—assuming you have different time blocks or helpers—that contributes to your overall one thing goal.

- **Business manager:** rebrand and re-release all existing fiction titles *wide* through PublishDrive to increase potential audience. (Her author assistant can help with this.)
- **Writer and creator:** complete drafts of two new titles—one full length fiction title written by Crystal, one non-fiction title co-authored with Donna and Eileen
- **Sales and marketing:** continue trend of at least 10 percent monthly sales growth of all existing titles through ads management. (Crystal contracted an ads manager to set up and oversee the Amazon ads.)

Once you know your priority area and the specific outcome you want to achieve, it's time to identify what items go on your to-do lists.

Break it down into pieces

When you have a goal like *write a book* written on the page in front of you, it's easy to see a mountain. But if you break it into smaller, more achievable lists of tasks then you can start moving forward. Sort of like climbing a mountain by telling yourself at each stage you just have to make it to the next resting point.

Writing a book can be broken down into sections and chapters. Editing can be broken down by numbers of pages, or hours spent editing. Finding an agent is really several tasks. Making a list of where to find possible agents, revising options and making a list of all relevant agents who might be open to your submissions, putting together your query letter, putting together your synopsis. Refining your submission package, and then actually sending out queries. Break the big things into bite-sized pieces, and they're easier to eat!

Your Turn

- Write each of the bigger tasks at the top of a page and then brainstorm a list of all the smaller steps needed to get you to that goal. Break everything into small, achievable chunks and action items.
- Not sure where to start? Ask in your community forums or show up at a mastermind session in The Creative Academy, and we'll help you figure it out.

74

IDENTIFYING YOUR METRICS

We get it. We're words people too. But if you don't track the numbers, look at hard data and examine the evidence in front of you, you won't know if you're spending your time, energy and money in the right places. Career authors know their numbers. They are brave enough to face the facts and use that information to level up.

While you are welcome to create all your own tracking sheets, you will find we've shared our favourites below. You will also find a number of tracking tabs already set up for you in the Business Plan Google Sheet.

Track your progress

To really see how those numbers are adding up to wins in your focus area, it's helpful to track your progress so you have a visual reminder to keep extra balls off the field! If your goal was to increase your mailing list subscribers from 500 to 1000, create a chart or tracking spreadsheet, and each week, make a note of how many new subscribers you've added. As part of your weekly to-do planning, identify any actions you could take to get even more subscribers next week.

Track time spent

If your current focus doesn't have a clear outcome attached to it, you may want to track cumulative time spent. Crystal does this often with a simple graph-paper-and-coloured-marker system (although there are apps like Harvest or Hours that handle time tracking if you prefer the tech approach). Basically, you make a grid of the number of time blocks you expect or plan to spend on your focus activity, and then you colour in one block for each unit of time spent.

Track days in the chain

One of the most common ways to form good habits is to set a consistent, daily goal and use a calendar or tracking app to monitor your progress. Your daily goal could be to write for an hour, or do your 15 minutes of website development, or send out one query letter to an agent. You circle each day you complete the task, effectively making an unbroken chain as long as you can. Each time you stumble, simply start a new chain and keep on going. Your goal is always to beat the length of your previous chain by focusing on one day at a time.

Track milestones achieved

This can take many forms, depending on your preferences. You might use a spreadsheet, notebook, or bullet journal to write down each action you take to move your priority project forward, highlighting every time you hit a milestone. Or you might place sticky notes on your wall and move them from one area to another as you complete them. It doesn't matter how you actually track this, just that you have a visual record you can look back on to see that you're making progress. This record is especially helpful when you feel tired or frustrated, or when it's taking a long time to see the results of all your hard work. Most things in the writing and publishing industry do not happen quickly. We are always playing the long game.

Your Turn

- Think about the goals you have set for yourself this quarter or year. How will you track your progress? How will you know you are achieving the targets you've set for yourself?
- Set up a system (or borrow someone else's), or use the Business Plan Google Sheet to track those milestones most important to you. Make sure to choose a system you will actually use.

75

LEVELING UP KAREFULLY

There are two main options when it comes time to level up in the area of your writing business. You can do *more*. Or you can do *better*. Our opinion? The ideal situation in most cases is when you are leveling up both quality *and* quantity, but that may depend on your personal goals.

We're going to dig into each area of your business model and evaluate some possible next steps for each. But first, let's talk about a KAREful approach to leveling up that you can apply to every area of growth.

No, that's not a spelling mistake. What do we mean by leveling up KAREfully? Crystal developed this acronym to remind herself of the proper series of phases that need to be part of every project she is working on, every new business idea and every single book that she writes and publishes. It's actually a great acronym to guide your approach to every stage and decision in your author life.

KARE stands for:

Knowledge
Action
Reflection
Evolution

For each and every big goal you set or change you consider, you're going to work through the following stages.

Knowledge

Your first step is always to stop for a minute and make sure you know what you're trying to achieve. Do some recon and google the heck out of whatever you're trying to do, and see how other people have already accomplished it. Put some time into getting as clear a picture as you can about what you're facing in this next step of your writing and publishing journey.

Once you know what you are going to do, how you're going to do it, and who is going to help you if you need it—then you can take action.

If your current goal is to write a murder mystery, for instance, you'll probably want to spend your walking or cooking times listening to podcasts about finishing a book, writing a murder mystery, and so on.

If your goal is to level up your income from $500 a month to $5000 a month, then you'll need to watch videos, listen to podcast interviews and read books by folks who have successfully pulled this off. You'll analyze what they did, how they did it, and how long it took them.

What if you don't know what you don't know and get stuck in the knowledge phase, overwhelmed by the flood of information? This is when you can reach out to your support networks for help. It might be that you have the resources you need in your own local writers' group, or in an online writing support community. Or you might do best with a one-on-one jump-start from a writing coach. You can always ask in our Creative Academy for Writers forums. We have a whole community who can direct you to the knowledge you need—or help you figure out what you don't know that you don't know!

You'll know best what your personality and your budget support. Don't be afraid to ask for help. It's much better—and usually cheaper—to get the help in the knowledge stage than it is to get help in the stages that follow.

Action

This is the part where you do *all* of the things that are needed to move you to your next step. Which you know, because you've researched it all in the knowledge phase. This is where to-do lists are your best friend and time management and budgeting all come into play.

Reflection

Once you've done a thing, you need to take a minute to reflect on whether or not it worked. Then you can adjust your process accordingly so that every single stage, every single book, every single cycle is better than the last. Even if the changes you're making only earn you a few minutes, a few dollars, or a few more readers, those changes will add up to very noticeable improvements over time. We firmly believe that it is this reflection stage that is most often missed by authors, perhaps in part because when we're dealing with creative works that are close to our hearts, it can be hard to acknowledge they could have been better in some way.

But you have an advantage over the author who writes only one book and checks that off their bucket list. What you are building is much bigger than just one book. You are building a *career*. That means every process flaw, every storytelling weakness, and every missed reader connection that you identify can be *corrected* for your next book or event. And those adjustments will ripple out and positively impact every single book you write in the future.

This is the true power of building a career. You're not starting over from scratch with every book you write. You're building on the successes of the previous book, and you're growing your skills, your expertise and your author life with every minute you spend on your projects.

Evolution

The final phase in this cycle is all about making changes and adjustments based on what you learned in the reflection stage. If the data shows you that not enough people downloaded your last book, then you know you need to change something about your process. In the reflection stage, you will have looked at your writing process, the effectiveness of your marketing efforts, the reach of your publisher, and the design of your cover. Maybe you noticed that you need a better cover or blurb to entice people to download it. This is your chance to make a course correction that will set you up for more success in the future.

We have found that making this KARE process a habit is one of the most effective and most efficient ways to make consistent incremental improvements in every area of your life—not just writing and publishing! And using it every time you level up will help you avoid costly mistakes and make the most informed choices you can.

76

LEVELING UP WRITING QUALITY

One thing that both Crystal and Eileen love about writing—and that occasionally makes us want to pound our heads on the desk—is that there is always more to learn. There are so many aspects of craft, and most of us have specific strengths and weaknesses in different areas. If you change genres, it may push you to learn more about a specific aspect of craft, from research to plotting, from character development to dialogue to world-building.

> *Writing is a craft. The road has been paved by many before you. Find their books. Study the craft. Learn from their mistakes, and your own. And always remember, the goal is not the finish line. The goal is to enjoy the journey.*
>
> — *Robert Dugoni, internationally bestselling author of the Tracy Crosswhite series*

Choose a focus area

There are lots of things you can do to figure out where to level up your craft:

Read your reviews

Yes, we know it can be very easy to go down a rabbit hole of reading, and then obsessing about, reviews. What we suggest here is to take a high-level view of those reviews. Are there recurring comments or feelings? Make a note of these—one column of things people love, and one column of things you will want to consider.

Read reviews in your genre

What are the reviews like for other books in your genre? Are there qualities that readers consistently express a love for, or things they consistently dislike? Do your book have these qualities?

Listen to your critique partners

If you swap manuscripts with fellow writers or readers, keep their feedback. When you're not in the middle of a deadline crush, revisit that feedback and look for consistent notes identifying areas for you to work on.

Review agent or editor feedback

Often when we get feedback from our editors or agent, we're in a time crunch to finish a book. When you're done with the book, take a look through any notes you were provided and see if there's anything you can learn. See if your agent or editor has time to speak with you about your craft. Tell them you're open to improving and want to learn about any areas where you should focus.

Read like a writer

One the best ways to learn craft is to read! Read books you love and figure out why they work. Read books you want to throw against the wall and figure out if you're doing any of the same things.

Choose your resources

Now that you've identified where you want to improve your craft, there are a number of ways you can learn how to level up:

Attend conferences

Online or in person, there are many writing conferences out there covering a wide range of craft topics. Be open about what sessions you attend and listen to recommendations about who is a great speaker. Take notes and look for places you can apply workshop wisdom to your own writing.

Critique others' work

It is a truth universally acknowledged that it is far easier to see what other people are doing wrong with their manuscript than to identify and fix problems in your own. Providing feedback to others helps you hone your eye so you can see and address issues in your own writing.

Consult craft books

Show of hands: how many of you have more craft books than you imagined possible? (Our hands shoot up in the air.) Whenever Eileen gets stuck on a manuscript, she fixes it by buying another craft book. The secret with these books is that while you won't use all their tricks, at times certain things will hit home. So pull out these books occasionally to see what catches your eye.

Take classes

There are lots of craft classes available both online and in person. Seek recommendations from writer friends about who offers a good course. We suspect there are two things in play when you take a class: you have a chance to learn some new tools and techniques, and—equally important—you are setting aside time and energy to focus on that area.

Explore master classes and learning hubs

The Creative Academy for Writers holds regular office hours and master classes on a wide range of topics. We have over three years of weekly content on there, and we keep adding! There is gold in them virtual hills. Grab your pickaxe.

Join writing communities

Yes, we're biased and think that The Creative Academy for Writers is the best writing community. But it certainly isn't the only one. Specific genres and geographic areas have specialized communities, and these groups often provide education and resources to their members.

Read like a writer

Look at that—reading showed up again! Good thing you likely enjoy this task. If you've identified a craft area to level up, focus on how authors tackle that particular area. When Eileen decided to write books with a thriller aspect, she knew she would have to up her plotting skills. She read stacks and stacks of other thrillers, taking careful note of how the authors unfolded the plot, created twists and red herrings, and kept the reader on the edge of their seat.

Your Turn

- Review the Writer's Self-Evaluation tool that you completed earlier and identify which craft areas you want to work on this year.
- Once you have identified craft areas for improvement, create a plan to address them. Will you take a course? Attend a conference? Read more carefully?
- Pull out a book that you love and really explore the craft that the writer used. Read it as a writer. Look at the POV they selected and how that impacted the story, how the plot unfolds, and how the character's motivations are explored.
- What is one practical take-away you can learn from that author?

77

LEVELING UP WRITING QUANTITY

We've discussed how creating better books can assist you in gaining fans and leveling up your career, but you can also increase the quantity of books that you produce. Readers can't buy books that exist only in your head. Many published authors find there is a "pivot" point at which they can create an ongoing income. This is when a reader who newly discovers them can also purchase a backlist of books.

We've identified three ways you can increase the quantity of your writing. But be aware there are a number of books designed to help you speed up your writing. *How to Write Fast: Better Words Faster* by Sean Platt and Neeve Silver, and *5000 Words per Hour* by Chris Fox discuss how to increase your output in more detail.

Increase your focus

Your first option is to get more bang for your buck from your existing writing time. Set up a dedicated writing space that is quiet and free of distractions. Crystal and Eileen have a writing friend who has a tiara. There's a rule in her home that when the tiara is on her head, she is *not* to be bothered unless the building is on fire. Others may post a sign on the door to let people know they can't be bothered.

Another option is to create routines that encourage writing. For example, Eileen often ends a day's writing in the middle of the scene and write a sentence or two about what she thinks will happen next. This way, when she sits down the next day, she can start typing right away instead of feeling that she has to warm up.

Regular writing dates with your manuscript often increase your focus. Because you're writing on a daily (or near-daily) basis, you don't need to spend time rereading work to remind you of the story. The Creative Academy for Writers holds regular online writing sprints that members enjoy because it keeps them accountable and earmarks a time to ensure they're getting writing done.

While there are no hard and fast rules, writing blocks of less than 30 minutes can make it a challenge to get into your writing groove. We're big fans of getting words in whenever and wherever you can, but if you need to focus, you typically need a block of time. So choose your block of time wisely. Maybe you need to write first thing in the morning before you open your email and distract your mind with other tasks. Others find their creative muse loves to party later in the evening when everyone else has gone to bed. If possible, block off your writing time when you are most creative.

Try something different

One of the most popular questions for authors at conferences and in interviews is "What is your writing process?" We suspect this question comes from a desire to discover a secret that will unlock the mystery of getting an idea onto the page. Alas, there is no secret. There is only what works for you. But you can try different techniques to see if some of them are a good fit.

Some authors swear by careful outlining and plotting, saying that it streamlines their writing and allows them to write faster without feeling "stuck." There are those who write by using dictation. It's well known that you can speak faster than you can type, and there are many programs that will transform your spoken novel into text. Some authors create vision boards that give them a new perspective on their novel.

Others start each writing day by brainstorming a list of what they want to write; this fires up their muse and keeps the words flowing.

There is no secret handshake or magical amulet that will unlock the words. It's up to every author to discover the mix of creative mojo that can get them turning out words. Talk to other writers and listen to podcasts. When you hear an idea that intrigues you, give it a try and see if it works for you.

Downsize other commitments

Despite our best efforts to create a device that can bend time and create more hours in a day, we've had no such luck. (We promise to keep you posted if this changes.) The last way you can improve the amount of writing you get done is to increase the amount of time you spend writing.

That sounds simple, but it hinges on a tougher task: you will likely have to downsize other commitments. You *may* have pockets of unused time in your calendar where you're just sitting around, but in our experience, most people don't. This means you'll need to look closer at your schedule. There may be time in your calendar that is not well-used. Social media is a common time stealer. Ever go online to post one thing and then enter a space-time vortex of kitten pictures and irritating political posts that drags you away, only to resurface hours later?

You may discover a few places where you can more easily claw back some time, but this won't always be the case. You may have to turn down opportunities or projects in order to have more time to write. You might decide to take a year off from being the classroom field-trip dad or put down the knitting needles for a time.

You don't have to remove everything you enjoy from your schedule. You should still have time for your hobbies, your family and, yes, even some mindless Netflix browsing. We all need to unwind, and there is no gold star for being productive *all* the time. That usually gets you a nasty case of burnout. However, if you want to increase your output by taking more time to write, something will have to come out of your schedule, even if it is only for a period of time.

Your Turn

- Do an 80/20 analysis on the tasks that are currently using up your time blocks. What are the 20 percent of tasks that are using up 80 percent of your time?
- Can you hire them out, remove them from your schedule or pause them temporarily so you can spend more time writing?
- What time of day are you most productive in getting your words written? Can you schedule more blocks of writing time at those "peak hours"?
- What could you change to make it easier to focus during those blocks of writing time?

Extra credit reading

Scrappy Rough Draft by Donna Barker has some great exercises to help you get that first draft of your book written.

And if you're confident in getting that draft done but you're hoping to level up your production schedule and outputs, know that Crystal has been hard at work on another book in this series called *Write More Books,* which digs deeper into topics like increased productivity, overcoming fear, unlocking creative blocks, and other things that may impact your ability to write more. This will be available in the second half of 2021.

When it comes time to level up your publishing, you'll focus on both external relationships and your own personal efficiencies. We're going to look at two vital relationships—with your agent and with your publisher—and we'll look at what you can do on your own be as efficient and productive with your publishing process as possible.

78

LEVELING UP RIGHTS MANAGEMENT

Review your contracts

We dealt with some specifics around rights and intellectual property in the Managing Your Assets section. But understanding what rights you have to leverage, and the contracts you have made with business and services providers, is extremely important. As we mentioned earlier, if you have an agent, it is a part of their service to help you understand. However, this is *your* career. Ensure that you're reading your contracts and noting key details, even if the agent is there to support you.

If there are restrictions on your contracts, or key indicators you should be watching for such as sales targets or out of print requirements, then you want to have notes made, or reminders set so you don't forget to act on things.

For example, if you have signed an agreement with an audiobook narrator that stipulates they get a percentage of your revenue for three years, set a reminder in your calendar for the end of that term. You could also write a "things on the horizon" list that you review each year when doing your business planning.

Things to think about:

- Are there any unsold rights that revert back to you this year?
- When does your KDP Select term renew? Is it set to auto-renew?
- When are you scheduled to receive royalties?
- What is the threshold of sales below which your rights can be reverted back to you?

Your catalogue is bigger than you think

There are several ways your existing products could earn you additional money without requiring you to do a lot of additional work. Some examples include:

Audiobook rights

You may sell these to an established audiobook publisher or consider producing and bringing the audio version to market yourself. If you're thinking about this, check out The Creative Academy's library of free master classes before you dive in.

Paperback or hardcover formats

If you're traditionally published, your book rights will specify if there will be hardcover, trade paperback or mass-market paperback editions. If there is a hardcover edition, a paperback version will often follow after approximately a year. If you are indie published, you have the option to create different print versions for your book.

Foreign sales

Foreign markets can be a lucrative way to earn additional income. If you're traditionally published, discuss with your agent if the publisher will retain foreign rights or if the agent will sell those rights. If you're indie published, you can pursue these rights on your own, although it can be difficult if you don't have the publishing and translation connections. There are agents who sell foreign rights only, but you often need a strong sales record to interest them.

Alternate formats

Depending on your book, it may make sense to have alternate formats. For example, we're aware of an author who has written a middle grade novel about a historical figure. She's also used her research to create a teaching guide for classrooms, non-fiction articles about the character and a picture-book version. If you've done significant work to develop your story, explore how else you might want to use it. A non-fiction writer can sell an article (say, on travel to Vancouver) to one venue, rework the article to sell to a parenting magazine ("Ten Things to Do with Kids in Vancouver"), write a focused article ("Best Vancouver Spas") and then turn it into a personal interest essay ("What I Learned While Travelling").

Rights reversion

If you are traditionally published (or an indie author who has sold subsidiary rights), you should clearly understand what rights you've sold and the limitations on these. Frequently your right to publish includes a reversion process. In this process, if the publisher has not sold a set number of copies or if a set period of time has elapsed, you can request the right to publish that book to be returned to you. Many authors have regained book rights and then reissued the book with a new cover.

Your catalogue is valuable. It's the body of your work. You need to keep clear records of what you've published, in what formats, and any rights restrictions on these.

You can use the Products-BOOKS tab in the Business Plan Google Sheet to help you track this information.

Your Turn

- Review your existing contracts and review the catalogue of products you identified previously.
- Do any unsold rights revert back to you this year?
- When does your KDP Select term renew? Is it set to auto-renew?
- When are you scheduled to receive royalties?
- What is the threshold of sales below which your rights can be reverted back to you?

79

LEVELING UP AGENT RELATIONSHIPS

Agents are a bit like unicorns. They may seem like mythical creatures who could take you to magical new destinations. Alas, many times it seems like they live to do nothing but stab you with their head horn—in other words, send you rejection letters. However, there is good news. Despite what you may have heard, agents are people just like us. They love books and stories and truly want to help authors build their careers.

Do you need an agent?

Short answer: no.

You don't need an agent to be published. You may choose to indie publish, in which case you don't require an agent to sell your work. You may be able to get your work directly in front of editors and publishing houses. You may also feel comfortable negotiating contracts or have a lawyer versed in the publishing industry who can do it for you.

Longer answer: no, but…

Agents aren't required, but a good agent can be a huge support and benefit to an author. Full disclosure: Eileen loves her agent. That agent has earned her percentage over and over, not to mention provided mental health support at no charge. Eileen wouldn't want to navigate this business without her support, and her agent's ability to negotiate has improved Eileen's ability to level up. A big part of the decision to pursue representation comes down to your career goals, your individual skill set and where you want to focus your time and energy.

Authors are not always the best advocate of their own work. We've worked on our book for so long and are so keen to have our work out into the world that we may be tinged by desperation. *"Yes! I'll totally take only a dollar for my book! In fact, I'll pay* you *for the right to publish my book. Just please tell me my story is pretty and you love it."* Eileen vividly recalls being in the middle of negotiations for one of her books and telling her agent, "I don't need more money. Mostly I want more of a marketing budget." Her agent responded, "What if we asked for more money *and* a bigger marketing budget?" Mind blown. That hadn't occurred to Eileen. An agent will make sure you don't sell yourself short simply because you are excited to have your story out in the world.

And if you're looking to sell foreign rights or subsidiary rights to merchandising, video games, film and TV as part of a leveling-up plan, you will likely need an agent to help you broker those deals.

What does an agent do?

There is some variation among agents, but an agent has three primary functions.

An agent's first function is to sell your manuscript to a publishing house and negotiate the terms of that contract. They will pitch your manuscript to editors, follow up and then review terms including advances, royalty rates, sub-rights, deadlines, option clauses and other aspects of the publishing house's offer.

Your agent's second function is to act as your representative during the publishing process. This may include dealing with conflicts along the way. Perhaps your publisher has picked a cover for the book that looks like your eight-year-old niece designed it. You're horrified. You'd rather dance naked in public than have that cover on your book. Maybe just looking at that cover makes you want to cry (and not pretty cry, either). An agent can be the one to raise that issue with the publisher and push back. They'll be the bad cop so that you can be the easygoing, lovely-to-work-with artist.

The agent can keep you abreast of what is happening on the publishing side, including cover design, release dates, marketing and promotion. They can explain parts of the procedure with which you may be unfamiliar and make sure you're able to make informed decisions.

Lastly, an agent will make sure you get paid per the terms of your contract. They'll follow up to make sure you're getting royalty statements and any money due to you. You may be thinking, *"What kind of idiot doesn't know when someone is supposed to send them money?"* Eileen is raising her hand here. And we know she's not alone. Publishing contracts are often paid in instalments, and keeping track of those dates, royalty statements for a larger backlist, contract bonuses if you sell more than a set number of books, foreign rights, and other subsidiary rights and bonuses is a lot to juggle—especially if you are writing multiple books on different timelines and prefer to spend time with your imaginary friends. An agent will keep on top of all this. And if there are any challenges, they'll wade into battle to make sure you get what you're entitled to.

What an agent *might* do

We've already established that agents are, in fact, people. This means there is a lot of diversity among agents with a range of strengths and interests. In addition to their primary duties, there are things that some agents do and others do not. You might consider the full range of an agent's role when choosing an agent.

Editorial feedback

Your agent may read and provide feedback on your manuscript. They may request revisions before submitting the manuscript to publishing houses. If your manuscript is getting passes from potential publishers, the agent may help identify areas to change before sending it out for another round of submissions.

Story brainstorming

Agents read *a lot*. They know the business. Some agents happily help their writers explore what to write next or act as a sounding board during the creative process. They are not your writing partner—as much as we might want them to, they will not write our books for us. However, they may be willing to give you the benefit of their experience.

Sub-rights negotiations

Sub-rights include things like foreign sales—the right to sell your book in other languages—film or dramatic rights, and audiobook rights. Maybe you're dreaming of action figures of your characters or related video games. Many agents work with co-agents who specialize in these areas. At the direction of your agent, these co-agents will attempt to make a sale in those areas.

Agents typically receive a different percentage for these sub-rights. While an agent's take is typically 15 percent, this rises to 20 or 25 percent for foreign and sub-rights, with 10 percent going to your primary agent and the other 10 to 15 percent going to the co-agent.

Marketing

Agents are not publicists. However, they've been knocking around in the business for a while and may have suggestions that assist you with the marketing and promotion of your book. For instance, they may connect you to another author to request a blurb for your book. Eileen's agent sits in on her meetings with her publisher's marketing and promotion department. Her agent is often more direct about asking for specific things to promote the book.

Career planning

When you sign with an agent, you will discuss if the agent will represent only the book you have queried or your full body of work. Many agents provide support as you navigate the publishing business over a period of time. This might include determining if you want to change genres, use a pen name or change publishing houses.

Your career planning, for instance, may reflect a desire to be a hybrid author. If you want to both traditionally publish and indie publish, you'll want to make sure your agent is looped into that plan. It is not up to them to give you permission, but they will consider issues you may not have, from competing deadlines to potential contract violations if you indie publish a novella related to one of your traditionally published novels.

If you're indie published and you've used an agent just to manage subsidiary rights, you may want to talk with them about your upcoming projects. They may recommend you consider traditional publishing for some of these ideas—and they may have great reasons for doing do.

Where can you find agents?

There are entire books on how to connect with agents and prepare a query letter. We won't repeat all that information here, but we do want to give you some high-level information to consider. If you've determined that you want to work with an agent, you might be wondering where you find them. There are a number of places to begin your search:

The Internet

What did we do before Google? There is a wealth of information online: interviews with agents, lists of agency websites, agents seeking manuscripts in particular genres, sites such as *Publisher's Marketplace* where agents post deals and job changes, and agent blogs. In our opinion, this is often your best source of information.

Conferences

Many writer conferences provide opportunities to meet and pitch agents and editors. Before meeting with that agent, be sure to look them up to see who they already represent and the type of manuscripts they are seeking. If you are able to have a conversation with them, open with something like "You represent Book *A*, which was my favourite book of last year," or "I saw you post on Twitter that you love werewolf motorcycle thrillers, and that's why I'm so excited to meet with you." It can be nice to meet an agent face to face—but remember to factor in the cost of attending the conference.

Agent listings

There are listings of agents both online and in print form. These include books such as the *Guide to Literary Agents* and *Jeff Herman's Guide to Book Publishers, Editors and Literary Agents.* These guides typically come out yearly, but because this business changes quickly, double-check their information with the agency website to make sure you have the most up-to-date information.

The *Writer's Digest* website has regular listings of agents seeking authors in particular genres. It also has a regular article forum on query letters, in which an agent dissects a query letter that drew their attention.

Books

When you read a book, go to the acknowledgements section. Most authors thank their agent. That provides you with a name you can search for online. See if they represent the type of work you produce and find their query guidelines. While you are on their website, check out other agents at that agency who might be a good fit for you.

Social media

Many agents are active on social media. They often post about the type of work they are looking for, and their posts give you a chance to "get to know" them. Hashtags such as #ManuscriptWishList can help you find agents. Remember: be on your best social-media behaviour, which means no agent stalking or pitching online unless they request it. Connecting with them online allows you to see their style and research their tastes online.

Referrals

If you know an author who has representation—and if you know that agent represents your genre—you can ask if they would consider referring you to their agent. Do not be offended if they say no. They may decline for a number of reasons: they know their agent doesn't represent what you write, they feel uncomfortable referring you to their agent because they haven't read your work, they've asked their agent a few times already, or they simply don't have time. However, if they do agree, include in your query that "author X suggested I query you."

You'll notice that we've listed referrals last. Many people think that you have to know someone in the business to break in. This is often said while grumbling about "the system" and drinking copious amounts of whiskey. And, yes, a referral can be helpful. Eileen knows what her agent likes, and if she knows of a great book, she's happy to tell her about the author and broker an introduction. However, you don't have to know someone to find an agent. The agents we've spoken to estimate that roughly 75 percent of their author list is made up of people they found in the query or slush pile. Eileen found both of her agents through querying.

> *Remember it is not called the Publishing Party or the Publishing Is-Everyone-Feeling-Okay it is called the Publishing Industry. It is a for-profit business and therefore, any author will want to treat their proposal like an in-person interview, making sure it's prepared to answer questions before they are asked.*
>
> — Barbara Poelle, Literary Agent and author of *Funny You Should Ask: Mostly Serious Answers to Mostly Serious Questions About the Book Publishing Industry*

How do you hire an agent?

If you've had interest from an agent, first take a moment to celebrate! Writing has plenty of ups and downs, so when an up happens, pause to enjoy it.

Typically, once an agent reaches out to say they are interested, you'll arrange a time to have a conversation and determine if you're a good fit for each other. You don't want just any agent—you want the agent that is *right* for you. We've created a list of questions that can help you make that determination. This is available as a downloadable checklist at https://creativeacademyforwriters.com/resources/fulltimeauthor.

An agent has reached out and now you're going to have "the call." But what should you ask before you agree to their representation offer?

Questions to ask about the book:

- What is it you like about my book?
- Do you feel the book is ready to go out now, or do you have revision suggestions?
- If you have revision suggestions, what are they?

Ask these questions to learn what they like about your writing and ensure you both share a similar vision of what the book will look like. And you'll want to know their suggestions for revision (if any) so you can determine a) if you are willing to make those revisions; and b) if the revisions they suggest feel like a positive direction for you.

Questions to ask about the submission process:

- What is your submission strategy?
- Do you share your submission plan with writers?
- How would you pitch this book to editors?

Ask these questions to learn if the agent feels your book belongs with one of the big-five publishers or a smaller boutique publisher. You'll want to understand their publishing vision and how they will approach it. Some agents share where they are sending the manuscript, and others guard this information. You might have a preference in this regard. Eileen knows one writer who wants to know where her manuscript is at all times and wants to hear all the responses. Another friend prefers to know nothing unless someone is making an offer.

Questions to ask about the agent:

- Do you offer editorial feedback to your clients?
- How will we communicate?
- How often will we communicate?
- What things will we communicate about?
- Are you a sole proprietor or part of a larger agency?
- How did you get into agenting? What were your last few titles?
- Do you work with the other genres in which I write?

Ask these questions to learn what tasks and roles your agent will take on so you can understand how your working relationship with them will function. And, if they are a sole proprietor, you'll want to know: What happens to your book if something happens to them?

Questions to ask about the money and the business:

- Is this offer for this book, or do you also want to represent my future work?
- Do you have a formal agency agreement?
- If either of us wants out of the agreement, how does that work?
- What happens if you leave the agency—or the agenting business altogether?
- How do you handle sub-rights?
- What is your fee? Do you charge for anything in addition to your standard agent percentage, such as copies and postage?

Ask these questions to understand how the relationship with your agent is structured, what aspects of your writing business they handle, and if there are any fees for this.

Note: Agents get a percentage of what you make when your book sells. While they may ask to be reimbursed for things like copies and postage, you should never pay your agent up front or outright to represent you. Anyone asking for money up front is *not* someone you want to work with.

Your Turn

- If you're unsure if you want an agent, review the list of supports they provide and determine how you would cover these on your own or with contracted help. Then evaluate if you prefer to work independently or with an agent.
- Create a list of what you are looking for in an agent. How do you want to communicate, what services are most important etc. Use this as a comparison when considering possible agents.
- If you are searching for an agent begin your research using the advice above and create a list of at least 50 possible agents.
- Create a list of the five most important questions you want to ask if you're considering hiring an agent.
- If you've been working with an agent for a period of time take time to reflect on your ongoing relationship. Are you pleased with how things are working? Are there things you'd like to change? Consider having an open conversation with your agent to check in and plan next steps for your career.

How, when and why do you fire an agent?

Those who are in the query stage may read this heading and think, *Fire an agent? Are you crazy? I'd give my first-born child for an agent!* However, there are a number of reasons you may choose to part ways with an agent as a part of your leveling-up plan:

You've made a career change

It's possible you started out writing children's books but now you want to write thrillers. Your current agent may not have the connections or know-how to take you in this direction. It should be noted that agents are often able to help you make these connections, even with another agent in their agency, but you may still wish to pursue options on your own.

The working relationship isn't working

Perhaps you'd prefer more communication or editorial support, or you don't like how your agent represents your concerns to the publisher. At any rate, if the relationship isn't working for you anymore, you may want to make a change.

You're not meeting your publishing goals

If you have publishing goals—like moving to a larger publisher—and feel that your agent is not supporting you in reaching those goals, you may wish to see if another agent can help.

Your agent has left the agency

While you sign with a particular agent, most agency contracts indicate that you are a client of the agency. If your agent leaves, you may have to sever your relationship with that agency to follow them or, if you want, seek alternate representation.

Before you channel your inner CEO and tell your agent, "You're fired!" here are some things to consider doing:

Take a deep breath

Ensure you understand why you're considering severing the relationship. It may be helpful to talk it through with another writer. Is there something with your agent relationship that isn't working, or are you simply frustrated?

Talk to your agent

Have you discussed with your agent what isn't working for you? Consider expressing what you would like to be different and have a conversation about whether or not it is possible for them to change.

Review your agency contract

Your agency contract will detail how to sever the relationship, but it typically entails providing written notification and 30 days' notice. Be aware there are different clauses that stipulate how your former agent may still be involved in your career. For example, if they sold previous books of yours, they are typically still the agent of record. If they recently submitted your manuscript to a publisher and that publisher later makes you an offer, they often still act as your agent for a period of time (typically six months).

If you end up doing the deed and ending your relationship with your agent, here are some guidelines to follow:

Follow the requirements of your contract

Make a list of what you need to do in order to fulfill the terms of your contract, such as sending written notice.

End your relationship with your current agent before seeking new representation

It's considered poor form in the business to start querying other agents while you're still being represented by someone else.

Give your agent a call

If possible, tell your agent personally that you are severing the relationship. Think of it like breaking up with a romantic partner: while you *can* break the news by text or email, a call is nicer.

Remain calm and professional

Even if you're angry at your agent, now isn't the time to burn that bridge. Publishing is a small world, and you never know who knows whom.

Keep records

If you have a manuscript that your agent has been submitting, ask your agent for a list of places it has been submitted already. Carefully file your former agency agreement, correspondence about previous sales, and a copy of your email formally terminating the relationship.

Take another deep breath

People change agents in this business for a range of reasons. Provided you've been professional in your interactions, it is highly unlikely there will be any hard feelings. This is your career, and no one will care about it as much as you. You need to take the steps to ensure you have the best representation for you.

80

LEVELING UP PUBLISHER RELATIONSHIPS

Depending on your career plan and process, you may wish to level up by working with a publisher in a traditional model.

What the publisher does

At last you've received "the call": a publishing house wants to bring your book out into the world. What do you need to know? Entire books have been written on this subject. One of our favourites—not the least because it's by Eileen's agent, but also because it's laugh out loud funny—is Barbara Poelle's Book *Funny You Should Ask: Mostly Serious Answers to Mostly Serious Questions About the Book Publishing Industry.*

This section will introduce you to just a few high-level concepts regarding publisher relationships.

The publisher did not buy your book

This is a phrase that writers use a lot: "XYZ Publishing House bought my book!" They didn't. They bought the right to bring your book out into the world in a particular format (hardcover, paperback, eBook, audiobook) in a particular place (North America, the world) for a particular period of time (often determined in your contract by how many books are still actively being sold).

In return for the right to publish your book, your publisher may provide you with an advance against royalties (a payment before the book sells to readers) and a set amount of royalties (laid out in your contract).

Show me the money—in advance!

An advance is the amount of money the publisher will give you before your book sells to readers. But before you go too crazy spending that cheque, don't forget that you pay your agent their percentage out of this money. You will also get regular royalty statements showing how many copies you've sold. Once you've sold sufficient copies to pay back the advance (known as *earning out*), the publisher will send you royalty checks. (And yes, there are few things better than money showing up in the mail!) The timing will be based on your contract, but often this happens twice a year.

How publishers spend their time

Eileen used to daydream about working in publishing. She imagined spending her time in a book-lined office, complete with large wooden desk and comfy reading chair. She'd chat with authors and attend a lot of swank literary parties where she would drink martinis. Having been to her publisher's office, she can indeed confirm that it is book lined. Books are everywhere. Stacked to the ceiling in many cases. But rather than sitting about reading, the staff seem to be working their tails off. They drag home manuscripts, take them on vacation, and have a never-ending to-do list. (However, some of them really do drink a lot of martinis.)

Typically, the person you will first have contact with is the acquiring editor. This is the individual who fell in love with your manuscript and convinced the editorial board to purchase the rights to publish it. This editor is charged with shepherding your book into the world. Most likely they will be your primary contact in traditional publishing. If you have any nerves about speaking directly with your editor, you can also go through your agent. If there is a contentious issue—you hate the cover, for example—it's likely best to start with your agent and then go forward.

A publishing house is a busy place. In addition to your editor, there may be an editorial assistant, a marketing and promotion team, designers, and a sales team. In most cases, these individuals will be in touch with you via your editor. Think of your editor as the conductor of the publishing orchestra: they make sure we all play well with each other. Typically, there is a meeting early in the book production process where you may get to meet—usually via conference call—the other people working on your book. Your goal in those early meetings is to be positive and to project the persona of someone other people will want to work with. Now is not the time to be a diva.

How to find a publisher

Publishing houses are both huge and small. We used to talk about the "Big Six" publishers: Random House, Penguin, HarperCollins, Hachette Book Group, Macmillan and Simon and Schuster. But there have been some mergers, such as the merger of Penguin, Random House and Simon and Shuster. (Crystal desperately hopes they'll call this mega-publisher Simon the Random Penguin. Stay tuned.)

But in addition to these large publishers, there are a number of medium and small houses, some that publish a wide range of books and others that may be very niche, publishing, for example, only cookbooks.

However, from a writer's perspective, there are two types of publishers: those that require an agent to submit your work for consideration, and those that will take un-agented submissions. The larger houses typically require an agent to submit your work (though exceptions may be made if you meet an editor at a conference, or if you have a connection inside the organization). If you want to work with one of these houses, you'll need to hire an agent or cross your fingers and hope to catch someone's eye inside the organization. This last is a lot easier to do if you have an established track record.

There are also publishers who take unsolicited manuscripts. In these cases, follow the submission process on their page to put your work forward. Just like when you seek out an agent, do your homework, learn where to submit and follow the guidelines they've provided to give yourself the best shot.

Leveling up with a publisher

Leveling up with a publisher will mean different things to different people. Some individuals will want to go to a bigger publisher because they are hoping for a larger advance. Others may hope to work with a specific editor, change genres or gain more support within a different house.

It is not uncommon for authors to change publishing houses. Much like changing agents, it's a process you should undertake with care and consideration. The advice we provided in the How, When and Why Do You Fire an Agent? section is relevant here. The primary difference is that if you are considering a publisher change, you can discuss it with your agent. It is not the agent's decision, of course—it is yours—but your agent can help ensure you're making informed and intelligent decisions.

Keep in mind that changing publishers may make sense for your career, but there is no guarantee that a change in houses will lead to you leveling up. Be clear about what you hope to accomplish with the change, research as much as possible to ensure you're making a wise decision. Afterward, reflect on your progress to determine if this move had the benefits you wanted.

Your Turn

- Schedule a "state of my career" meeting with your agent. Where are you with your long term goals. Share your career plan with them. Get their feedback on things you could be doing or things that may have worked for their other clients.
- Review and create a list of who you are working with at the publishing house. You likely know your editor, but do you have the names of your publicist, marketing director, sales team? Is there a way you can reach out to them so that they know you beyond just a name on a book cover?

81

LEVELING UP YOUR INDIE PUBLISHING PROCESS

There are two main ways you can improve your publishing processes:

1. Utilize tools, level up your skills and streamline your processes to help you accomplish more in less time and with less money.
2. Add to your team and outsource your tasks to level up your skilled help and free up more of your time.

How can you level up your own process?

If you are indie publishing, you will be managing a lot of moving parts each time you publish a book. It may be weeks or months or sometimes even years between book releases, and even though you *think* you will remember what you did last time, usually that strategy doesn't work. And that's assuming nothing has changed since you last published a book—which is rare. If you've been following along with us so far, we've drilled into your brain that change is the only constant in publishing.

In order to level up your process, you first have to know what steps you actually take and how you take them. Making a checklist of all your publishing tasks, tools and workflows in some kind of editable format (word doc, asana, google sheet) is the first step. And then you can review that list at the end of each round of publishing and refine or revise it, based on what you've learned this time around. These are the "reflection" and "evolution" steps from the KAREful approach.

Once you have a process recorded, you can review it, and think about the following areas:

Streamline your process

Take a look at all the steps you have in your publishing process, and the order in which you do those tasks, and try to see a more efficient way of doing it. Maybe you could set up a pre-order just a few days before your actual release date so that you have time to update all your author profiles and check all your publication details *before* launch day. Maybe you could rearrange your file management system so that everything you needed for your publication process was in one place. Maybe you could review the costs and benefits of publishing direct to each eBook outlet versus using an aggregator like Draft2Digital or PublishDrive. Maybe if you did all the same things—just in a different order—you would save yourself a great deal of time and energy. You know yourself, your schedule and your own process. Reflect on it, and then evolve along with it.

Level up your tools

It's easy to get settled into using tools we know and love (or love to hate, in the case of some older eBook formatting tools!). If you learned to format your book files using Indesign, that took a lot of time and energy. It's easy to feel committed to that tool and that process. But when something new comes on the market, like Vellum or Draft2Digital's free formatting tool, the idea of learning it can seem like it's not worth the effort or expense—at first. But what if using it could save you an average of 12-14 hours *per book* you publish for the rest of your career? What is that worth to you in writing time? And in the reduction of your stress levels?

Whenever you're trying to decide if a new tool is worth it, ask yourself:

- How happy are you using the existing tool? How long does the task take you now?
- How long will it take to learn this tool?
- How much time will using it save you for each book (once you know how to use it)? How much time will that save you in one year? In 5 years?
- How much does it cost to purchase this tool? Is this monthly, annual or a lifetime license?
- In what ways will this level up your publishing game? What are some benefits of that leveling up?

Level up your skills

Sometimes you don't need to change your tools or your process. You just need to get a bit better at doing whatever tasks you're tackling. It can feel like a waste of time to hit the pause button and spend more time learning how to use something you already *mostly* know how to use. But if you could get faster at typing, or get better and faster at making those promo images, or make less grammatical errors in your writing that then needed to be fixed, how much time could you save? How much energy? How much money? How much faster to produce or better would each book be? And what would those small improvements add up to over a lifetime? Small changes produce big results over time.

If you want some more in-depth help leveling up your indie publishing game, you can take advantage of the free resources offered in The Creative Academy for Writers, and get your hands on a copy of *Strategic Indie Author* when it is released in early 2021, where we will deep dive all the way into these details. Oh, and work your way through each and every book that David Gaughran has written. *Seriously.*

Your Turn

Can you make your publishing processes more efficient by changing your process? Look at all the steps in your current publishing process:

- Is there anywhere you can streamline things, remove steps or decrease the time or energy required to complete a certain step?
- Is there a skill or software you could invest in that would speed things up? For example, investing in Vellum software and spending a couple of days to learn it could save you dozens of hours in the layout process on *every* book—and save you hundreds or even thousands of dollars in professional layout help.

82

LEVELING UP YOUR CAPACITY BY OUTSOURCING

The second way to level up your publishing game is by outsourcing some of your tasks to other people or companies.

If you are traditionally publishing, you'll have the opportunity to actively choose some of your team members, while others will be chosen by your publishing house. But for indie authors, building your team is 100-percent your responsibility as well as being a very cool perk of being the boss.

You may want to stay at your current level. If you're making a living you are happy with and love where you're at, then there is zero pressure to level up! Each person you add to the team, each cog you add to your writing and publishing machine, makes things more complex. It increases the communication energy and time you need to use and increases the possible stress points in your business.

But you will reach a point in your career where it will become very difficult to develop further and still do everything yourself. And it's often well worth expanding your team to reach the next level. It is also extremely effective and efficient to have a team of specialists at your disposal.

The magic questions to ask yourself:

- How many books do I have to sell to make this expense worth it?
- How many hours do I have to work elsewhere to pay for this expense?

How do you know it's time to add someone to your team?

It's best to focus on the stuff that only you can do. The Pareto principle—most commonly known as the 80/20 rule—states that roughly 80 percent of your returns will come from 20 percent of the activities you do.

Your first mission is to pare down the stuff on your to-do list to the 20 percent of things that will get you 80 percent of results. Once that to-do list is as lean as you can make it, do the same thing again—but instead of *removing* items from the list, *outsource* them. What on that list will get you the most results if you outsource it to someone who can do the job well? How could you leverage that additional time if you had it available to reassign?

The other time this makes sense is to overcome resistance. If there is something you can't do yourself—and you don't have the time or desire to learn—or that you just don't want to do, it makes sense to find the money to contract out the task so you can keep things moving forward.

When does it make financial sense to add to your team?

It's a simple rule: Paying someone to help frees up your time. If you can make more from that time than it costs you to pay for the help, then hiring someone makes financial sense.

It can be hard to wrap your head around this at first. Sometimes we set income-level restrictions on our spending—*I can't hire help until I'm making more than $50,000 per year,* or *until I have $10,000 in the bank.* And while it's important to set limits on your spending, it helps to look at what can you make with the time that you save and how you can increase accelerate production, sales and revenues by doing so.

Let's use an example to illustrate this idea.

Crystal has tracked her time and revenue over several projects. She knows that at her current rate of sales and mailing list size for her CJ Hunt brand, the publication of an additional novella in a year is worth a minimum of $5,000 profit the first year that novella is available (after paying to produce that book). She also knows that right now, each novella takes her about 50 to 60 hours to write and publish in eBook, print and audio formats. But only about 35 of those hours are actually spent writing, which is the part that only Crystal can do. The other 15 to 30 hours are made up of tasks related to preparing that book for publication and promotion.

What if she invests in an author assistant to help reduce the time it takes to get that novella to publication stage?

The author assistant could do the following tasks:

- First round of proofreading so final copyediting is quicker and cheaper
- Layouts of the finished book in various formats
- Uploading of the final files to the distributor
- Listening to the audiobook recording for accuracy
- Updating the website
- Preparing newsletter content
- Preparing social media posts for launch promo
- Adding the new book to author profiles around the web
- Making sure that all the info on characters, settings and events are updated in Plottr software so that the series bible is up to date and correct for the writing of the next book

In theory (and once the assistant's initial training period is over), this will free up Crystal to focus on producing more content, which could double the number of titles she could write and release in a year. It will also help keep her focused and in writing mode because she won't have to switch to the business management side of her brain as often.

And the benefit of leveraging your additional available time has long-tail effects as each book continues to earn well past its first year. In fact, if you leverage your assets well, a single title can continue to earn throughout your lifetime and beyond.

A word of caution: If you're just starting out you won't have enough solid data to make this decision because you won't know how much you will earn per title. And even if you think you know, things change. If you're taking this approach, ensure you set aside enough money to pay for support for a set period of time, after which you will evaluate the effectiveness of your approach and adjust plans as needed. Crystal, for example, in addition to tracking and analyzing data from her past releases, has been saving for two years to take care of her budget for the full year's production and publication costs. At that end of that year, a cost-benefit analysis will be conducted to decide if this approach worked, or if adjustments need to be made for the following year.

Your Turn

- Look at your list of all the recurring tasks, or project-based tasks that take up your time during the indie publishing process that you created in the previous step. What are the items that you can't make any more efficient on your own?
- What on that list will get you the most results if you outsource it to someone who can do the job well?
- How could you leverage that additional time if you had it available to reassign?
- How many books do you have to sell to make this expense worth it?
- How many hours do you have to work elsewhere to pay for this expense?
- Which tasks will you look into outsourcing immediately?
- Which tasks will you look into outsourcing in the near future?
- Which tasks will you look into outsourcing eventually?

83

LEVELING UP YOUR TEAM MANAGEMENT

It's no good to decide you're going to hire help and just assume it'll be an amazing experience. You need to take steps to ensure that a) you hire the right people, and b) you build and maintain good relationships and systems that will work for all parties involved. Spending a bit more time up front to establish solid working relationships will mean less turnover of contractors, less time you have to spend on training and orienting yourself to new systems, and less frustration for all parties involved.

How do you know who to hire?

The first step is to identify candidates who have the skill set you're looking for and the rates you can afford. It is generally a good idea to interview them as you would in any other hiring situation, although this doesn't have to be a formal process with a lot of set questions. It is a good idea to brainstorm a few things that are important to you in a working relationship and ask questions to determine if this person is the right fit for you.

Personality

One of the reasons Crystal has such a good relationship with her editor and doesn't put off doing her edits or revisions is because her editor is very approachable, uses informal language to explain suggestions and puts emojis in the comments when she has a strong reaction to something. If you hate it when people you work with are overly comfortable or familiar, this might not suit you at all. So you need to make sure that your working style aligns with that of the candidates you are considering.

Preferences

If you write in Google Docs and do everything virtually, but the editor you are considering only works off paper manuscripts, that may not be a good fit for you. And if your author assistant uses only a PC, while all your programs run on a Mac, you may have trouble developing consistent systems and processes that work for you both.

Priorities

If the person you want to hire does this work as a side hustle, will they be in a position to prioritize your projects when you need them to? What else do they have going on? Do they have certain days of the week or weeks of the year when they are completely unavailable?

If they're doing this job full-time, is the bulk of their time already contracted to long-standing clients while they squeeze you in around the edges? There's no wrong answer here. But understand that if you want to be someone's priority client, you'll likely have to pay for the privilege—or else gradually build a history with them to get you to that point.

Price point

Can you afford this person now? Will you be able to afford them in 6 or 12 months? Often if someone is very affordable, it's because they are building up their business and client list. But what happens once they have built to a certain level and are no longer in the learning phase of their career development? You will want to get a sense of how long they have been in business and how often they raise their rates. Are they willing to sign a contract guaranteeing a certain flat rate so you don't get surprised with a big fee increase partway through a project or a budget year? It's not reasonable (or fair) to assume the costs for a particular service will never go up. But it is reasonable to agree on a price for a specific number of completed projects or a specific time period so that you can budget appropriately. And, yes, if you have negotiated an agreement like this, make sure that the specific terms of your agreement are documented on paper and signed by both parties so you know everyone is on the same page.

If someone proposes a price increase that will put them outside your budget range, you can be open with them and explain why you won't be able to use them anymore. This *will* likely happen at some point, and that's okay. Either they will make an exception because they love working with you—and perhaps you can agree on a future date when you will begin to pay more—or you'll move on and hire or train someone else to take over those tasks.

Do you know what you want and need from your team?

The best way to get what you want out of any collaborative working relationship is to know what you want. If you aren't clear about what you are trying to achieve or how the work needs to be completed, you can't expect people to magically do it the way you want or need it to be done.

Here are some questions you should be able to answer:

- What are you trying to accomplish with a specific task?
- What outcomes or deliverables do you expect to see from that person?
- Are you contracting for a specific amount of time? Or a specific outcome?
- How will you track that time or those outcomes?
- How will they invoice you?

- How will you pay them? This is especially relevant if you're working with someone in another country. Don't assume that your preferred payment method (PayPal, or direct deposit from your business account) will work for them. You need to *ask*.
- What tools need to be used for each task? Will you provide them with those tools, or do you expect they will supply them?
- What are the timelines associated with each task? Are those timelines flexible?
- Who pays costs associated with errors? (For example, if another proof needs to be printed because of errors that were made.)
- Who is responsible for the final quality check? (*Hint:* You are the boss. The answer here is *always you* unless you have specified otherwise or put someone in place to quality check for you).

Part of the reason to hire an expert is to benefit from the skills and experience they bring to the table. Expect to do as much learning as you do teaching in any collaborative situation! You have hired this person for their expertise, so be open to adapting to their tools or systems if those will ultimately save you time or money or get you a better end product.

How do you set up effective systems for collaborative working arrangements?

There are four main elements of any collaborative project.

1. Work tools and programs
2. Communication streams
3. File Storage and sharing
4. Account and password management

These are no different from what is involved in basic project management—but you need to be able to share access to these elements, and they need to work for all parties.

Now let's look at options and our recommendations for each area.

Work tools and programs

Break down your work process into its main phases and identify which programs you use and when. The breakdown below is the case study for the creation, editing, and publishing of this book so you can see how all the pieces come together.

Writing: Google Docs

Eileen uses Microsoft Word for writing, while Crystal generally outlines and writes in Scrivener. But for our collaborative projects, we are using Google Docs because we can both access the shared document anytime, and we can work in the file simultaneously without worrying about reconciling multiple versions of the manuscript later.

Editing: Microsoft Word, Dropbox

Our editor prefers to work in Microsoft Word with track changes. Because we want to discuss suggestions and easily import our final file into Vellum (and Word format works great for this), we will export the Google Doc to Microsoft Word and save it to a shared Dropbox folder, where Amanda, Eileen and Crystal can all access to the documents. Amanda will make corrections and leave comments. Once we've made all the desired corrections and tidied things up as much as possible, then we're ready for formatting.

Publication prep: Vellum, Photoshop, Dropbox

To prepare for publication, we use Vellum to prepare our book layouts (interiors), Photoshop to handle cover design, and Dropbox to store and share files among team members.

Promotion: BookFunnel, BookBrush

When promotion time arrives, we use BookFunnel to deliver review copies to our ARC team, and BookBrush to prepare both three-dimensional book covers for our website and images for newsletters, social media and other promotional media.

File storage and sharing

It's important that everyone has access to the same file-sharing and storage options in a way that works for your process. We use Dropbox or Google Drive for file sharing, depending on what is being shared and which team members need access. Just make sure things are stored in one place so you don't risk creating multiple versions of the same files. Confusion and wasted effort will be the result if someone ends up working on the "wrong" version.

Communication streams and times

It's important to reach an understanding about how and when your team members work, and to figure out a process that works for everyone with minimum disruption to your focused work time. If you use a project management tool (like Slack, Asana or Basecamp) to organize your tasks, you may want to confine all project-related communication to that tool, so everything is in one place when you need to refer back to something. Or maybe you're on a mission to spend less time on your phone, so you only want messages to go to your email.

Make sure that whoever you're working with knows the most effective way to get a hold of you and let them know if there are times in the day when you are unavailable so they won't be waiting around for you to respond to a message.

For example, these are the communication guidelines Crystal has established with her team:

- Crystal has her phone in Do Not Disturb mode every day until noon so she has a guaranteed, uninterrupted, four-hour work block first thing in the morning.
- Her team members know that, and they will put questions into the group WhatsApp chat so that as soon as she *does* turn her phone back on, they can get answers to their questions while she's between focused work blocks. If one of the other team members *is* online, they can give answers as they are able.

Because some team members are involved in multiple projects, this also helps separate streams of conversation into relevant areas. For example, there are separate chat streams for the Strategic Authorpreneur podcast, The Creative Academy, and Thigh High Ink (her romance publishing company).

- Emails are reserved for incoming opportunities, business inquiries and account statements.
- Text messages are for social planning (non-work chat)
- Phone calls are for urgent issues or emergencies. Crystal has programmed in her team members' (and family) phone numbers so that if they actually phone, the calls will come through even if she is in Do Not Disturb mode. That allows her to relax, knowing that if there's an actual emergency, she's still reachable. And because she doesn't have to worry about missing something urgent, there is no driving desire to check her phone or email messages until her work block is finished.

Separating different types of communications into different channels means it's easier to take breaks and filter inputs during focus times.

Account and password management

If you have helpers to manage your ads, complete publication tasks, schedule your social media, manage your website or even respond to some of your fan mail, you'll need to make sure they can access your various accounts as needed. But you may not wish to give away complete control over your accounts or hand over access to your personal info. The access levels you grant will depend a great deal on your history with that team member, how much you know and trust them and how much information is available inside the account.

Many services will allow you to grant different access permissions by adding people to your account. When you can, this is the best option. Then if you need to remove them from your account, revoke access or change permissions, you can do that easily. For some things, though, that won't be an option. If you do need to grant someone access, a team-based password app might be good to try. There are several, but something like PassCamp (which Crystal uses) is a good option. It allows you, for instance, to give team members permission to copy and paste your passwords and username without actually *showing* them the passwords and info. And you can remove sites and tools, or revoke access, if you switch up team members.

Your Turn

- Make a list of any personality traits, skills or characteristics you are looking for in a team member or contractor.
- What is your budget for contracting out these tasks?
- What are you trying to accomplish by outsourcing this specific task?

For each team member you are looking to add, or task you're planning to contract out, make sure you can answer the questions below:

- What outcomes or deliverables do you expect to see from that person?
- How much will it cost for them to complete this task?
- Are you contracting for a specific amount of time? Or a specific outcome?
- How will you track that time or those outcomes?
- How will they invoice you?
- How will you pay them?
- What tools need to be used for each task? Will you provide them with those tools, or do you expect they will supply them?
- What are the timelines associated with each task? Are those timelines flexible?
- Who pays costs associated with errors? (For example, if another proof needs to be printed because of errors that were made.)

- What does the review process on completed work look like? Who is responsible for the final quality check? (*Remember:* You are the boss. The answer here is *always you* unless you have specified otherwise or put someone in place to quality check for you).

84

LEVELING UP PRESENTATIONS AND WORKSHOPS

One of the great things about being a writer is that you know a lot of things. You know how to write, but you also know a million random things you learned doing research. (For example, more people are killed by falling vending machines than by sharks. Think about the *Jaws* theme next time you go to score a Diet Coke.)

If you enjoy sharing this knowledge, writers have opportunities to speak about what they have learned. Your audiences may be made up of other writers, people interested in reading and writing or people who just like to learn more about different topics. Opportunities and venues for speaking include:

- Writer's conferences
- Library talks
- Literary and book festivals
- School talks
- Writer organizations
- Continuing education classes at colleges and universities
- Courses at community centres

Speaking opportunities take different forms

When you give a presentation, for instance, you speak to an audience (up to hundreds in size) with limited interaction. Workshops tend to involve smaller groups in a give-and-take format. Be aware that these aren't hard-and-fast definitions, and people may use them interchangeably. When you're invited to speak, talk with the organizers about what type of experience they're hoping to provide for attendees.

Speaking opportunities may or may not be paid

For example, many writer's conferences do not pay their speakers. They consider the exposure to be the true compensation. On the other hand, many schools have budgets to bring in speakers. Some children's writers make a significant portion of their income from these school presentations. If you're seeking to be paid, you should know the going rates so that you can price yourself comparably. When in doubt, reach out to your writer network.

> *Being a full time author very likely won't mean only writing, that is if you want to put food on the table. For example, as a writer of middle grade fiction, a significant slice of my yearly income comes from doing school and library visits. Charge at least Canada Council minimums; remember, your time is worth something, as is your experience. Work up a good, entertaining hour-long presentation and promote it on your website. It can be a sweet financial boost while you wait... and wait... for that next royalty cheque.*
>
> — Susin Nielsen, author of *We Are All Made of Molecules* and *No Fixed Address*

How to level up your speaking opportunities

Be prepared

Come to any speaking opportunity prepared. Don't expect to just "wing it" based on audience questions and answers. Choose a clear topic and prepare sufficient material—but not too much—for the time period.

Know your audience

Are you speaking to experienced writers or to people who are interested but haven't written before? Know who your audience is, and tailor the talk to them.

Practise, practise, practise

Practice your talk until you feel comfortable and relaxed. If you're using tech such as PowerPoint or showing videos, ensure you know how they work. Confirm with your organizer that the equipment will be available and the space will be appropriate for what you have in mind. If possible, bring your own cords and connections instead of assuming the organization will have this already. (This is especially important if you are a Mac user.)

Hydrate

Make sure you have a glass of water and possibly some cough drops handy in case you need them. Crystal has been known to spill any container of water that doesn't have a lid, so she always brings her own water bottle that has a sealable top and is hard to spill.

Leave time for questions from the audience

It's up to you as a speaker to decide if you want to take questions during your talk or wait until the end. Be sure to tell your audience your preference up front.

Mention your own books

You can do this either as a part of your introduction or at the end of your talk. We often bring a physical copy of our books to prop up on the podium during the talk. You may also want to bring business cards to pass out to people.

Find out in advance if there will be an opportunity to sell your books

Some events have a bookstore set up on site—usually you have to arrange this ahead of time—and sometimes they just provide a table at which you can sell and sign your own books. If this is the case, you will need to bring copies, and that requires advance planning! If it's a school visit, some classes will send home order forms in advance so you know how many books are needed.

If you've created handouts, be sure to feature your name and website on the bottom of each page.

Engage with your audience

Don't stand in front of the room and just read your notes or slides to the participants. Look up, engage with your audience and use notes simply to *guide* your talk.

Give your audience value

It's fine to mention your book as an example, but don't make it the only example. And make sure that you are providing value to your audience with the information you are sharing, not just using the opportunity as a sales pitch. Always ask yourself, "What is the benefit to my audience?".

Don't allow someone to hijack your talk

On occasion, you may have an attendee who wants to either discuss their own project in detail or lead a discussion of their own. It can feel awkward to interrupt someone or shut them down—especially for us introvert types—but remember that you're in charge of this talk. People have come to hear *you* speak.

Your Turn

- Generate a list of conferences that you've attended in the past. How would you describe the "personality" of the conference?
- Take—or review—notes on your favourite speakers. How to they engage the audience? How do they handle the flow of information? What can you learn from them?
- Pull a list of popular conferences and look at what type of sessions are offered. Are there any gaps? Topics that come up frequently? What could you offer?
- Create an outline for a workshop session including: what you would cover, how long those sections would take to teach, and any prompts or audience interaction planned. Decide if you need a handout. It may help to have more than one workshop idea to pitch to conference organizers.
- If you haven't spoken before, identify an opportunity to do this with a smaller crowd to determine if you enjoy it.
- If you are ready to pitch your workshop, identify which conferences are open to submissions from prospective speakers and submit your information.
- Make a list of all the events you are interested in speaking at. If there is information about the process on the event's website, review their guidelines for submitting presentation ideas and note their application deadlines. Often events are planned a year or more in advance, so you will need to be proactive.
- The larger and more prestigious the conference, the more likely they will want you to have had experience speaking. Volunteer to do speaking engagements at your local library or with your local writers groups to gain experience. Brainstorm a list of places you could volunteer.
- When you propose a workshop to conference organizers, provide clear details: the topic will you cover, the intended audience, the duration of the talk, the degree of interaction with the audience.

- Solicit feedback from attendees and organizers when you speak.
- Collect testimonials and references that you can provide to other conference organizers.
- Research and apply to a speakers bureau if you would like someone else to help you find speaking opportunities.

85

LEVELING UP KEYNOTES

Giving a keynote address is a weighty responsibility. If you've been asked to give a keynote, you should take it as a compliment. Keynotes are generally something you are invited to do, not something that you apply for. You are chosen because the organization or conference feels that you would be good at helping to set the tone of an event. Unlike other talks that are focused on sharing information or providing education, a keynote is typically more about eliciting an emotional reaction from listeners.

Learn about the organization's expectations

To give a good keynote, take time to learn more about the organization, its mission, and the audience expected to attend the event. Even if it's an organization you're familiar with, take the time to talk to the organizer about what they hope to see in the keynote, in addition to specifics like where the talk will take place, how long you should speak and how large the audience will be. Eileen finds it useful to ask, "What emotions do you want people to feel at the end of the speech?" She uses those emotions to guide her talk.

Provide a concise bio

Most keynote speakers are introduced by the MC or another person from the organization. They may ask you for a bio, but even if they don't, it's a good idea to send them some bulleted points that you hope they will hit. They may mention your awards, recent books or fun details about you.

Remember that a keynote is not about you

Although you may share personal details, a keynote is not the place to sell yourself, your services, or your writing. A keynote is like a well-written novel. In your books, you're likely trying to convey a point, lesson or theme, but if you're too heavy-handed the reader—or listener—will lose interest.

Consider personal examples that can help make your point

A well-done speech is like a well-told story. There are highs and lows. Know where you want to pack an emotional punch. It's possible that telling the story will bring out emotion in you. This is okay. Listeners are touched if they see that you're also emotionally engaged. However, if you're broaching a subject that is very hard for you to speak about, ensure you practise often enough that you can get through the talk with composure.

Write down the words

While you will not want to spend your keynote staring down at your paper, it's wise to have your talk written out so you can quickly glance down and ensure you're on track. A wandering keynote is never a good thing. Printing out your speech in a larger font (such as 16 point) can be helpful. As you practise, you may write in breaks to remind yourself to breathe and pause. You can also underline thoughts or sentences you want to emphasize in your talk. Maybe you'll speak that line in a louder voice. Or maybe you want to ensure That. Each. Word. Is. Distinct.

Engage the audience

You may ask them to raise their hands if they've ever done something similar, or encourage them to stand or repeat a line after you. Author Robert Dugoni once gave a keynote at the Surrey International Writers Conference in which he modified a call to war from *The Lord of the Rings* into a call to keep writing. He repeated "this day we write" as a call to action for all the conference attendees. By the end of the speech, he had the entire audience yelling it along with him. You could feel their energy and excitement. They were ready to run out of there and *write all the things*. That's a good keynote.

Decide on visuals

These could be pictures you hold up to illustrate a point, or slides with images or quotes. Keep in mind that most people don't plan to take notes during a keynote—heck, by the time you get to the podium, they may be eating dessert and on their third glass of overpriced wine from the cash bar. Any visual should add to your talk, not drive it.

Learn from the masters

TED Talks are available online and provide a range of inspiring keynote-style presentations on just about every topic you can imagine. Watch several and make notes about what engages you. Consider even writing out what they say and looking at how they "performed" the words. And make notes about what didn't engage you or diverted your focus from the point they were making. Then put those onto your "don't" list.

Practise, practise, practise

This seems obvious, but it merits repetition. You'll want to practise your talk. Deliver it to the mirror, deliver it to your loved ones. Eileen's dogs are always willing to listen to her speeches, provided she offers the occasional liver treat to keep their interest. You want to feel comfortable when you're speaking. Practise any words that are tricky to pronounce, or swap them out. The more you practise, the more natural you'll appear in front of the group. If you're really nervous, it's okay. You can even let people know off the top that you are—it might endear you to the audience.

Less is more

Very rarely do people say, "Gee, I wish that keynote had gone on even longer." Write your speech like you're drafting a scene: enter the action at the latest possible point and leave a bit earlier than you might expect. Speeches benefits from being tight and concise.

Once you've made your point and built the audience up to a climax, it's time to exit stage right. You'll typically end with a "thank you" or other signifier that you're done, and then you can step back from the podium. If they (hopefully) burst into applause, feel free to stand there a moment and enjoy it. You deserve it.

Your Turn

- Watch recorded keynotes or TED Talks and determine what aspects you enjoy and would be a good match for your personality.
- Record yourself delivering your keynote. Watch your performance and identify where you can improve. Record it again and have it as a resource to show conference organizers if asked.

86

LEVELING UP MENTORSHIP

What is mentorship?

Mentorship is the process by which a more experienced individual provides guidance and support to someone with less experience. Most writers practise unofficial mentorships by reaching out on occasion to people they know, or people who are connected to them, for suggestions and advice. However, some writers are willing to pay for a more formal, structured and consistent mentoring relationship.

What is included in mentorship?

There are no formal rules about what needs to be offered in a mentorship except those that you and the other individual agree upon. But here are examples of services that could be provided:

- Feedback and suggested improvements on manuscript pages
- Guidance on craft issues
- Feedback on specific projects such as reader newsletters, advertising strategy, website content, query letters, responding to editorial letters

- Discussion of specific issues the individual is working through such as challenges with craft, publishing, the agent search, advertising, reader engagement
- Regular accountability meetings to assist a person in staying on track with their manuscript or project
- Recommending resources such as books, software, contractors (e.g., a cover designer or author assistant) or classes and learning opportunities

Dos and don'ts of mentorship

Don't make promises you can't keep

Make sure you are clear about what type of support you can provide, and don't indicate that working with you will ensure anyone a book deal, bestseller status or any other outcome that is not directly within your control.

Provide clear timeline expectations

With mentorship, someone is essentially paying for your time and expertise. Be very clear about how much time you will be dedicating to this project. Will you meet them weekly for 30 minutes, once a month by phone, or only by email? Will you respond to questions within a set amount of time? Are you charging them for all your time (for example, the time it takes to respond to email)?

Don't surprise anyone with a bill

People should have a clear idea of what mentorship with you will cost. You may have a set service fee, or you may bill for your time hourly, but if you're billing hourly, you may wish to set a ceiling with the client—stipulating, for instance, that if they go over $500, you will let them know before you bill anything additional.

Clearly outline what services you will provide

Just as you provide clear guidelines about your time, you'll want to make sure your client knows what they can expect from you. Will you be preparing lessons for them to work on, or are you simply available to answer questions in the moment? If you are reading their manuscript, what kind of notes can they expect to get from you?

Don't oversell your own abilities

It's okay not to know everything. In fact, no one trusts a know-it-all. If someone asks you a question, and you don't know the answer, it's okay to say so. (In fact, it's the right thing to do.) You can then either promise to get back to them later, when you've had a chance to do some additional research, or let them know they need to approach someone else for help in that area. Never pretend or make up answers. This almost never goes well except in romantic comedies.

Maintain a record-keeping system

You will need some way to track a) who you are working with; b) what they are working on; c) next steps; d) what has been billed; and e) if they have paid. You may do this with file folders, a paper calendar and a cork board with invoices tacked to it, or you may utilize a software solution like Google Sheets or an app like Hours or Harvest. The system is less important than your commitment to using and maintaining it.

Don't be inflexible

A client's needs may change, so stay flexible and check in with them on a regular basis to make sure the mentorship is still meeting their needs. You are much more likely to have a long-term relationship if you can adapt with them to address their identified priorities.

Ask for feedback

The best way to improve your services is to ask for feedback. What did mentorship clients like about your mentorship program? Was there anything they would like done differently? You may want to modify how your mentorship program is offered, or you may determine that you need to screen more diligently to ensure people are a good fit for what you're offering.

Ask for testimonials

If clients are happy with your service, ask them if they would consider writing a testimonial that you can use on your website or in marketing materials.

Don't assume everything always works out

You might consider consulting with a lawyer to ensure you've covered any risk to yourself. A clear working agreement or waiver may be helpful, and you may want to consider purchasing insurance.

How to level up mentorship

If you want to add mentorship to the services you offer consider doing the following:

- Ask writers you know if they've worked with mentors before, and get feedback on what they liked and disliked about this service.
- If you've practised through an informal mentorship with anyone, ask them for a testimonial.
- Word of mouth is one of the best ways to build a client list, so tell writers in your networks that you offer this service and ask them to please pass on your name and contact information to anyone who may be interested.
- Provide information about your mentorship services on your website and include a way for people to reach you.
- Consider offering writing advice on a blog or a newsletter to give people a taste of your style of support.
- If you do any teaching or write articles online, list or mention this experience in your description of mentorship services.

Your Turn

- Make a list of areas in which you feel you could provide mentorship. Note what makes you an experienced individual in this area.
- If you have mentored people before on an informal basis, reach out to them to discuss what worked and what they would have liked done differently. Ask if they are willing to act as a reference for you or collect a written testimonial you can use on your promotional materials.
- Add information about these offerings to your website, and share that you are taking on mentorship clients on your social media and in your various writing groups as appropriate.

87

LEVELING UP GROUP INSTRUCTION

The cliche is that "those who can't do, teach," but it should be "those who want to learn more about what they do, teach." The process of explaining a concept, be it craft or publishing knowledge, includes several stages:

1. Understanding the concept yourself
2. Explaining the concept to someone else
3. Explaining the concept in different ways because people learn in different ways

Both Crystal and Eileen adore having the chance to teach. We know that we have learned far more helping other writers than we would have learned on our own. So let's explore how you can level up through different forms of teaching.

What is group instruction?

When you consider teaching, what might jump to your mind is the classic image of a person in front of a classroom, imparting their knowledge to a group of rapt students. Eileen has taught for many years and she is disappointed to report that she has never had Indiana Jones's experience where a student has written *I love you* on their eyelids. On the upside, she *has* gotten high reviews for her teaching, so she keeps coming back.

Teaching may take place in either a live classroom setting or online. Classes may be offered through an accredited educational program (such as a college or university) or privately through writing groups, associations or individuals offering group courses and mentorships.

What does group instruction include?

You'll be teaching to a group that can range in size. An in-person class typically has a minimum, often 10 or 15 students, and a maximum depending on room size. An online class may have upward of 100 students.

Instruction will take place over a set number of weeks or months, depending on the program.

The class may or may not have education or experience requirements or prerequisites. For example, students may be required to take certain courses or acquire certain practical experience first. Admission to a program may be on a competitive basis, with students submitting applications and writing samples in order to be considered.

As the instructor, you'll present materials and information. The amount of interaction you have with students, or students have with each other, depends on the course. Eileen teaches with Simon Fraser University. The students in The Writer's Studio are working on their own manuscripts, but they also participate by critiquing each other's manuscripts in a group workshop format. Class structure may be determined by the program, the school or the instructor.

How to level up group instruction

Some educational programs require instructors to have specific education in order to teach. Colleges or universities may require a master's degree, but they may also waive this requirement depending on the author's experience, for instance if you are a successful, multi-published author.

Many community colleges offer adult education courses. If you don't have a teaching background, you may find it helpful to enroll in a course or courses in this area. These courses will teach you how to adjust to different learning styles, work with students, address ethical issues and create and deliver a learning program.

Many community colleges offer continuing education programs, and this is an excellent way to get your foot in the door. Approach them with a course proposal. This could include a description of the course you want to teach, learning objectives for students, your teaching experience and often a sample lesson plan.

If there is a particular program you are keen to teach with, reach out and ask what they look for in instructors. If possible, shadow a class they currently offer and seek out a chance to chat with people in the program.

You can also tell your networks that you are looking for teaching opportunities and ask them to pass along any news they come across.

Your Turn

- Give some thought to what mediums you might be interested in teaching in. Are you interested in teaching online? In-person classes? A mix of both?
- Are there specific age groups you feel most comfortable working with?
- Review the current offerings at local community colleges in your area to see if there are gaps.
- Identify topics you feel confident teaching. Brainstorm what you would include and why you're the ideal instructor for this topic.
- List what skills you have that make you a strong candidate for group instruction.

- Explore different learning styles and decide what approach you would take with your teaching style.
- Identify any possible opportunities within your geographical area, or within your online networks.
- Find out how to submit your application to your chosen programs, and pitch yourself!

We covered the most common three areas to level up if you're looking to see a boost in income—writing, publishing, and teaching—but there are other ways to accomplish this as well. In the following sections we dig into three other areas where you can level up your income, not directly through your own writing but in ways that will potentially benefit your writing career in the long term.

88

LEVELING UP PATRONAGE

If you have a patronage model where your readers and fans are providing support directly, then you can approach leveling up one of two ways. You can focus on getting more fans to subscribe to monthly support via Patreon or whatever platform you are using. Or you can try to increase the income from existing patrons by asking for a time-limited or project-specific increase in funding, or by providing more value to your existing patrons.

If you don't yet have a patronage program, it can be a way to supplement your income. Be aware that this is a whole new industry to develop for yourself and there is a learning curve. Like anything else, it will take time to build up your followers and generate a consistent source of revenue from this approach. So if you are exploring this route, make sure that your financing needs are not immediate, and remember that it will take time away from your other writing activities.

Your Turn

- If you're considering a patronage model, visit Patreon.com and look for different writers who are doing a good job of building up a following there. How much are they making per month? How long have they been on Patreon? What are they providing to their supporters in exchange for their support?
- Sign up with one to three writers in your genre and follow them for a month or two. What do they send out to their patrons? How do they interact with them? How much time per month do you think they are investing?
- If you're still interested in adding this income stream after your analysis, then brainstorm a list of things you have to offer to patrons and write a pros and cons list of adding this income stream to your business model.

89

LEVELING UP GRANTS, SCHOLARSHIPS, WRITERS-IN-RESIDENCE

If you want to increase your revenue from sources like grants and scholarships, we discussed these in "Financing Your Business Growth".

Many writers organizations provide lists of grants, residencies, and scholarships that may be available. This is a good place to start your search, in addition to using everyone's favourite research tool, Google.

The number of opportunities and their requirements will vary. Here are some tips and suggestions to assist you in navigating them:

- Do your homework by reading the guidelines and applications carefully. Create a list of the information you will need to gather as well as noting deadlines.
- Take advantage of any information sessions or supporting documents available to you.
- If there is a list of past successful candidates, you may reach out to past winners and see what you can learn from their experience.
- When you respond to the application questions, attempt to express not only how you can use this financial help to further your own creative goals, but also how your work will benefit the

grant-awarding organization or the writing community. (For example, many writer-in-residence programs include organizing events for the community.)

- Have your information handy. Having a list of your publications (including publisher and publication date), awards, and teaching and conference experience means that you won't spend time scrambling for those details at the last minute.
- Organize your references in advance. Many proposals ask you to include letters of support. If you've been collecting these in your career, you will have some ready. If you are using people's names and contact information, be sure to reach out to them first to let them know and ensure they are willing.
- If you've missed the submission deadline, put it in your calendar because many of these opportunities are yearly.
- If you aren't successful, many programs provide an opportunity for feedback on individuals applications. If this is available, take it! Take notes and learn how you can improve your chances.
- Understand that there will be more applications than funds given out through these opportunities. Don't be discouraged. Many writers apply multiple times before receiving support.

Your Turn

- Create a writing resume. Often funding sources request a writing resume, and having one ready to submit or update is a time saver. Writing resumes typically list your publications any speaking experiences, awards and any relevant courses you have taken.
- Research and make a list of opportunities being advertised in your area. If there are any programs you know of that might be possibilities, contact the organization and ask when the next round of applications will open up.
- Set a reminder in your calendar for any you would like to apply for.

If you aren't sure what a writing resume might look like you can download Eileen's example resume at

https://creativeacademyforwriters.com/resources/fulltimeauthor.

In the next few sections, we're discussing income that you generate by doing writing-related tasks *not* directly connected to your own creative projects. If you're looking for an additional stream of income, it seems reasonable to use your skill set as a writer to generate that money. Why not use your superpowers for good—and moolah—after all? You already have transferable skills in this area, and presumably you enjoy writing, so this may be a perfect strategy for you.

Before you pursue this route full speed, however, consider if you want your income stream to be related to writing. There are some who would rather use their creative energy for their own writing. They find they have only so much "creative juice" in the tank and don't want to spend it on other people's projects. Others love having a chance to work in writing in any capacity. You may want to dip your toe in this work before committing to it to ensure it's a good fit for you.

We'll consider four different types of writing-related income. This isn't meant to be an exhaustive list but something to get you thinking about what might be possible. The ability to express yourself in a written format is a huge skill! If this area interests you, brainstorm different ways you might utilize your writing and publishing knowledge to generate income.

90

LEVELING UP EDITING

Are you the queen of the critique group? Do you have an ability to look through someone's writing and provide guidance? If yes, you might consider freelance editing. Editing services are required by everyone from other writers to students to organizations and companies.

Editing typically comes in three formats: developmental or structural editing, copy editing and proofreading.

Developmental edits: If someone is requesting story edits or developmental editing, they are seeking assistance with the various story components. This includes issues such as character development, pacing, plotting, dialogue and setting.

Line and copy edits: Someone requesting edits in this area wants help with issues such as consistency—if your protagonist has brown hair in Chapter One and blond hair in Chapter Five, you may have a problem—technical consistency, factually incorrect statements, sentence structure, punctuation and spelling.

Proofreading: A proofreader is checking the final copy of the manuscript (or a printed proof) for quality before it goes into production. They may correct awkward word or page breaks, formatting issues or the occasional typo.

The growth in indie publishing means that an increasing number of people are seeking editorial support to ensure their books look as professional as possible. Even writers seeking traditional publication often contract freelance editors to make their manuscripts as strong as possible before submitting to agents or publishers.

There are also editing opportunities with students preparing papers or thesis manuscripts, and organizations seeking editorial support for their marketing materials and website content.

As an editor, you will need to determine how you charge for this service: per word, per page, per hour or per project. You may decide to take on only certain types of projects. Eileen has a friend who specializes in developmental edits for middle grade, YA and contemporary romance manuscripts. This editor doesn't take on horror or hard fantasy because she doesn't feel she can offer suggestions in genres she is not familiar with. Another editor only takes on non-fiction projects because she writes fiction and finds that editing anything close to her own genre messes with her creative process. You will be the best at determining what type of work you can take on.

How to level up with editorial services

- Many universities and colleges offer formal editorial courses and continuing education classes, online and in the classroom.
- Depending on your experience and education, you may be able to join a professional editing association
- If you don't have formal education but do have teaching experience, the formal feedback you provided to students can demonstrate capability in this area.
- You may consider offering services to people you know for free, or at reduced rates, in order to gather testimonials and build word of mouth.

Your Turn

- Which editorial areas do you already have skills in?
- Are there any areas you need to improve with additional training? Identify some courses or resources that could help you improve those skills.
- Are your skills at a high enough level to begin charging for those services?
- Do you have a proven track record with clients and testimonials or references to support your skills?
- If not, consider offering your services to a small number of clients either for free or at a reduced rate to gain enough experience and references to move to the next step. What are you willing to offer, and where could you share this opportunity?
- If you are ready to start charging, draw up a rate sheet and post on your website and in your author networks that you are offering editorial services for a fee.

91

LEVELING UP AUTHOR SERVICES

Writing may be a solitary activity, but running and operating an author business can take a team. Many authors seek out help with a range of tasks:

- Booking appointments
- Arranging travel
- Monitoring and directing advertising
- Organizing mailing lists, sending out newsletters and holding contests
- Formatting books
- Uploading titles
- Bookkeeping
- Research
- Cover design
- Creation of marketing materials
- Website maintenance and updating
- Managing email and reader engagement

Individuals who offer these services may be called assistants or virtual assistants. They may offer their services as a package, as a one-time service, or on an hourly basis. They may offer all the services outlined above, or only select services.

How to level up with author services

- There is no formal education or training available in this area, but many people have administrative skills and experience.
- Depending on what services you plan to offer, you may take courses or get training in a specific area, such as bookkeeping.
- Your own experience may qualify you to offer these services, but be prepared. People will want to know what you've done and what outcomes you've achieved.
- Commit to ongoing learning. Many of these areas—such as formatting and advertising—are in constant flux. Ensure you're staying on top of the most current trends and requirements.

Your Turn

- Which areas have you developed skills in?
- Which of these skills would you potentially be interested in hiring out?
- Do you have access to any tools that other authors may not have or not want to learn to use?
- Which services could you offer without it interfering with your writing time?
- Are your skills at a high enough level to begin charging for those services?
- Do you have a proven track record with clients and testimonials or references to support your skills? (This could include examples of your own projects)

- If not, considering offering your services to a small number of clients either for free or at a reduced rate to gain enough experience and references to move to the next step. What are you willing to offer, and where could you share this opportunity?
- If you are ready to start charging, draw up a rate sheet and post on your website and in your author networks that you are offering author support services for a fee.

92

LEVELING UP WORK-FOR-HIRE

Publishers and individuals hire writers to write—or ghostwrite—books. A publisher, for instance, may have a celebrity who has a book idea but is not be interested (or capable) of writing it themselves. At other times, the publisher may have an idea or series concept and hire writers to make it a reality. You may already know that the Nancy Drew series, for example, was actually written by a number of different writers. In fact, there are organizations known as book packagers that solely prepare ideas they feel are marketable and then seek authors to write them.

Individuals may hire writers because they want to write a family history, their memoir or a non-fiction book about sales techniques. They may want a book to record a memory or use as a part of their business, but they do not want to write it. That's where you can come in!

Both Eileen and Crystal have done work-for-hire projects. Crystal was hired to write a series of books for an educational publisher. Some published under her own name, and some published under a variety of pen names. Eileen wrote two novels for a publisher who had a concept and outline but needed a writer to bring it to life. There are a number of things to be aware of in these cases.

Credit

You may, or may not, be listed as the author of these books. The term "ghostwriting" refers to the idea that the real author is a ghost to the name that goes on the front. In some cases, the real author's identity is designed to be a secret. You might have to sign a contract indicating that you won't come forward in any public way regarding this work. Other work for hire may get published under another name, but you will be allowed to publicly acknowledge you are the author and may even be listed on the cover.

Payment

Work for hire and ghostwriting contracts are paid in different ways. Some individuals are paid a one-time fee for the book. Other contracts may resemble a standard publishing contract with allowances made for earning some type of royalties or sub-rights. If you are paid a one-time fee, you are likely to get more money up front, but be aware that if the book becomes a runaway bestseller, you won't be sharing in that windfall. On the opposite end of the spectrum, if your arrangement involves a more modest advance in combination with royalties, you may not get paid any additional money if the book doesn't earn out. Read your contact carefully.

Creative flexibility

The amount of control you will have over the end product varies from contract to contract. In some cases the contractor may provide the writer with only a brief outline; in others, they may have very clear guidelines and expectations about characters, plot and voice. It is important to understand that you are writing to prepare a product that reflects the client's desires and not your personal creative goals. You will need to flex your personal ideas for the project to fit theirs. You will also typically be writing on a deadline, so you will be expected to deliver the product on time.

How to level up with ghostwriting

Ghostwriters are typically authors with publishing experience. People often want to look at your existing work and have confidence that you can deliver books on time. If you have an interest in this area, it will help if you have a publishing track record.

If you have an agent, let them know you are interested in work-for-hire opportunities. Publishers often reach out to agencies to see if they know anyone who might be a good fit for a particular project.

If you are working with an established publisher, you can also let your editor know that you're interested in ghostwriting in case they are aware of opportunities.

You, or your agent on your behalf, can approach a book packager to let them know you're interested in this type of work. They may request writing samples from you to have on file.

If you are approached for a book-for-hire situation you may be asked to submit work samples. This could include your ideas on a project or sample chapters. In these cases, you will often sign a nondisclosure agreement promising to not share this idea with others. These sample chapters may or may not be paid. The more experience you have, the more likely you are to be paid for a sample chapter even if they don't hire you for the project.

Your Turn

- What appeals to you about ghostwriting or a book-for-hire situation?
- What do you think would be challenging about ghostwriting or a book-for-hire situation?
- Reflect on how time spent on writing projects that are not your own will impact your own creative energy.
- If you are ready to seek out this type of work, speak to your agent about opportunities, or post on your website and in your author networks that you are open to work-for-hire opportunities.

- Research book packagers, and search for work-for-hire situations online. Make a list of possibilities.
- Ask your networks if anyone has worked with any of the companies you identified, and see if they are willing share what that experience was like. Make notes of any concerns you have, and any advice or contact information they share with you.

93

LEVELING UP COPY WRITING

Similar to ghostwriting, there are a number of paid, writing-related work opportunities. These don't include writing on your novel, or even necessarily book length projects. These can include the following types of work:

- Selling articles or short stories to magazines or online publications such as *Medium*
- Writing website copy for organizations
- Writing copy for marketing materials, catalogues, or brochures
- Speech writing
- Blog writing
- Writing short, human-interest stories for charities

Similar to work for hire, you will likely have less creative control over many of these projects compared to your own creative work.

How to level up with copy writing

- Indicate on your website, or on a separate website, that you offer copy writing services.

- Have a portfolio of work samples available so people can see the range of work you can do.
- You may seek out either paid positions in organizations or offer to do this work on a freelance basis.
- Request a testimonial for completed projects when the client is happy.
- If appropriate, let the client know that you are seeking similar work so they can pass on your name to appropriate people.

Your Turn

- What skills or experience do you have in copywriting?
- Review open copywriting positions on sites such as LinkedIn. Look at what skills and experience they are seeking for different positions. Consider the tasks and projects. Can you see yourself doing this type of work?
- Reflect on how time spent on writing projects that are not your own will impact your own creative energy.
- If you are ready to take this on, make a list of any open positions that interest you, and start submitting applications.

94

LEVELING UP AFFILIATE AND ADVERTISING REVENUES

You can supplement your income with money from affiliate referrals. Affiliate referrals are where you receive funds for recommending particular products (software for example) when another individual purchases them—usually via a customized URL. This strategy can work if you maintain a blog or an active online community, if you teach or coach other writers or if you're pursuing online marketing efforts on your own books. You may also generate revenue from ads that appear on your website or blog if you are sharing creative content with the world.

It is very important that you understand the guidelines and restrictions of each affiliate program contract you sign and that you follow those guidelines when sharing your affiliate links.

Your Turn

- Brainstorm a list of any tools you use in your author business that you might recommend to other authors in your networks.

- Make a list of where you could share these links with other authors or your readers (if appropriate).
- If you are blogging, or writing non-fiction, are there any products or services you write about that may have affiliate programs?
- Find each tool or company's website and determine if they have a referral or affiliate program. If you don't find an answer on their website, email them to ask. Often there is a program that just isn't posted publicly.
- If you have service providers that you regularly refer people to, ask them if they have any kind of referral program or bonuses.
- Make yourself a spreadsheet to track any programs you sign up for, what their terms, conditions and restrictions are, your login information if they use a specific affiliate platform, and make a note of what link to share to ensure your referrals are tracked.
- Make sure you understand the rules about disclosing when you use an affiliate link, and that you follow best practices.

95

LEVELING UP NON-WRITING INCOME

Many writers have a business model in which income is not entirely dependent on writing and publishing income. Especially in the beginning, this can be a key element of sustainability over time as you build your career. You might be funding yourself if you inherited some money, won the lottery or if you have kept your day job either full- or part-time. You may have a spouse or family member who is helping pay household bills so you can grow your career without drawing income from your writing business.

How do you level up in this area? There are two primary ways: you can increase your revenue from non-writing-related income, or you can decrease the amount of money you need to bring in by reducing your expenses.

Increasing your income might mean working more time at your day job or getting a better day job. The upside of this approach is the chance to set aside cash to grow your writing and publishing budget, which can help you take that leap to the next level. The downside is that it may slow down your progress in your writing career because you are spending more time and energy at work.

So look at your lifestyle and see if you can—and if you want to—reduce your ongoing expenses. If you rent your home, is it worth moving to a cheaper place? If you own your home, do you have the option of temporarily pausing mortgage payments or remortgaging at a better rate? Some authors we know move to a less expensive place to keep their expenses low and their stress down as they build up to a career-level income. Even the small things make a difference—is there anything in your lifestyle that isn't serving you, or that you could give up for a while?

Your Turn

- Brainstorm ways you could increase the non-writing-related income available to you right now.
- Do a pros and cons list for each of the ideas you come up with, and list how much money you might be able to generate from each one.
- Brainstorm ways to reduce your expenses so you don't need as much income. Which of these things might even help you move your writing forward? (For example, if you cancel your cable subscription, you may spend less time watching TV and more time writing). Remember to ask your spouse, family members or writers group to share their ideas. They'll likely have some good ones you haven't thought of.

96

LEVELING UP YOUR OPPORTUNITIES

The saying goes that luck is when preparation meets opportunity. And when people talk about important tipping points in their careers, they often say things like, "It was really lucky timing for that book to come out," or, "It was such a lucky break when I met so-and-so [fancy director] at that screenwriting conference. It totally changed everything when my book got made into a movie."

But these writers were taking an active part in living a "writerly life," generating opportunities for themselves by learning new skills, connecting with other industry people, and just writing their darn book. So, when the moment arrived, that book was ready to go off into the world.

Create your own opportunities

Outside of fairy tales, you likely won't hear a story about someone who was just sitting around, *thinking* about what they wanted to happen, when—poof—some fairy godmother appeared to grant their every wish.

A wish is a desire or hope for something to happen.

A goal is the object of a person's ambition or effort: an aim or desired result. It's far less fun than magic and fairy dust, but it's a lot more likely to produce results.

Wishing is a pretty passive act. Have you ever heard someone say, "I wish I were as lucky as so-and-so?" Well, that's the problem right there. They'd probably be a whole lot "luckier" if they took some steps to prepare themselves for any opportunities that arise. Often just taking action—any action!—opens up doors we'd never have even noticed if we weren't moving ourselves toward our goals. Opportunities arise *because* we take action.

Have or build a community of working authors around you so have an "office" of co-workers to help answer questions, bounce ideas off, or just to kick around with by the virtual water cooler.

— ELIZABETH BOYLE, *NEW YORK TIMES* BESTSELLING ROMANCE AUTHOR

When it comes to helping you create or level up opportunities for growth, your writing community and networks are your best and quickest pathway to results. In fact, we love community so much we built one just so we could have a place to play! Your community can provide support, opportunities, and education.

Here are some great ways to create opportunities:

- Be clear about what you want
- Identify places you may be able to find information and opportunities
- Ask your networks to share with you any opportunities they come across
- Be proactive in suggesting what you have to offer

- Take advantages of any opportunities you get and make sure you deliver value and quality
- Reflect on what went well and what could be improved next time
- Be patient—growth doesn't happen overnight

In her day job as a counsellor, Eileen used to provide career counselling to individuals making career shifts due to injury or illness. One thing that she would stress about this process was network, network, network. Why? Because you never know where opportunities can come from, and those who do best in their profession are often those who have a broad network. She discovered that this is even more true in the writing profession.

Now, you might think, *But I'm a writer—do I really need a network outside of my imaginary friends?* You do. A strong network can help with any or all of the following.

Writing opportunities

You may hear about writing opportunities or introductions to editors at different publishing houses.

Agent contacts

Knowing other writers may give you referrals.

Insider information

You can learn what it's like to work with different organizations, publishers or agents.

Resources awareness and deals

Other writers will tell you about resources they use and love. They may also have coupons or templates that help you learn the tool or save money.

Blurbs and editorial reviews

You may be able to ask other writers for blurbs that can help sales of your new release.

Reviews

Reviews influence sales by helping potential readers determine if your work will appeal to them. When you have a solid community, you can ask them to leave a review if they feel comfortable.

Signal boost

A strong community can boost any news or social media you'd like to share with the world by retweeting or reposting news of book launches, sales or newsletter sign-ups.

Opportunities

Fellow writers can connect you with opportunities to speak at conferences, to teach a workshop or to be included in an article or media opportunity.

Book research

A strong community can connect you with research resources, including people who work in specific industries represented in your own book.

Cross-promotion

You can help each other by cross-promoting your work through newsletter swaps or contributions to a box set project.

Collaboration

You could write with a friend in a shared world, or author books together, or even just be critique partners or accountability buddies so you're not in this alone.

Find opportunities through your writing community

Now that you see the value of having a strong community, how do you build one?

Participate in writing groups

There are so many! Groups include The Creative Academy for Writers, Sisters in Crime, the Society of Children's Book Writers and Illustrators, Romance Writers of America and many other national and international genre-focused groups, as well as local writing groups and chapters.

Create a business card and website

This gives you a way to easily establish contact when you meet other writers.

Attend writing events

This could be everything from public book readings to library discussions and conferences where writers are likely to attend.

Volunteer at book events

The best way to be involved is to give your time and energy. Remember those healthy boundaries, though!

Introduce yourself

This can seem like an introvert's nightmare, but there's something to be said for reaching out to an author and just letting them know that you like their work.

Signal boost other writers

If you have an author you like and you see them post something about their book, boost it for them by sending it out over your own social media.

So you want a favour

You've been building a community for a period of time, and now you want to reach out and ask something of them, like a blurb, a review or an introduction. Here are some things to keep in mind:

This is a relationship, not a transaction

The other person does not owe you anything. There may be a number of reasons they are unable to help you at this time. If someone turns down your request, be gracious and understanding.

Don't open with a request

Imagine that someone moves in next door to you. They come over the first day, introduce themselves and ask if you'd mind shovelling their driveway for them. You'd likely be put off. But if you'd spoken several times, and they'd picked up your mail when you were out of town, and *then* they asked if you'd mind shovelling for them because they'd been sick, you'd likely be glad to do it. (Or have your teenager do it. Isn't this why people have children? Free labour?) No one likes to feel used.

Be aware of the scope of the ask

Asking someone to read your manuscript is a *big* ask. To read a full manuscript and provide notes is a lot of work. Many writers do this on a freelance basis as an income generator. If you're asking someone to do it for free, either to give you feedback or in the hope that they'll provide a blurb, be aware that you are requesting a huge favour. Asking for an introduction to an agent or editor is a similarly big ask. It may require less time than reading a manuscript, but it puts the author in a place where they are requesting a favour of someone else they know. There are only so many of these requests they can make of their own connections.

If you're making a request, make it possible for the person to say no without putting a strain on things. For example: *I was hoping you might be willing to read my book and potentially offer a blurb if you like it. I know you're quite busy and likely have lots of requests, so I understand if you don't have the time or the book doesn't fall within your interest area.* Making someone feel obligated can be off-putting.

Provide a reasonable time limit

If you're already requesting a favour of someone, don't put them under the added pressure of doing it within a tight turnaround. At the very least, understand that the tighter the timeline, the less likely they are to meet this demand. However, you also want to be honest. If you need a blurb by a set time let the other author know so they can determine if they can meet it.

Explain why they can help

It goes a long way if you've read the author's books and can explain why they would be uniquely helpful.

Don't be "that person"

No one wants to be *that* person. You know the one. You see their name in your inbox, and your soul shudders. Ugh. You can avoid being that person by doing the basics: be polite, be kind and be willing to return favours. Don't be obnoxious, entitled, demanding or rude. Part of this is being aware that some humour may not translate well into online forums. Unless you know the person, you should be careful with sarcasm.

Do your research

Don't ask people for information that you could easily get on your own with a bit of work. We're surprised by how often we're asked questions that can be answered with a simple Google search: "What should be in a query letter? What does a literary agent do? Can you self-publish on Amazon from Canada?" We get that you have questions. But before you ask someone to spend their precious time gathering information for you, see if you can gather it by yourself. It demonstrates a respect for the other person's time. Save your "call a friend" credits for when you are really stuck!

Know who you're speaking to

Eileen—a multi-award-winning YA author—was once asked, "Do you know anything about writing for teens?" It's not that Eileen expects people to know who she is, but to reach out and ask for writing advice when you clearly haven't even looked at an author's website makes it feel like you don't want *their* help, just help from *anyone*.

Publishing is a smaller business than you might expect. It's unwise to burn bridges because you never know how people may be connected. The writer you disparage or accidentally insult may be the client of the agent you're pitching. The book you slam on a panel may have been written by the moderator's good friend. This doesn't mean you have to be endlessly plucky and like everything, but it does mean choosing your words carefully and being respectful of other artists. If you're ending a relationship with someone, try and do it in a professional way. You may not wish to be friends with that person, or to work with them again, but ideally, you'll leave the relationship with some positive feelings still attached. If a relationship does end badly, consider very carefully how much of that dirty laundry you want to air publicly.

The summary of this section could be the golden rule: treat others as you'd like to be treated. Seems simple, but it's a good goal.

Your Turn

When you are ready to gather knowledge about leveling up to the next stage of your career, here are a few questions and tasks to tackle:

- What do you already know about this topic? Make some notes.
- Do you know anyone who has done this before, and who may be able to answer some of your questions? Perhaps they can even help you flesh out your list of questions—by pointing out all the things you don't yet know that you don't know.
- Brainstorm a list of search terms you can put into Google to find some answers for yourself.

- Which companies or tools might provide people or resources that can help you? For example, if you're in the editing stage, you will want to check out the blogs and help tutorials from companies like ProWritingAid and Grammarly. They offer up a ton of free information about the editing process.
- Create a list of people who are already in your network. Identify if you'd like to grow your network in any particular area. Would you like to know more authors? Librarians? Conference organizers?
- Look at your calendar and pencil in time to spend on building and maintaining your network. How you build it is up to you. You could send written notes to individuals, reach out on social media or participate in more conferences or writer meet-ups.
- Identify those priorities you could use some help growing. If you want to arrange a couple of newsletter swaps to support a new release, for example, make a note of all the things you need help with in order to level up.
- Now make a list of which networks might be able to help, and brainstorm ways to approach your networks for help without breaking those golden rules. What do you have to offer in exchange for your request?

97

LEVELING UP BY OPTING OUT

When you first start your author career, you're thrilled anytime you're asked or invited to do anything, whether it's to guest blog, judge a contest or speak at an event. As people who have been through this ourselves, we suspect this excitement is a mix of wanting to give back, being overjoyed that someone thinks you're important enough to be involved, and being afraid that if you don't participate, you'll miss out.

> *Take care not to sell yourself short: don't do things for free without asking if there's a way you can barter for a benefit that helps support your writing life and your writing community.*
>
> — Renee Sarojini Saklikar, award-winning author of *Listening to the Bees*

Many of these offers come with a promise of "exposure." And while these opportunities may indeed put you and your books in front of an audience, not all offers of exposure are equal. Writers, especially those early in their careers, tend to assume that if they don't take advantage of every opportunity, they'll miss the magical one that would have vaulted them to stardom. But the writing and publishing world is filled with opportunities, and while some will legitimately benefit you in one way or another, others are just going to distract you from your priorities.

Audition your opportunities

In order to evaluate those opportunities, get a sense of what the opportunity provides to *you*. It's not typically just about money (or even the exposure). It may include a chance to work with people you really admire, or attend a conference somewhere you wanted to visit anyway, or do some good that makes you feel warm and fuzzy.

If it doesn't? You need to learn to say no. And yes, we are both recovering "yes" addicts, and we are still learning how to put those two little letters together—and say them out loud—on a regular basis. So we understand exactly how hard it can be to say no. But it has a direct, positive impact on your ability to level up your writing career.

> *Leave time quarterly to think about your long term goals. Ask yourself, 'Are the items on my to-do list moving me toward my goals?' You might be surprised how many projects you've taken on that will move you sideways, rather than forward. You can still choose to do them if they are fun or fill the well, but prioritize the activities that actually get you closer to realizing your dreams and let most other things go.*
>
> — CORA SETON, AUTHOR OF *ISSUED TO THE BRIDE, ONE NAVY SEAL*

One effective strategy to avoid getting overwhelmed and overloaded and distracted from your just one thing is to understand when saying no to an "opportunity" is the right choice. (*Hint:* No is the right choice more often than you think.) *Opportunity* is in quotation marks here because not all opportunities are created equal. And not all of them will actually help you on your journey.

When some new and shiny and exciting opportunity comes your way—an offer to be part of a box set with other authors, an invitation to present at a conference, or a nomination for a volunteer role in your favourite writing organization—you need to weigh that opportunity against what it will cost you to say yes.

At some stages of your career, it makes sense to say yes to more things. For example, if you have decided that the next phase of your career growth includes moving into speaking at events and teaching workshops, then you might say yes to all opportunities that come your way for a while in order to build up your skills, your resume and your references. But if the next phase of your career journey includes some aggressive writing and publication goals, then clearing your schedule to focus on that number-one priority project is extremely important.

We have found the following four questions to be helpful in selecting only the opportunities that will give you extra kicks as you move those balls down the field.

1. Is it a *Hell, yes?* If something is being pitched to you, and your response is not an immediate *Hell, yes!* then you probably want to pass. (The exception here is that sometimes in order to pay our bills, you can take on things as needed and ease your way into better opportunities that are more likely to rate a *Hell, yes!* on the scale).
2. Is it going to help you achieve what you have identified as your short-term priority focus—for example, setting up your author mailing list and growing it to your first 1,000 readers?
3. Is it going to help you achieve what you have identified as your longer-term priority focus—for example, attaining a certain monthly income or publishing your fifteenth book?
4. What will saying yes to this opportunity cost you in terms of time, energy, money, and focus? Are there any other "costs"

associated with this opportunity? (Will it negatively impact your brand, confuse your readers or make your family upset with you because you are ignoring them on weekends?)

And always remember: saying yes to *this* opportunity will use your precious resources of time and energy—which might mean you'll have to say no to the other cool opportunities coming your way in the near future.

How to say no

This is hard. Like, *really* hard for some of us. (Both Crystal and Eileen are nodding and raising hands here, although Eileen wants it known she finds it very easy to say no to kale.) Learning to say no is one of the most powerful and effective ways to help yourself achieve your career goals and avoid burnout and frustration. There are a few different strategies that we've found to work quite well, even for those of us who really struggle with saying no. Using all of these in combination is the most effective approach.

Immediate no

If at all possible, say an immediate, and polite but firm, "No, sorry, that's not something I can take on right now." You don't waste their time, you don't waste your own time, and you don't end up agonizing over something or, worse, being tempted to say yes for the wrong reasons.

If you know someone who is trying to level up in the area of the opportunity, this is the perfect time to suggest them. But do your friends a solid: only pass along this opportunity to those you are quite sure are actually interested. Otherwise, you're just putting your friend or colleague in the tough spot of having to say no as well.

Let me sleep on it…

If you are like many of us, it's much harder to say no when someone catches you in person or on the phone, even when you know it's the right thing to do. If someone does catch you like this, and you feel yourself faltering, tell them you need to sleep on it before you make a commitment. And ask for more details about the opportunity only if it scores a *Hell, yes!* on your enthusiasm scale. Then you can look at your punch card and reply via email the next day with your carefully prepared script—tools that you will learn about below.

The punch card method

Imagine you have a punch card. You are allowed to say yes to only a limited number of commitments that do not directly advance your priority focus project before you will fill your available slots. Maybe you decide to devote two slots on your punch card to presenting at conferences, one slot to attending a conference and one slot to volunteering. Maybe you have only five "yes" slots for your whole year, with each one representing a commitment of three hours or less. It's up to you how you set up your punch card. But the goal is to initially give yourself fewer slots than you would like. That way, when an "opportunity" comes your way, you have to decide if it's really worth giving up one of those precious slots.

The super polite no script

Crystal got this idea from the book *Deep Work* by Cal Newport. It's a great read if you're looking for something to help you refine your focus mode and really dig into things. In it, he shares a response from Seth Godin, who was turning down the opportunity to be involved in a Tim Ferris project. It was so clever and such a great idea. Basically, you write up a scripted response for yourself that you can use anytime you're invited to do something that you might actually want to do but that doesn't fit on your punch card or get you closer to your primary goal. Then you copy and paste that response anytime someone emails you about an opportunity you have to decline. Having a script means having a response at hand so you don't lose time hemming and hawing and trying to craft the perfect response. Here's an example script that Crystal has written for her upcoming Just One Year experiment. You are welcome to steal like an artist and adapt this for your own use.

Dear [insert lovely person name],

Thank you so much for the invitation to be part of your [project/event]. It looks like a wonderful opportunity, and I love that you think I would be a good fit.

While normally I would jump at the opportunity, I'm in the midst of an experiment where I have given myself Just One Year to completely focus on my creative projects and see what magic can happen with an intense level of dedication.

That means I'm in write-like-the-wind mode, and even though it's hard (really, really hard) to say no to great invitations like this one, I'm going to stick to my plans for this year. However, if you're doing the event again next year and still think I'd be a good fit, feel free to reach out after February 1, 2022, when I will emerge from my hermit cave!

Possible addition: If you're looking for someone else to fill that spot, I would highly recommend [name of referral] as they are [awesome because of x, y, z]

I have no doubt your event will be a smashing success…

xo Crystal

Your Turn

- Considering your current career goals and priorities, what criteria need to be present for an opportunity to make sense for *you*?
- What hypothetical opportunities would make you react with a *Hell, yes!*?
- What hypothetical opportunities would take you away from your focus?
- Choose one or two of the strategies above—or brainstorm a list for yourself—to help you say no in the moment when unfavourable opportunities arise.
- Write your own polite "thanks, but no thanks" script.

PART IX

REWRITING YOUR AUTHOR CAREER

98

STAYING IN THE GAME

Get some multi-published, full-time authors talking about their careers, and you'll hear some war stories that may turn your hair white with fear. People who have been in the business for a while can vouch that it has ups and downs.

We're not saying this to discourage you but rather to give you a clear sense of what's ahead. Once you start writing with the intention of making money it goes from being your art, the thing you do for fun, to your job. And jobs aren't fun all the time. (Except maybe ice-cream taster —we'd still like to give that one a go.)

Being a full-time author and joining the grizzled-veteran crowd—hey, we *do* have great parties—means understanding that this is a long game. You don't want to become caught in short-term thinking or allow short-term problems to pull your focus away from your priorities.

You may think that you won't ever need to bounce back because you're going to plan and be strategic and careful as you level up. Planning and making wise choices can save you a lot of heartache, but it's important to remember that you can't plan for everything. Remember in 2019, when we all made plans for 2020? Ha ha ha. Yeah.

There are things that are outside your control: a publishing house closing down the line you write for, Amazon changing its business model, your spouse losing their job, or a global crisis upending the best-laid plans. It's important to remember that being a full-time author isn't just about avoiding problems and challenges—it's impossible to avoid them all—it's about knowing that you can cope when they *do* appear.

We love the term *bounce back*. It sounds so perky, when by its very definition, it involves first slamming to the ground. So how do you become a ball that bounces back in the air instead of a water balloon that goes splat?

That bounce is what we call resilience. When psychologists use the term, they mean an individual's ability to adapt to trauma, stress and challenges. Resilience is a handy trait to have because, in this life, it's impossible to escape challenging, sad, traumatic experiences. We've tried to avoid these painful situations for years, and it never works.

In the sections that follow, we'll cover some common situations that can arise during the course of an author career and offer some specific, actionable things to try when you hit those speed bumps along your path to success. These responses will also help build your resilience so when things get tough again, you'll stay on the road.

99

PICKING YOURSELF UP

When things go awry, there are steps you can take to assess the situation and see what you can do to mitigate any major issues that could hold back your career growth.

Pause and take stock

Did everything fall apart, or does it just feel like it? We ask this because we love you, and we're also writers. Are you being a bit dramatic? One of the best things about being a writer is that your imagination knows how to take things to the extreme. One of the worst things about being a writer is that your imagination knows how to take things to the extreme. It can be easy to fall into fling-yourself-on-the-sofa mode while wailing that you've *ruined your career*. In the middle of a crisis, it's important to pause and take a nice, deep breath.

Try and write down what has happened without using emotion-laden words. Instead of *I'm an idiot, and I uploaded the wrong version of my book so everyone thinks I'm an incompetent loser and is mad at me,* try *I uploaded the wrong version of the book. Other people are upset because they didn't get what they expected or needed.* Instead of *I sent a really nasty, vile email to the wrong person, and now everyone knows what a horrible person I am and will never speak to me again,* try *I sent an email I shouldn't have, and I stated things publicly that have hurt or damaged others as well as my own reputation.* If you're going to address the problem, you have to be able to clearly state what's happened.

Recognize your feelings

Above, we asked you to be objective, to state the problem without going down the road of emotion. But you do need to recognize the emotional impact of what happened. If the problem was something you caused, you may be feeling sadness, guilt or shame. If someone else caused the problem, you may feel betrayed, hurt or angry. What you feel is up to you, and those emotions are valid. You're entitled to them.

But you can't allow those feelings to become a barrier to action. Write them down, journal your feelings, talk with friends, family or a therapist. A healthy response to feelings is to feel them and then move through. If you find you're getting stuck in the feels, you may need support to keep going.

A word of caution here: try to keep your personal feelings and reactions in the private zone and off social media or other public forums at this point in the process.

Determine the damage

Eileen had a cousin who worked in insurance damage response. It was his job to go to a home after a hurricane, earthquake, flood, or zombie attack and assess the damage so that the claim could be filed and rebuilding could begin. You can't do anything until you know the state of the damage, and this is true in a writing career as well. Can something be repaired, or is it a total write off? What were the losses? If your career has taken a big hit, begin the same evaluation process. Have you burned bridges with individuals or organizations? Have you lost readers? Social media connections? Are there financial losses? Are there projects you need to walk away from? Pen names that you may need to abandon?

Take responsibility where needed

When we've made a mistake, it's human nature to explain that we never meant to make that mistake or that someone else is really more to blame. Remember as a kid, when you got caught lying to your parents about where you spent the weekend? They'd say something like, "Are you *sure* you were at your friend's place?" Part of you *knew* you were busted, but the desire to avoid that pain was strong—and, after all, there was always the slim chance that they really *didn't* know. So you'd try denial. Then, when confronted with your lie, you'd start spinning your wheels, trying to explain why you not only lied about where you were but also lied about lying. This is never a good look.

If you've made a mistake, the best thing you can do is recognize your part in the situation and take the path of accountability. "I didn't check my quotes to make sure they were attributed properly, and that's on me." Or "I didn't make the deadline, but I didn't tell you in advance because I was embarrassed. I know that wasn't the responsible choice." It's okay to mess up; we all do it. But learning the art of a sincere apology goes a long way to fixing those mistakes.

Create a plan to fix things and to avoid making the same mistake again

There's a school of thought that believes making mistakes and failing is a gift, because the sooner you make those mistakes and fail, the sooner you can learn from them and move forward. The key part here is that you need to learn. Sit down and create a strategy to move you forward from your current situation. And look carefully at how you got into the situation so you can take steps to prevent it from happening again.

One thing Eileen had to learn early on is that she's a people pleaser. She would say yes to projects and tasks that she didn't have the time to do because she didn't want to let anyone down. The problem was that she still ended up letting people down because she couldn't keep all those balls in the air.

Lesson for Eileen: You are the master of your time and schedule. You may disappoint people with what you can't take on, but better that than to take it on and not complete it properly. And here's another lesson: When Eileen says no, people aren't nearly as devastated as she thinks they will be. They just ask someone else. The disappointment is often more in her head than in reality.

Ask for help as needed

Just because you got *into* the problem on your own doesn't mean you can get *out* of it on your own. When things go wrong, it's important to seek help from the right kind of people. Getting an outside perspective on a problem can really help you brainstorm a solution or at least possible next steps. Reach out privately to members of your network who may have had similar experiences, or talk the situation through with a friend or family member. They might see things that are not visible to you at the centre of the storm.

Depending on how intense the situation is, you may also need to reach out to experts: your agent, image consultants, lawyers or counsellors. Their job is to help you navigate tough situations. Asking for help before you make things worse by blundering around on your own can save time, money and heartache in the long run.

Take care of yourself

Stress in your creative career can have ripple effects that reach much further than your business plans and bottom line. Your mental and physical health are extremely important because they directly impact your ability to write, create and publish. You need to handle difficult situations in a way that will protect *your* mental and physical health and the health of the other important people in your life. When you're dealing with extra stressful times in your career, ease up the pressure on yourself and really take it back to the basics. Eating healthy, walking in nature, staying off social media and resting more may not directly solve the problem, but they will help recharge your energy and contribute to your resilience. (Remember resilience? It's that thing that allows you to bounce back instead of break.)

Know you might have to step back before going forward

We'd all like to see our sales go up, up and further up with each book. We'd like to see our mailing list grow daily. We'd like to see each publishing contract stipulate a larger and larger advance. We'd like to see the income line on our tax returns grow steadily every year.

But there may be times when you have to step back in order to move forward. You may have to start over in a new genre, or with a new agent, or with a new software, which means redoing some tasks to keep everything consistent and systematic. Career growth rarely happens in a straight line. Often you have to back up and look at a historical average to know what is really going on.

Zoom out for the bigger picture... and regroup before the next big charge. When you're trying to hike up a mountain, you have to pause every now and again to rest, recharge, and check your map. You may even have to circle back if you took the wrong path. It's going to be the same with your career.

And while basically everyone we know has had to step back at times, we've got a couple of specific examples to share so you can see what all this metaphorical circling back might look like in the real world.

An example from Crystal

Crystal is a lover of charts and graphs. Not only can she make a sharp-looking spreadsheet, she can read them too. It's one of her superpowers. And Crystal's graphs of her fiction publishing career look something like what happens when you pull out your Christmas decorations to find three strands of Christmas lights all tangled up in the box: nary a straight line to be seen, and plenty of tangly messes to unwind one strand at a time. Not to mention the occasional burnt-out or broken bulb. On the fiction side, she is currently working through a rebrand and reboot of all her products, systems and processes after learning some major lessons from the publication of her first few romance novellas. Her tasks included:

- Pausing all new releases and trying to get enough stories written that she will have a consistent release schedule in the future, even when life smashes a bulb or two
- Changing mailing list service providers and setting up a re-engagement campaign for more than 5,000 subscribers after a long period of no sending
- Making adjustments to the content of the books in response to specific suggestions in reader reviews
- Revising covers based on reader feedback and leveled-up skills and budget to increase click-through rates and sales from ads campaigns
- Refreshing website design, focus and content
- Adjusting newsletter focus and schedule to reflect feedback from readers and industry stats
- Redoing all print files in Vellum instead of InDesign to remove InDesign as a monthly expense and to delegate formatting and layouts to an assistant, thus reducing production time
- Acknowledging that she is happiest when 100 percent of her income is not dependent on fiction sales, and accordingly diversifying income streams by publishing non-fiction and retaining her group coaching platform through The Creative Academy
- Assessing what was holding her back from achieving her writing goals, and redesigning her life to ensure that she has fewer commitments of time and money so she can do less contract work and have more clear, unstructured time to find that elusive state of writing flow

That reinvention phase has taken Crystal approximately two years to complete. She had to reinvest a chunk of her royalty income, and a great deal of self-control, to take that step back and wait for all the pieces to be in place before relaunching. It's not easy to assess your business with a critical eye—and then pull it all apart. But when you put it back together using everything you've learned along the way, the result will be stronger, and you will be that much more likely to achieve success in the long term. Sometimes these transformations are fairly minor things we can do in a few days, weeks or months. Other times, it can take years to fully transform your author career.

An example from Eileen

Eileen had been in the trenches, trying to get published, for several years. She experienced lots of rejection. (Lots and lots.) She'd written and queried multiple books. She didn't give up. At long last, she secured an agent! Her agent sold her book!! There were film rights optioned!! It sold in multiple countries!!! (Eileen is building exclamation marks to illustrate her growing excitement.)

Now, we're not saying that Eileen was hanging out with Oprah, but she felt a bit like she'd arrived. She was busily working on her next book and imagining how quickly she might be able to give up her day job and spend her days with her imaginary friends full-time.

Then her editor called. Cue doom-and-gloom music.

The publisher liked Eileen. They liked her books, but romantic comedy—what she'd always written—was on the way out. (Or so they honestly thought at the time. Good news: it's back now!) They weren't going to publish anything more in that area. They didn't need Eileen's second book after all. *Thanks. It's been fun. Don't let the door hit you on the way out.*

There were tears. (Understatement.) Then, acting on advice from her agent, Eileen started to look at the young adult (YA) market, which was growing. The light comedic tone of her first book would work well in that space. She spent time reading and studying YA books, and then she began writing her own. She would later sell her first YA and go on to build the bulk of her writing career—at least so far—in that genre.

Your Turn

- One of the best ways to learn is to explore what you've done before. Do a deep dive into a past experience when things seemed to fall apart—either with writing or in another area of your life. How well did you identify the problem? What solutions did you consider? What action did you take? In hindsight, would you do things the same way? What would you change?
- You can also prepare for mistakes by looking at what others have done. The Internet provides us with lots of examples of authors behaving badly or tripping over bad behaviour. What steps did they take that led to the error? What would you do differently if you were in that situation? Compile a list of things to avoid as you grow your career.

100

PUSHING THROUGH WHEN IT'S HARD

What do you do when it gets hard? You keep going, because the only way you can guarantee you won't succeed is to take yourself off the playing field. But how do you do that? First off, it can help to understand that the desire to give up is human nature. Our brains are hardwired to avoid pain. The trick is figuring out how to persist.

Give yourself a break

No one can give 110 percent all the time. This is a damaging myth. We sometimes hustle with the sense that if we don't work around the clock toward our dreams, we "don't really want them." But all people need balance. Time for work, but also time for ourselves and our family and friends. Taking time to recharge is valuable, and it can often allow us to see our challenges in a new way. It's more than okay to take a break—it's a healthy move that also allows you to spark fresh creativity.

Identify the real problem

When Eileen teaches conflict in her writing classes, she uses the term "placeholder conflict." This is the idea that what two characters are fighting about is standing in place of the real issue. For example, you may yell at your spouse for leaving their socks on the floor. If you're angry, it's unlikely about the socks. It's more likely because you feel you're being treated as a maid or you're unhappy with the household work distribution.

The same placeholder conflict happens inside you. You may be upset about one thing, but is that what is the *real* problem? Take some time to reflect on what is bothering you. Is it a recent rejection letter, or what you think that rejection means? Is it that you don't know how to fix your website, or that you feel a certain way when confronted with tasks you don't know how to do?

Remember your purpose

In fiction, we know it's important that the characters have very clear and strong motivations. If they don't have a strong reason to keep pursuing their goal, they would quit, considering how much we throw at them. So what is your motivation for becoming a full-time author? What does it mean to you? What will happen if you stop? You need to know your priorities. This doesn't need to be life and death.

For example, Eileen once asked the group in The Creative Academy what would happen if they didn't finish their book. One person responded, "Nothing, really. There's no publisher who wants it." Well, no wonder it can be hard to finish! However, Eileen then started talking to the writer about why she wanted to write that story. What it meant to her. Why she felt that story mattered. The author then reframed her answer to address why that story needed to be in the world and what it offered to readers.

Identify your priorities

Being overwhelmed is a real thing. If you are feeling stuck, it's possible that you have too many balls on the field. Take time to identify your just one thing that needs your focus and time at this moment.

Break down large projects

It may be that you haven't gone far enough in breaking down your bigger goals and milestones into smaller, more achievable parts. If you're struggling with this, review the section on Identifying Your Next Actions and drop into a mastermind group in The Creative Academy for Writers. We'll help you figure out your next move.

Ask for help as needed

One of the best coping skills you can learn is to ask for help when you need it. You'll likely be surprised how many people are happy to help if you simply indicate where you need the support. But this means being specific. Do you need a writer friend to sit down and help you brainstorm? Do you need feedback on pages or a project plan? Do you need someone to help with dinners or household chores so you can focus?

Take care of yourself

This shouldn't even need to be said, but given that both Crystal and Eileen have dealt with challenges, clearly we can all use reminders from time to time. Your body has a way of reminding you to take care of it—and the consequences of ignoring those cues are typically unpleasant. You get ill, you have trouble sleeping, you wake up with those weird kinks in your neck and can't even turn your head fully so you walk around like a stick figure. Yeah, those things. You have to take care of yourself, both body and mind, in order to produce your best work. This means eating food that fuels you, moving around every so often and taking care of your mental health.

Celebrate small victories on the way to those big goals

Can you tell we like a good celebratory party around here? Crystal even has a bell on her desk that reads, *champagne, please!* (Eileen wonders why she hasn't invested in one of these for herself.) It may seem silly, but by celebrating those small wins, you're training your brain to believe that you're a winner. That you do succeed. It helps refill the energy well when things are challenging. (We discussed this in greater detail in the sections Playing the Long Game and Celebrating Success.)

Your Turn

- Look at your writing in general or the particular book you are working on now. What is your motivation to write? Why does it matter? Clarify this, and post your reasons where you can see them.
- Who can you call on for cheerleading or support when you're having a rough day?
- Write a letter from a future fan telling you what your books have meant to them. Post this where you can see it as a way to drive you forward when things get hard.
- Write your own self-care plan. Identify what you're going to do to ensure you're taking care of your health. Put these to-dos in your schedule.
- Did you make your happy file that we suggested in the Celebrating Success section? Pull it out and take a look. Read and repeat as often as is necessary until you get your mojo back. If necessary, write nice things on sticky notes and put them up around your office or your home.

101

REINVENTING YOURSELF

As a kid, Eileen lacked any and all athletic talent. (Who are we kidding? This has extended into her adult years—she can still trip and fall when walking on a flat surface.) Often, when she swung wildly at a baseball, missed completely and knocked herself in the head with the bat, she would declare, "Do over!" In kid-speak, this meant the last attempt didn't count. It didn't happen. She got to try again.

We feel there should be a do-over function for adulthood, where you can marry the wrong person and then loudly declare, "Do over!" You can mess up at work, stand up in the boardroom, and yell, "Do over!" prompting your co-workers to pretend that you hadn't just sent the wrong email to everyone in the company. Alas, for many things in life, the do-over function does not exist.

But there *is* a do-over in writing! Writers reinvent themselves and their careers all the time. You may want to reinvent or reboot your career for a number of reasons. Perhaps you had kids and stepped away from the business for a while. Maybe your sales in a particular genre tanked. It's possible you stepped into a publishing mess and want to create as much distance from that mistake as possible. Maybe you are changing genres, and you want to sever all connection to the previous version of your author self. For example, if you want to write picture books but previously you wrote erotica, you need to make significant changes to ensure those two reading groups don't mix.

Even a technical issue can prompt a career reboot. You may not mind folks knowing you write in two different genres, but you don't want to confuse the algorithms—or your readers—on your author pages. Let's take a look at different ways to reboot and refresh.

102

REBRANDING EXISTING BOOKS

We are all learning as we go, and book styles change just like clothing styles do. Sometimes your book needs a bit of a cosmetic makeover to liven up your sales. Maybe your cover doesn't quite hit the right tone for the genre or subcategory. Maybe you have gotten your rights back from your publisher, and it's up to you to re-release a new version of your title. Sometimes you need to take a good, hard look at your existing set-up and do a strategic rebranding of your content.

How do you know if branding is the thing that's holding you back? There are clues. One is if you have great reviews, but your sales aren't as high as you'd like. Another is if you sell well to your newsletter list, but when you pay for promo slots or run Amazon ads, you don't see much click-through or sales. You may even get disappointed reviews from readers who didn't realize from the cover what kind of book they were getting.

If you are indie publishing, you have direct control over the covers on your books. And you can make a change if trends change, or if you have learned a lot since you started publishing. For example, Crystal has redone the covers on her MacAllisters of Rivers End series twice in the last five years, and each time it has attracted more of the right readers, increased the effectiveness of her ads and leveled up her sales.

Although you won't always have direct control over your covers if you are traditionally published, there are still options you can discuss with your publisher. Eileen's book *The Hanging Girl* came out to strong reviews. It would go on to win the John Spray Award for best YA mystery in Canada that year. But sales… yeah, those weren't setting the world on fire.

The idea for the title had come from the fact that the main character reads tarot cards, and the card for the Hanging Man is all about change and the need to see things in a new way. So she cleverly called the book *The Hanging Girl*. This idea was so clever that most people didn't get it and thought the book was about suicide. The dark appearance of the cover didn't help either. For the paperback release, the book was given both a new title—*One Lie Too Many*—and a different cover. And while it is unusual to re-title a traditional book, it is much easier to get the publisher to consider a change in cover.

Whether you are indie or traditionally published, the most important thing is to let existing readers know that you have changed your covers so they don't think it's a new book and get frustrated when they realize it's not. This is easily accomplished with an email to your mailing list. And, assuming you haven't changed the ISBN or title, most eBook sales platforms will inform customers if they have already purchased the book.

Your Turn

Take a good hard look at each of your existing products and your catalogue as a whole and ask the following questions:

- Do your covers accurately represent your genres and the types of stories you have written?

- Are your covers professional and similar to other books in your subcategories? (*Note:* If you are in Kindle Unlimited (KU), check your covers against other bestselling books in KU. If you are wide or traditionally published, check the top sellers on other platforms like Kobo and Barnes & Noble.)
- Scan your reviews for comments from people who felt misled by the cover or disappointed that the story didn't live up their expectations based on the cover or category listing.
- Review the chapters "Your Author Brand" and "Your Market" to help you identify issues, and actions to take to fix these issues.

103

RE-RELEASING NEW EDITIONS

If, as an indie author, you *are* switching the title or publishing the book in a new format (e.g., hardcover instead of paperback), you will need a new ISBN. If you are doing a complete rewrite and re-release under a different title or author name, you will need to publish a whole new edition, not just switch out your files. This will clear the reviews from your title—yes, you will be starting from scratch! It will also clear up any garbled "also-bought" messaging so your new and improved book will really have a chance to fly.

How do you know a new edition would be helpful? Take a hard and honest look at your reviews. Are there lots of negative comments about the quality of the story or content? If it's non-fiction, are there comments about the information being out of date?

Do folks who offer to review it end up not posting anything at all? Yes, sometimes people get busy. But people are often hesitant to post negative reviews. If people keep offering to review your book and then say nothing, it may be that the content is not quite up to snuff and you need to re-evaluate your product.

Did you write the flagship first book in your series before you really settled into your groove? You've learned a ton since you started writing, and if the first book in your series doesn't really grab people, you won't be able to turn them into fans. Sometimes a full rewrite and re-release of your earlier books does make sense. Or perhaps you can clean it up and get a high-quality edit without a full rewrite, and slowly turn things around that way. The only way to clear those reviews, though, is to publish a new edition and start fresh.

A good rule of thumb is that if you are updating more than 10 percent of the content, you should think about publishing a new edition of the book. So if you're polishing up typos and fixing your formatting, you can keep the same edition. If you give it a new ending and totally rewrite the book, a new edition is the way to go. If you are doing a huge overhaul to try to counteract some early negative press, and you're using a pen name to do it, you probably want to go as far as unpublishing your existing book and starting from scratch with a full relaunch and re-release! If you are going to tackle a full relaunch, the book *Relaunch Your Novel* by Chris Fox can help.

Your Turn

- Read through your reviews. Are there complaints that your book needs professional editing or that the content is out of date?
- Reread your earlier titles with a critical eye. What could you do to improve quality without rewriting the book entirely?
- How much of your book would you need to change to level up the quality? Is this enough to justify a new edition?

104

SWITCHING OR ADDING PEN NAMES

Adding a pen name (or three) to rebrand, untangle your also-boughts and un-confuse your readers is a viable option. Think about this carefully, however, because each pen name you add can also increase your workload, depending on how fully you embrace that new name and your reasons for doing so. Do you need a separate website? New social media accounts? If you are implementing a pen name because of a scandal, public mistake or major meltdown in your publishing career, or if you hope the pen name will protect your privacy, you may want to wipe the slate clean, keep your social media accounts completely separate and not tell your existing newsletter list.

If you are switching or adding pen names strictly for business reasons, you don't necessarily need to reinvent yourself from the ground up. For example, if you want Amazon to promote more effectively to your readers or help readers distinguish among your subgenres, it may be enough to simply separate the identities on the publishing end while maintaining a single website for all your pen names.

You may, however, want to consider keeping separate email lists, or at least separate groups within your list. Readers are more likely to stay subscribed and interested if you send them only content tailored to their interests.

Your Turn

Take a good look at your books and your brand and ask the following questions:

- Do all your books fit into the same category, or at least related categories? Or would it be easier for the algorithms and your readers if you divided your writing between a couple of different pen names?
- When you go to your book listings on Amazon.com, are the "also bought" items at the bottom of the listing similar in genre and category to yours, or is there a huge mixture of different kinds of books?
- Are you thinking about using a pen name to protect your privacy? Or just to distinguish among your genres?
- Would you be comfortable with readers in one of your genres knowing that you write in your other genre or genres?
- Are you working with a publisher? Be sure to check with them about their policies around pen names, what gets printed on copyright pages, and any suggestions about how to handle your pen name when publishing in partnership with them.

105

SWITCHING GENRES

Writers typically write in a single genre at a time so they can build a brand and readership in a particular area. However, it's not uncommon for writers to branch out. Eileen's written in the genres of adult romantic comedy, YA contemporary, YA thriller, middle grade fantasy and non-fiction. And in case you think only Eileen is flighty, Crystal's written non-fiction, picture books, middle grade books, contemporary romance, romance with a touch of magic, and she's now working her way into romantic suspense and experimenting with other ideas under various pen names.

A great reason to write in alternate genres is because you're interested in those genres. Maybe you have a great idea or a passion for a particular story. Or maybe one genre is more lucrative, but you adore the less lucrative one as well. There are many reasons to stick to one genre, but an author planning a long career can—and should—feel free to explore where their muse takes them.

Things to consider when changing genre:

- Are you planning to write on an ongoing basis in two or more genres? If yes, are you confident that you can meet the demands

of the publication schedule (e.g., completing two books in a year)?
- If you work with an agent, discuss your desire to write in multiple genres early on so that you can talk through any possible ramifications.
- Do your genres work well together (like romantic suspense and paranormal romance) or are they wildly different (like romance and horror)? How will this impact how you market these books?
- If you're changing genre because your current genre is oversold or waning in popularity, keep those past works! Things have a way of coming back around, and you may end up switching back at some point.
- Don't switch genres only to jump on the bandwagon of what is popular right now, or what you think will be popular in the next year or two. Make sure you're also really excited to write in that area. Readers can sniff out authors who aren't really interested, and writing and publishing takes longer than most people realize.
- Take time to read widely in the new genre you're considering. Make sure you understand the tropes and clichés in that genre.

Your Turn

- If you're considering a genre change, list the qualities you like about the new genre and what excites you about writing in that field.
- What would be involved for you to make a genre change?
- Make a list of pros and cons of changing genres.

106

TAKING A BREAK

Sometimes, pushing through isn't the right answer. Sometimes what you need is a little time and space to process what has happened, take stock of what you really want at this moment in your life, and make some decisions about the right way forward—for you.

It's okay to quit, as long as it's for the right reasons

There's a myth out there that you can never quit. That the difference between "real" artists and those who are simply pretending is nothing but persistence and grit. But here's the thing. You *can* quit. Writing is like any other career: if you don't want to do it anymore, if it's no longer satisfying, or if something else will make you happier, you don't have to keep doing this.

Take a moment and let that sink in. You don't *have* to be a writer. At least, you don't have to be a writer with the goal of publication or revenue generation. You could choose to write just for you. No deadlines. No pressure. No branding or genre worries.

That can be an incredibly freeing thought. It puts you back in control. Yes, things may be hard or unpleasant, but if you choose to stay in the game, that's different than feeling like you can't leave. Think of it like a long-term relationship. You've invested a lot of time and energy into it. It will be difficult to walk away. There may be others in your life who will be disappointed. However, if the relationship—or career—has run its course, there is no reason to stay in it.

What you don't want to do is threaten to quit as a way to urge others to be your cheerleaders. Look, we've all been there. You look at yourself and declare loudly, "I look horrible!" Then your friends rush in to tell you that's not true. "You look great. You look better than great!" And a wave of relief flows over you. You're using their compliments to prop up your self-esteem.

In this business, you need to be able to prop up your own self-esteem. You can't rely on others to do it. That doesn't mean you can't ask trusted friends and family to share what they like about your writing, or read the happy file of all your best reviews. Go on, do it. It feels great. Just don't threaten to quit in order to gather that feel-good energy.

Not sure what you want? Give yourself a break

If you're truly considering quitting, take your time making that decision. Consider if what you really need is just a break, or a change in genre or routine. Consider what is making you want to walk away. Is it a temporary problem, or have events in your life shifted? Do you still enjoy writing? Ask anyone who has been in a long-term career if they've ever thought of doing something else. I guarantee they have. Career-change statistics shows that the average person pursues five to seven different careers in their lifetime. Why do we feel that writing would be any different?

Evaluate your other job options. There are a lot of books out there on changing careers and figuring out what you should do. *Designing Your Life* by Bill Burnett and Dave Evans, and *Pivot* by Jenny Blake, are just two examples. You may choose to do something related to writing, return to an earlier career or pursue something completely different. You get only one glorious ride in this life. If you aren't enjoying the ride, it is up to you to change it.

If you decide to take either a permanent or temporary break from writing, take time to wrap up loose ends. Think of it like going on short-term vacation, taking a longer sabbatical or giving notice at a traditional job. Inform people who will be impacted. Tidy up your desk. Organize your materials so that if you decide to return one day, you know where things are and can put your hands on important documents and contacts.

Mark the occasion

Lastly, consider having some kind of ceremony or party to mark the occasion. If writing has been your job, it deserves recognition for its importance in your life. Invite people to talk about how your writing impacted them, take time to read your past work and be impressed, revel in the accomplishments you made and the work you created. Have a cake and a party. What you did, what you created, mattered. It was important.

And that creativity never goes away. It will be right inside of you if you ever want to access it again. Right where it always was—next to your heart.

Your Turn

- When you think about taking a break from writing, how does that make you feel?
- If you're thinking about quitting your author career, try starting with a holiday. How long feels right to you? Mark the start and end date on your calendar, and give yourself permission to be on vacation from writing during that time.
- At the end of that vacation, reassess how you're feeling. Do you wish the break were longer? Remember earlier, when we said you're the boss? Yep. Still true. Extend your vacay. Are you missing writing? What about it are you missing?

- Are you getting the urge to write again? If so, is it an urge to write the same kind of books—or different formats, genres or lengths? What is it that feels fun and exciting to you?
- If you're considering leaving writing permanently, create a pros and cons list for staying in the industry.
- Write a journal entry about what your day-to-day life might look like if you stopped writing and worked in another field.
- If you're considering other careers, reach out to people in that occupation and ask them what they like or dislike about it.

PART X

YOUR NEXT STEPS

107

IMPLEMENTING YOUR PLANS

AND CELEBRATING YOUR SUCCESS!

You still with us? Fantastic! You've re-committed to leveling up your writing and publishing career this year, and it's time to apply what you've learned and put all that planning to good use. Time to start working towards that next milestone. First things first: a quick pre-flight check.

Have you completed your business plan for the coming full year?

If you followed along with the Your Turn activities in the Google Doc or your journal as you went, your business plan should be mostly filled in now. Congrats! If you read through the exercises but didn't actually complete them the first time through, no judgment. But you'll probably want to head on back to the beginning and fill out the Full Time Author 'Your Turn' Workbook and the Business Plan Google Sheet so you have a clear direction for your next steps. Find these and other resources at https://creativeacademyforwriters.com/resources/fulltimeauthor.

Have you created your job descriptions?

We've identified three very important and distinct roles that you will play within your writing and publishing business: creator, business manager, and sales and marketing director. The exact composition of these roles will vary depending on whether you are indie publishing, traditionally publishing or going the hybrid route.

It can be helpful to break down your calendar and your budgets into these different areas and roles. Making the role clear, and the job description very specific, will help you envision those aspects of your business and budget your time. Distinguishing clearly among those roles will also help when you decide to contract out parts of your business.

Review your answers to the Your Turn questions in the previous sections, and write a job description for each of the roles you have chosen:

- Job description: Creator
- Job description: Business manager
- Job description: Sales and marketing director

Are there any additional roles or positions determined by your business model? Maybe teacher? Or affiliate marketer? If your business plan includes additional components, decide if those tasks fit into one of the existing job descriptions or merit a job description of their own.

Once you've finished writing the job descriptions, make sure you block time into your calendar to carry out the demands of each of these positions.

Have you set three goals for this year?

Set yourself three specific goals—or one for each of the roles in your author business as you determined above. Try to summarize each goal in a single, simple, straightforward sentence.

1. What is your primary goal for this year as a creator?
2. What is your primary goal for this year as an author business manager? (This might be to increase sales of your backlist, republish your older series with new covers, manage publication of the three new books you are writing this year, or get your financial tracking systems in place.)
3. What is your primary goal this year as the sales and marketing director for your author brand?

Have you made a quarterly action plan for your next 12 Week Year?

Decide what to tackle in the first quarter of the year and make a specific plan. If you need some help with this, you can sign up for the next 12 Week Year virtual planning retreat in The Creative Academy for Writers, or you can watch the last one we recorded. We also have weekly motivation and accountability sessions, as well as monthly marketing mastermind sessions, to help you set those regular, smaller goals and break things down into bite-sized tasks.

Have you taken a deep breath?

Seriously, you got this. We know you do. And we're right here, cheering you on. You have a plan. You know what you want. You know where you want to be at the end of this year, or this quarter, or this week. We can't wait to see what exciting things are on the horizon for you.

Have you put a celebratory post in The Creative Academy for Writers?

At the beginning of this book, we talked about the wee versions of ourselves: the kids with pigtails and a library obsession who dreamed of making writing a full-time career. We've walked you through our journeys, trying to give you a lot to consider so you can determine if this is the job for you. We've let you know what things to put into place to begin your journey or take it to the next level.

Our hope with this book is to inspire you and get you excited with all the sparkly opportunities out there—and also to give you pause to consider all the possible challenges. As a writer, you know there's no epic journey without highs and lows. There will be times when you're in uncharted territories, and that means possible encounters with trolls or dragons… but also magic.

The upside—and downside—of the author career journey is that there is no finish line. There are only endless chances to set out on new and more exciting journeys.

We've got a few last (optional, but appreciated!) Your Turn exercises before we send you on your way.

Your Turn: Leave a review

We hope you found this book and the accompanying resources helpful. We'd be forever grateful if you took a moment right now to post a quick review wherever you bought your copy, and also on Goodreads and BookBub if you have accounts there.

Your review will help other writers find the book. It also lets us know what you found most helpful. This book is part of a series, and your feedback will ensure our next books give you more of what you liked—so let us know in your review. We'll see it and take note!

Your Turn: Share with a friend

The only thing better than writing and reading books is sharing books with friends. If you know others interested in developing their writing into a full-time author career, please let them know you enjoyed this resource and found it helpful.

Your Turn: Join The Creative Academy for Writers

Having a community that understands what you're going through as a writer makes all the difference between getting stuck and getting it done. Join our fabulous free community at https://creativeacademyforwriters.com/join-us and get access to a wealth of our best resources.

Your Turn: Check out the Strategic Authorpreneur podcast

For more great info on saving time, money and energy as you level up your writing career, check out the Strategic Authorpreneur Podcast at https://strategicauthorpreneur.com.

Your Turn: Check out the other books in this series

It's always sad when you come to the end of a good book. But the brilliant part about a series is that the fun doesn't *really* have to end! So put away your Kleenex. We've got more books in this series to help you along your writing and publishing journey. Be sure to check out our other titles at https://creativeacademyforwriters.com/books.

More Creative Academy Guides for Writers

We've got a whole series of books to help you along your writing and publishing journey.

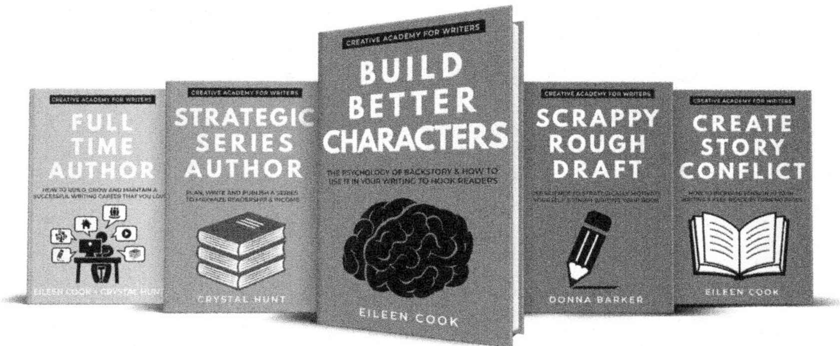

Available in eBook & print

Scrappy Rough Draft by Donna Barker
Build Better Characters by Eileen Cook
Strategic Series Author by Crystal Hunt
Create Story Conflict by Eileen Cook
Full Time Author by Eileen Cook and Crystal Hunt

Come visit us...
www.creativeacademyforwriters.com

Want to access our collection of FREE courses and resources for writers? Visit us online at creativeacademyforwriters.com/resources.

ABOUT EILEEN COOK

Eileen Cook is a multi-published, award-winning author with her novels appearing in nine languages. Her books have been optioned for film and TV. She spent most of her teen years wishing she were someone else or somewhere else, which is great training for a writer. She's an instructor/mentor with The Creative Academy for Writers and Simon Fraser University's Writer's Studio program, where she loves helping other writers find their unique story to tell.

Eileen lives in Vancouver, Canada, with two very naughty dogs. You can learn more about her on her website at https://eileencook.com or connect with her on social media.

facebook.com/EileenCook.author
twitter.com/Eileenwriter
instagram.com/eileencookwriter

ABOUT CRYSTAL HUNT

Crystal Hunt is the author of over forty books in a variety of genres and formats. She writes non-fiction for authors as Crystal Hunt, contemporary romance as CJ Hunt, and children's books as Crystal Stranaghan (and a variety of other pen names). No matter what name she's using, she is living her dream life as an instructor/mentor with The Creative Academy for Writers and a full-time author.

Crystal lives in Vancouver, Canada, with her husband. You can learn more about Crystal on her websites: https://crystalhuntauthor.com and https://cjhuntromance.com.

She's a bit of a hermit where social media is concerned, but if she is online, she can be found on...

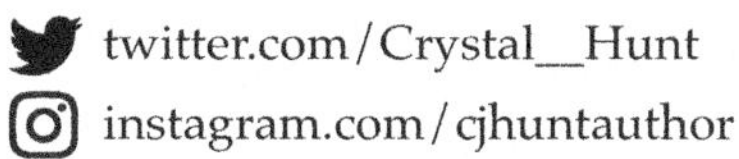

twitter.com/Crystal__Hunt
instagram.com/cjhuntauthor

ACKNOWLEDGEMENTS

First, thank you to all the people who supported our personal goals of becoming full-time writers: family, schoolteachers, friends, readers and all those along the way who believed in us—even when we didn't.

To our author friends who generously contributed quotes and wisdom—you're an inspiration to all of us, and we thank you.

Thank you to the team at The Creative Academy for Writers. We built the community to help other writers on their writing journey, but we never imagined how much we would gain. We appreciate everyone's questions, suggestions and support. Our members very generously helped us test the resources, and they helped us decide what needed to be in this book by sharing their questions and frustrations along the way. With the past year being challenging (understatement), we are so grateful for the community we share.

Hugs and gratitude to Donna Barker and Michele Amitrani, our beta readers who offered their time and energy to make this the best book it could be. To our editor Amanda Bidnall, who ensured we put our best words forward (and in the right order). Any errors you find are our responsibility alone! Thank you to Stephanie Candiago for assisting us with all things related to layout and administrative support. We couldn't do what we do without you.

All of these people have earned our deep gratitude, and we eagerly await a time when we can all meet together in one place and raise a glass together.

Thank you to readers of our previous books—*Strategic Series Author, Build Better Characters,* and *Create Story Conflict*—who offered their thoughts and suggested new topics they wanted to explore.

Lastly, we want to acknowledge and thank *you*. We're aware there are many books out there for you to choose from, so we appreciate your time and focus. We hope this book assists you in creating a plan to reach your personal author goals, and we hope it's something you can come back to year after year as you level up. If you have ideas that you'd like to see covered in future books, please feel free to reach out to us.

We look forward to sharing the shelves with you and hearing all about your various successes.

xo Crystal & Eileen

RESOURCES

Books

The 12 Week Year: Get More Done in 12 Weeks than Others Do in 12 Months by Brian P. Moran and Michael Lennington, Wiley, 2013

5000 Words per Hour by Chris Fox, Chris Fox Writes LLC, 2015

Amazon Ads for Authors 2020: Tips and Strategies to Sell Your Books by Deb Potter, Fairytale Factory, 2020

Build Better Characters: The Psychology Backstory & How to Use It in Your Writing to Hook Readers by Eileen Cook, Creative Academy for Writers, 2019

Create Story Conflict: How to Increase Tension in Your Writing & Keep Readers Turning Pages by Eileen Cook, Creative Academy for Writers, 2020

Deep Work: Rules for Focused Success in a Distracted World by Cal Newport, Grand Central Publishing, 2016

Designing Your Life: How to Build a Well-Lived, Joyful Life, by Bill Burnett and Dave Evans, Knopf, 2016

Funny You Should Ask: Mostly Serious Answers to Mostly Serious Questions About the Book Publishing Industry by Barbara Poelle, Writer's Digest Books, 2020

Getting to Yes: Negotiating Without Giving In by Roger Fisher, William Ury, and Bruce Patton, Penguin Books, 2011

Guide to Literary Agents 2020 by Robert Lee Brewer, Writer's Digest Books, 2019

How to Write Fast: Better Words Faster by Sean Platt and Neeve Silver, Sterling & Stone, 2019

Jeff Herman's Guide to Publishers, Editors & Literary Agents (28th edition), by Jeff Herman, New World Library, 2018

Newsletter Ninja by Tammi Labrecque, Larks & Katydids, 2018

Pivot: The Only Move that Matters Is Your Next One, by Jenny Blake, Portfolio, 2017

Relaunch Your Novel: Breathe Life into Your Backlist by Chris Fox, CreateSpace Independent Publishing Platform, 2017

Resolving Everyday Conflict by Ken Sande and Kevin Johnson, Baker Books, 2015

Scrappy Rough Draft: Use Science to Strategically Motivate Yourself & Finish Writing Your Book by Donna Barker, Creative Academy for Writers, 2019

Start With Why: How Great Leaders Inspire Everyone to Take Action by Simon Sinek, Portfolio, 2011

Strategic Series Author: Plan, Write and Publish a Series to Maximize Readership & Income by Crystal Hunt, Creative Academy for Writers, 2019

StrengthsFinder 2.0 by Tom Rath, Gallup Press, 2007

The Enneagram Made Easy: Discover the 9 Types of People by Renee Baron and Elizabeth Wagele, HarperOne, 1994

The Four Tendencies: The Indispensable Personality Profiles that Reveal How to Make Your Life Better (and Other People's Lives Better, Too) by Gretchen Rubin, Harmony, 2017

The Illusion of Money: Why Chasing Money is Stopping You from receiving It by Kyle Cease, Hay House, 2019

The One Thing: The Surprisingly Simple Truth Behind Extraordinary Results by Gary Keller with Jay Papason, Bard Press, 2013

You are a Badass at Making Money: Master the Mindset of Wealth by Jen Sincero, Penguin, 2017

2021 Creative Academy Guides for Writers

Create With CoAuthors by Donna Barker, Crystal Hunt and Eileen Cook

Strategic Indie Author by Crystal Hunt

Write More Books by Crystal Hunt

Sell More Books by Crystal Hunt

Find the latest releases at https://creativeacademyforwriters.com/books

Podcasts

The Strategic Authorpreneur podcast

The Self Publishing Show podcast

The Creative Penn podcast

Six Figure Authors podcast

Additional resources

TED Talks are available online on just about every topic you can imagine. https://www.ted.com/talks

Made in the USA
Las Vegas, NV
08 February 2022

43439417R10275